P9-DCI-561

Jim Hunt
A Biography

Opposite page
Governor Jim Hunt in 1996
PHOTO BY CHARLIE JONES

Jim Hunt
A Biography

by GARY PEARCE

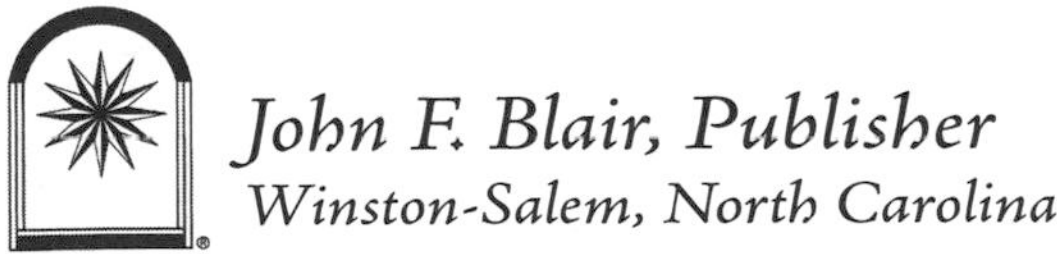
John F. Blair, Publisher
Winston-Salem, North Carolina

1406 Plaza Drive
Winston-Salem, North Carolina 27103
www.blairpub.com

Manufactured in the United States of America

COVER IMAGE

Jim Hunt, November 1996
Cover photo by Dan Crawford Photography; www.dancrawford.com

Library of Congress Cataloging-in-Publication Data

Pearce, Gary.
Jim Hunt : a biography / by Gary Pearce.
p. cm.
Includes bibliographical references and index.
ISBN-13: 978-0-89587-388-0 (alk. paper)
ISBN-10: 0-89587-388-5
ISBN 978-0-89587-394-1
1. Hunt, James B., 1937- 2. Governors—North Carolina—Biography. 3. North Carolina—Politics and government—1951- I. Title.
F260.42.H86P43 2010
975.6'043092--dc22
[B]
2010031894

DESIGN BY DEBRA LONG HAMPTON

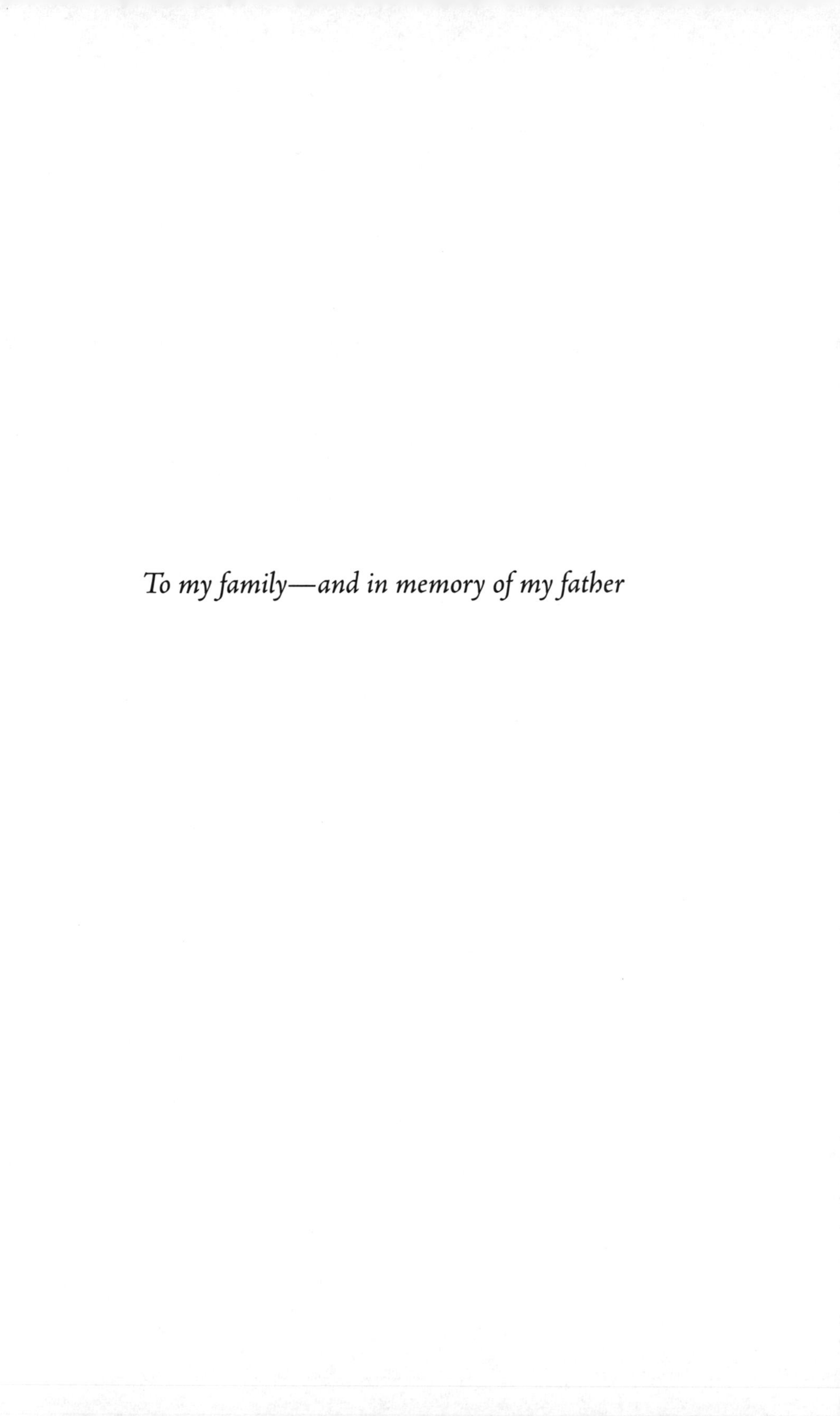

To my family—and in memory of my father

Contents

Author's Note

This is an authorized biography of James B. Hunt, Jr., North Carolina's longest-serving and arguably most influential governor. It's also an account of what I saw and learned as an aide and adviser to Hunt through four gubernatorial administrations and five statewide campaigns.

Clearly, I am not an unbiased observer of Hunt. But I sought in this book to be candid and objective, for much is to be learned from studying his life and the times. Hunt was a remarkably successful politician with the exception of his one campaign for the United States Senate. And the fifty years in which he has been active in politics—from 1960 through this writing in 2010—constitute one of the most volatile, exciting, and transformational eras in the history of North Carolina, the South, and the nation.

Governor Hunt was extraordinarily generous in the time and cooperation he gave me during the almost four years I spent researching and writing. I conducted more than thirty-five interviews with him, which I taped and transcribed. He made his papers, personal files, and photographs available. He encouraged friends, family members, and political associates to talk with me, and they did. I interviewed more than fifty people involved in the events of those years.

Except when Hunt is quoted, this book reflects my viewpoint and conclusions, not the governor's. He read the manuscript and offered minor corrections and suggestions, but he neither asked for nor exercised final approval over what I wrote.

It was my decision to avoid making this book a lengthy recitation of every single initiative and issue of the sixteen years Hunt was governor. Accordingly, many good people and the good things they did were left out. I focused instead on what I regard as the central story. How did a farm boy without wealth or a big political name go so far, so fast, and for so long? How did he get elected governor—and subsequently become the first North Carolina governor in modern times to be reelected? Why did he lose to Jesse Helms in 1984? How—and why—did he come back to be reelected governor a third and fourth time? How did he navigate the stormy political seas of his time and steer North Carolina on a progressive course when much of the South and the nation went in another direction? And how did he deal with the ever-present and ever-troubling issue of race?

In answering these questions and telling this story, I hope my book might give encouragement to some young man or woman who believes that politics can be a noble calling. So many people today are cynical about politics and politicians. And so many politicians have given them reason.

After all my years in and around politics and with Jim Hunt, I'm still an idealist. If good people go into politics, they can make the world a better place. And they can have fun along the way.

Prologue

Jim Hunt campaigned down to the last minute on Election Day, November 6, 1984. Polls showed him losing to Jesse Helms at the end of their long, bitter battle for the United States Senate. But Hunt believed that if he just worked hard enough, he could still win.

He always outworked his opponents. He made more stops, gave more speeches, and shook more hands. He had built the biggest, deepest, and broadest county-by-county, precinct-by-precinct organization in the history of North Carolina. That was how he had won three straight statewide elections, one for lieutenant governor and two for governor.

Hunt was a driven man with relentless energy. He had a burning desire to beat Helms, a two-term senator whom Hunt considered an embarrassment to North Carolina. A demagogue who pandered to the worst in people. An out-and-out racist, Hunt believed.

Early in the morning on Election Day, Hunt was campaigning at precincts along Interstate 85 in the textile-manufacturing counties near Charlotte. Jerry Falwell's Moral Majority was working hard there to reelect Helms and President Ronald Reagan. Buses from conservative evangelical churches were hauling in voters. In the past, Hunt had always done well in those blue-collar precincts. He knew they would be crucial this time.

Outside one polling place, he greeted a young woman, prim and plain, who had her husband and two children in tow. He asked for her vote. She was polite but told him, "I'm sorry, Governor Hunt. We like you, but we're voting for the Christian."

Voting for the Christian? Hunt was dumbfounded. He was a Christian. He took his faith seriously. He was raised that way. He had two great-grandfathers who were circuit-riding Methodist preachers. His father was Sunday-school superintendent at Marsh Swamp Free Will Baptist Church in rural Wilson County in eastern North Carolina. He and his father sang in the choir. His mother was the most Christian-spirited of women. The Free Will Baptists were strict. No working, dancing, or fishing on Sundays. No smoking or drinking ever. Hunt was baptized in the Farmer's Pond near Bailey—a full-immersion baptism—when he was thirteen. He, his wife, Carolyn, and their family had been regular and active church members all their lives, even when they lived overseas.

People of religious faith, Hunt believed, were required to act on what was morally right and wrong. Words weren't enough. Deeds were required. He grew up believing that deeds were what politics should be about—making a difference for people, like country people who didn't have good schools, good roads, and good medical care. Hunt felt called to politics the way some men were called to the ministry. Politics was a way to get things done. And Hunt was good at it.

His was a remarkable rise. He was a farm boy from modest circumstances. He had no personal wealth. He wasn't from a well-known political family. But he was elected lieutenant governor at age thirty-five and governor at thirty-nine. He was a popular and successful chief executive. He earned a national reputation for education reform. He was a tireless recruiter of industries and jobs. He appointed women and minorities to key positions in state government.

Hunt was the first modern-era North Carolina governor elected to two four-year terms. His first year as governor, he had pushed through a constitutional amendment allowing governors to serve two terms. He won reelection in a landslide in 1980, even as Ronald Reagan was beating Jimmy Carter and Democrats were losing in North Carolina and all across the South and the nation.

But now, for the first time, Hunt was losing an election.

The Helms campaign had hammered Hunt for eighteen months with ads mocking him as a pandering politician and a "flip-flopper." On Election Day, when the young woman told him she was voting for "the Christian," Hunt realized that Helms's assault had cost him the support of voters he had always done well with, even the kind of rural people with whom he had grown up.

For the first time, Hunt could not pull off the tightrope act he had always managed before, keeping his balance between city people and country people, conservatives and liberals, old-style political bosses and young reformers, business and labor, and, most of all, blacks and whites.

Race. The oldest and bitterest issue in the South. That's what the campaign had come down to. Even religion took a backseat to race. Hunt had started the campaign 20 points ahead in the polls. Then the United States Senate took up a bill to make Martin Luther King's birthday a national holiday. Helms took to the floor to filibuster against the bill. He ran television ads taunting Hunt: "I oppose a national holiday for Martin Luther King. Where do you stand, Jim?"

Hunt supported the King holiday. A year before the election, one of his closest advisers had warned him that his stand could lose him the election. "In that case, I'll just have to lose," Hunt said.

He did. Helms won another term in the Senate and went on to become North Carolina's best-known and most controversial politician. It was a crushing loss for Hunt. For months, he was numb.

If Hunt had beaten Helms, he might have become president. Hunt, not Bill Clinton, might have been the moderate Southerner elected to the White House. Instead, he went back to Wilson County, to the family farm where he grew up and still lived. He took a job with a law firm in Raleigh and began commuting back and forth daily. He and Carolyn started raising beef cattle and grandchildren. He twice considered running again for the Senate but passed both times.

Then, in 1992, the shifting tides of politics moved his way. Republicans, who had held the governor's office for the eight years after Hunt left, seemed poised to assert their long-term dominance over North Carolina politics. Lieutenant Governor Jim Gardner, a Helms-type conservative who had led the GOP's resurgence in North Carolina in the 1960s, was now the Republican candidate for governor. Democrats fretted that they had no candidate who could beat Gardner.

Hunt thought about what he had done as governor—and what he had left undone. He considered what he might do if he had another chance. He had spent much of his time out of office serving on national study commissions on the issues that were his passions as governor: education and economic growth. Hunt always loved learning. And he had loved being governor. Now, just like when he first ran for office twenty years earlier, he saw an opening. He seized it. He ran for governor again. He swept the Democratic primary. He defeated Gardner in a tough, bare-knuckle campaign. He won his third term as governor.

And he went on to a fourth term in 1996.

Hunt was a different governor the second time around. He was more mature. He no longer had any national ambition. He had eight years of experience as governor. He had eight years out of office—time to think, learn, and grow.

He had one more chance to put his stamp on North Carolina.

In 1950, the state was—in the words of Bill Friday, longtime president of the University of North Carolina—"poor, rural and segregated to the core."

Most people worked on farms or in factories. The economy was based on textiles, furniture, and tobacco. The work was hard, and little money was to be made. Most students dropped out of school before graduating. They didn't need much education to work on the farm or in the mill. The schools were segregated—just like the stores, the restaurants, the neighborhoods, the factories, and the offices. Most people lived in small towns or in the country. Charlotte, Raleigh, and Greensboro were small, sleepy cities—no skyscrapers, no sprawling suburbs, no Research Triangle Park. North Carolina was just another slow, sometimes-backward Southern state.

Then it changed.

By the beginning of the twenty-first century, North Carolina had become one of the most progressive, prosperous, and fast-growing states in the nation. Tobacco, textiles, and furniture were replaced by new technologies and new industries—by pharmaceuticals, health care, biotechnology, computers, electronics, automotive parts, and food products.

Science, research, and technology brought a new economy, and the new economy brought new people—millions of them. Between 1970 and 2010, North Carolina nearly doubled its population, from five million to almost ten million. In the 1990s alone, the population grew by a million people.

They transformed the cities, the towns, and the countryside. Charlotte became a national and then an international center of banking and finance. The Research Triangle Park brought an economic boom and explosive growth to Raleigh, Durham, Chapel Hill, and the once-tiny crossroads of Cary. The coast, the mountains, and the area around Pinehurst became coveted retirement and vacation destinations.

Arguably, no one individual had more to do with that transformation than Jim Hunt. He wasn't the only one to play a part, by any means. Dozens, hundreds, thousands of people brought about the changes that swept the state.

But it was Hunt who held statewide office through twenty years, sixteen as governor and four as lieutenant governor. It was Hunt who was the dominant progressive political leader of his time, who

Hunt firing up the crowd at a Democratic Party rally in downtown Raleigh in November 1996. He loved nothing better than speaking at high-energy campaign events. He was still at it in the 2008 campaign.

Photo courtesy of the *News & Observer*

dramatically expanded the powers of the governor's office. And it was Hunt who—through the vigorous exercise of those powers, through sheer longevity in office, and through his personal force and persuasiveness—set a new course for his state.

Earlier than most North Carolinians, he had seen economic change coming. He relentlessly prodded politicians and the people to embrace that change, to seize the opportunities it offered, to adapt to new technologies, and to take a larger view of the world. He pushed North Carolina into fields like biotechnology and computers. He recruited to the state companies and people from across the country and around the world.

Every schoolroom in North Carolina felt Hunt's impact. He launched a decades-long pursuit of better education—the Smart Start early-childhood program, statewide kindergartens, reading programs, higher standards and higher salaries for teachers—and thereby improved student performance all the way through high school and into college. He preached a message of economic growth through better education that dominated the state's agenda for years.

He changed the face of state government—literally. He systematically brought African-Americans, women, and young people into leadership positions. He appointed the first black cabinet secretary, the first black North Carolina Supreme Court justice, and the first black chief justice. He patiently and determinedly knocked down racial barriers. And when a growing Hispanic population became a hot-button political issue, he was a passionate advocate for fairness and opportunity for those immigrants and their children.

Politically, Hunt defied the tide that swept most every other Southern state. He was the Democratic bulwark who kept North Carolina from going Republican. He developed a political formula that, well after he left office, kept the governor's office and the legislature in the hands of his style of progressive, business-friendly Democrats.

A decade after leaving office, he remained vigorous and influential. He founded two university-based "think and do tanks," as he called them, one on education and one on emerging issues. He traveled widely, spoke often, and was routinely sought out for counsel by young people and old hands alike.

And he stayed active in politics. In 2008, at age seventy-one, he campaigned across the state for Democratic candidates like Beverly Perdue, who was elected the state's first woman governor, and Kay Hagan, who was elected to Jesse Helms's old Senate seat.

Hunt also campaigned for Barack Obama. And nearly a quarter-century after losing a campaign that turned on racial attitudes, he had the satisfaction of seeing North Carolina vote—albeit narrowly—for an African-American president.

Jim Hunt lost the battle to Jesse Helms in 1984. But he won the war for North Carolina's future.

Part I
Rise

Hunt speaks at "Jim Hunt Appreciation Day" in his home community of Rock Ridge in November 1975. The event was an early kickoff to his first campaign for governor.
Photo from Governor Hunt's personal collection

Chapter 1

Farm Boy

The first time Jim Hunt ever called me at home was on a Saturday morning in November 1975. I was a political reporter for the *News & Observer*, the state capital newspaper. Hunt was lieutenant governor, and his office was part of my beat.

That Saturday was "Jim Hunt Appreciation Day" in Rock Ridge, the little farming community where Hunt grew up and still lived. "We're too small to be a crossroads," Hunt would say. "We just have a T-junction." Everybody knew he was planning to run for governor in 1976, and this was a hometown kickoff. Not a formal announcement, mind you. But the folks in Rock Ridge knew Hunt wouldn't be spending a lot of time with them in the months to come. They wanted to show they were behind the boy who had always been headed for bigger places.

Hunt called me because he wanted the *N&O* to run a story about Jim Hunt Appreciation Day. I knew it wouldn't be a big story. But it was hard to say no to Hunt. Besides, it wouldn't hurt to know more about a man who might be North Carolina's next governor. So I made the drive east to Wilson County.

It was the first step in my decades-long journey with Hunt. And it was the first of what seemed like thousands of times he called me at home.

It was a crisp fall day. And a big celebration. The neighbors piled on the food. Eastern North Carolina barbecue. Chicken, biscuits, deviled eggs, potato salad, and slaw. Dozens of pies and cakes.

All afternoon, Hunt, his wife, Carolyn, and their four young children shook hands and talked with old friends, family members, and neighbors. He gave a little speech: "It's too early for me to announce, but I promise you that Rock Ridge will have a candidate in the governor's race next year."

Hunt pulled me aside for a quick tour. "That's the field where I played six-man football," he told me. Rock Ridge High School was too small to field an eleven-man team. At halftime, still in football uniform and pads, Hunt joined the marching band on the field. He played trumpet until the second half started.

After leaving Rock Ridge, I drove back to the *N&O* newsroom in Raleigh and wrote a short story that ran on an inside page.

A few weeks later, Hunt called me again. This time, he asked me to join his campaign as press secretary.

It might sound better to say I abandoned journalism because I was so impressed by Hunt. But the truth is that I was bored at the newspaper. I liked politics. I was tired of being outside the room trying to find out what happened. I wanted to be inside. So I joined Hunt's campaign for governor at the beginning of 1976. I was twenty-six years old.

For the next twenty-five years, Hunt gave me a front-row seat. I worked with him through four terms as governor and five statewide campaigns. I was with him in the lowest times and the highest moments. After 1984, I shared his shock and bitter disappointment. I shared the satisfaction of his comeback in 1992. After he left office in 2001, I watched as he became a respected elder statesman—"the Eternal Governor," one observer called him. Over those years, often inspired by him, sometimes frustrated by him, I thought about that first trip to Rock Ridge. I came to see how Hunt was the product of where he grew up, and the political tradition he grew up in.

At Jim Hunt Appreciation Day, I met Hunt's mother and father, who lived on the same farm where "Jimmy" and his brother, Robert, grew up. Jim and Carolyn had built a modernistic A-frame house for their family on the farm. James Baxter Hunt, Sr., was a flinty farmer, stern and serious. He also worked as a soil conservationist for the United States Department of Agriculture, teaching farmers to prevent soil erosion. He was so frugal that when he gave his grandchildren chewing gum, he would split one stick into even pieces for each of them. He once ran ads looking for "the sorriest farmland east of Raleigh." He wanted to show how good soil-conservation practices could rescue farmland. He found a farm that suited him and paid bottom dollar. Sure enough, he turned it into productive land.

Because he had a federal job, Mr. Hunt couldn't be too overtly active in politics. But he never hesitated to express his opinion about issues, agricultural and otherwise. He always carried a wad of newspaper clippings in his shirt pocket. He would pull out the right one to make a point.

Robert, the younger brother, later described their father as "domineering and dogmatic." Robert and his father had conflicts. Robert rebelled. "I would get in my dad's face." Not Jimmy, Robert recalled years later. "Jim said, 'Yes, sir,' but then went ahead and did what he wanted."

Their cousin Carl Henley, who spent summers with them and later was Jimmy's college roommate, said Mr. Hunt was "very bossy" and a "slave driver" when it came to chores on the farm. "He'd give you an assignment and check on you every five minutes," Henley recalled. Later, as governor, Jim Hunt had the same habit.

Mr. Hunt was from the little community of Pleasant Garden outside Greensboro. James Baxter Hunt, Jr., was born in Greensboro on

May 18, 1937. His mother, Elsie Brame Hunt, was from Wilson County. The Hunts soon moved there to a farm that had been in the Brame and Renfrow families so long it was recorded in Wilson County Deed Book Number One.

People said Jimmy Hunt inherited his father's determination and self-confidence. But they also said he was more like his mother. They invariably described her as a "saint," kindly and generous. When Jimmy and Robert were little and times were hard, hobos would show up at the back door. Elsie Brame Hunt always fed them.

She and her husband both had college degrees, a rarity in a rural area. Mr. Hunt had worked his way through North Carolina State College, getting up at three in the morning to peel potatoes at a boardinghouse. Elsie had gone to Woman's College in Greensboro. In those days, women who wanted to work had two choices: nursing or teaching. She became a schoolteacher. Jim Hunt remembered her spending afternoons and nights at home tutoring students, especially the poor kids who sometimes came to school barefoot and couldn't afford to buy lunch. She believed every child could learn, if you just gave them enough help and time.

Like his mother, Hunt loved reading and learning. He did well in school, except for his habit of talking too much when he finished his work. His fifth-grade teacher cured that by giving him Zane Grey Westerns to read when he finished early. Pretty soon, Hunt had read everything Zane Grey wrote.

Hunt worked hard on the farm, doing chores under his father's precise instructions. Carl Henley said Hunt was "a typical teenager—quite the ladies' man. He always had a girlfriend." Hunt liked sports—and was good at them, according to Henley: "We were the same size, about five-ten. That wasn't that short then. And we both were real fast." Hunt played football and basketball in high school. He dreamed of playing basketball in college but wasn't *that* good.

Through his school years, Hunt was usually the best student in class and the class president. His son Baxter said years later, "If they'd had a student body president in kindergarten, he would have been it."

Above: *Sixteen-year-old Jimmy Hunt, rear, with his father, mother, and brother, Robert, thirteen, on Easter Monday in 1954. In front is Polly Renfrow Brame, Hunt's grandmother, who lived with the family.*

Photo from Governor Hunt's personal collection

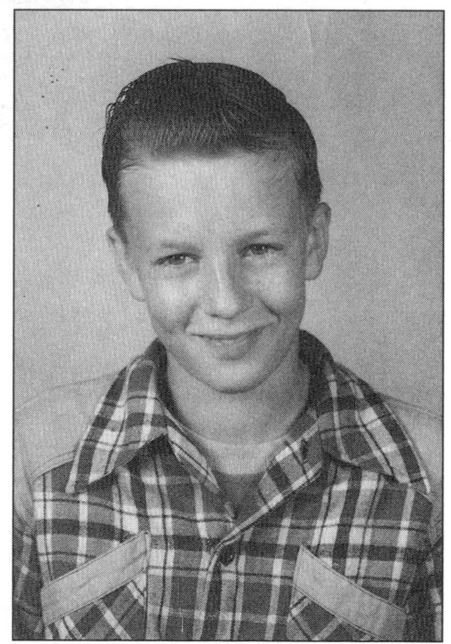

Left: *Jimmy Hunt's grammar-school photo, age nine*

Photo from Governor Hunt's personal collection

D. B. Sheffield congratulates Hunt after his election as state president of the Future Farmers of America in June 1955. Sheffield, Rock Ridge High School's vocational agriculture teacher and FFA adviser, was an early mentor to Hunt.
PHOTO FROM GOVERNOR HUNT'S PERSONAL COLLECTION

He was quarterback on the football team and point guard on the basketball team. He edited the yearbook and was the lead in the class play.

He found a mentor in D. B. Sheffield, the school's vocational agriculture teacher and adviser to the Future Farmers of America (FFA) chapter. Being the "vo-ag teacher" was an important job in rural communities in those days. "D. B." made a big impression on the young man. "He was a man's man," Hunt recalled years later. "He would go out and help the farmers whenever they needed help. If they needed help castrating pigs, he'd go out there and castrate the pigs himself."

Like Elsie Hunt, Sheffield loved learning. He had a way of exciting his students. He pushed them all to excel. Especially Jimmy Hunt. Sheffield spotted something in the boy. He called him "a diamond in the rough." He coached Hunt in the FFA's parliamentary-procedure and public-speaking competitions. "He wanted to win everything," Hunt said. "Every time Rock Ridge was in a contest, he wanted and expected to win it." Hunt already was competitive at sports. He got that from his father. One hot August day, he came home from football practice, tired and sweaty, and announced he didn't want to play anymore. "Hunts aren't quitters," his father told him. Hunt stayed on the team.

Now, Hunt found another outlet for his competitiveness. The boy who loved to talk took to public speaking. In FFA, he said later, "you learned how to speak. You learned how to articulate, you learned how to connect with the audience, you learned how to watch for their reaction, you learned how to develop a good message, and you learned how to try to make it interesting to people, all of which of course has served me throughout the years." Like any good politician, Hunt developed one basic speech that he gave throughout high school. It was about the importance of federal agricultural programs for farmers. "I had written it, and I memorized it. I can remember countless hours driving a tractor, mowing pastures, getting up hay, plowing land, and I'd be reciting that speech. I knew it cold."

He practiced the speech in the school auditorium. Sheffield would sit in the seats, an audience of one, listening and offering suggestions. Hunt gave the speech to his parents at home. He worked on it and constantly improved it.

He won several speaking contests. His school team, with Hunt as president, won the county parliamentary-procedure contest. Then it won the district competition and went to the state finals. It lost there because it went over the time limit. But Hunt won D. B. Sheffield's respect. When Hunt was elected state FFA president in 1955, Sheffield was in the picture beside him, proud as punch.

Just outside Rock Ridge is a two-lane road that became an important part of Jim Hunt lore. It was the road past his family's farm. When he was a boy, it was a dirt road, dusty in summer and hubcap-high in mud when it rained. When Hunt was thirteen, Governor Kerr Scott paved the road. Not personally, of course, but Hunt about thought he did.

Hunt's parents were Democrats, big supporters of Franklin Roosevelt and Harry Truman. In 1948, the Hunts supported Kerr Scott in the Democratic primary for governor.

Kerr Scott was a cigar-chomping dairy farmer from Alamance County. He had been master of the North Carolina Grange, where the Hunts met him. He was elected state agriculture commissioner in 1936. In 1948, he ran a populist campaign for governor against the conservatives who had run the Democratic Party for nearly fifty years. Scott was the candidate of farmers and country people—people like James and Elsie Hunt. Scott called his supporters "branchhead boys"—meaning they lived at the heads of creeks. He promised to get the country people paved roads and electric lights. They voted in droves, and Scott won.

Scott was a real rural populist, the kind of politician who became rare as North Carolina grew more urban and suburban. But he remained a hero and a touchstone for a generation of progressive Democratic politicians, including Jim Hunt.

As governor, Scott pushed a series of progressive reforms through a reluctant legislature. When he met resistance, he gave radio addresses appealing for public support. The legislature gave in. It passed his $200 million road bond program to pave farm-to-market roads and a $50 million school bond issue. Scott pushed the utilities to extend electricity and telephone service to rural areas.

Governor Scott appointed Elsie Hunt the first woman on the North Carolina Board of Health. And he paved the Hunts' road. Hunt always remembered the day the paving machine came. "It dawned on me that if you work in politics, you can change people's lives."

Hunt, left, *age thirteen, and Junior Grangers from Rock Ridge with Governor and Mrs. Kerr Scott at the Executive Mansion in October 1952. Scott was Hunt's first political hero.*
Photo from Governor Hunt's personal collection

Hunt's parents had been involved for years in organizing farm people to do just that. Mr. Hunt organized local Grange groups across eastern North Carolina. Getting into politics was built into Jimmy's DNA. In FFA and the Grange Youth, he discovered that he liked politics—and was good at it.

Even as a boy, Hunt resented how country people got the short end of the stick. Like waiting to see a doctor. When his mother took him to the doctor in Wilson, they sometimes had to wait hours. One day when he was thirteen, Hunt timed the wait. It was three hours. Sixty years later, remembering that day, he pounded the table angrily: "Three hours to see a doctor! That's just wrong! It's wrong to mistreat people like we were mistreated. We weren't getting equal treatment, like people in cities and wealthy areas."

When he got to North Carolina State, he found that even though he was valedictorian of his seventy-two-member high-school class, he was academically behind the boys from the city schools in Raleigh, Greensboro, and up north. That was wrong, too, he thought.

At college, he realized that country people weren't the only victims of discrimination. The worst discrimination was against African-Americans.

Hunt never thought about segregation when he was a boy. He sang "Dixie" at school rallies. He graduated from high school in 1955, one year after the Supreme Court's *Brown v. Board of Education* decision, which declared segregated schools like the ones he went to unconstitutional. Hunt wrote his senior paper about the decision. He argued that the court was wrong and that "separate but equal" was okay.

Wilson County was a racist place. Karl Fleming, who later covered the civil-rights revolution for *Newsweek*, worked for the *Wilson Daily Times* in the 1950s. He wrote in his memoir, *Son of the Rough South*, that, among many whites in the community, "it was assumed that colored people were just slightly elevated animals. . . . Among the proofs cited that they were of a sub-order was an alleged peculiarly pungent body odor. What's more, it was a 'known fact' that there was no use hitting them over the head with a blackjack. Their skulls were so abnormally thick that they were impervious to these blows. And they were perpetually in heat."

Hunt's parents, especially his mother, didn't think like that. They called blacks "Negroes," the polite term at the time. They forbade their boys to say "niggers." Robert recalled years later that he once used that epithet. He said, "Mother took me into the house and told me about how blacks had been slaves and how children had been taken away from their parents." He never used the word again.

At college, Hunt said later, "I got my eyes opened." He met people whose views were worlds apart from what he had learned in Wilson County. He heard professors talk about the evils of racism, segregation, and discrimination. He heard Allard Lowenstein, a student activist and later the leader of the movement to dump Lyndon Johnson, lecture about apartheid in South Africa. Lowenstein had been student body president at UNC–Chapel Hill and an instructor at N.C. State. Hunt remembered when Lowenstein spoke to a National Students Association meeting in Columbus, Ohio: "He told about his experiences in South Africa and the terrible injustices and cruelties of a segregated system. And he spoke about segregation here in America and the South. I was absolutely persuaded that a segregated system was wrong, morally wrong."

He became convinced that segregation was contrary to his religious beliefs. As a boy, he learned in church how Jesus fed the hungry and healed the sick. "I saw my parents do it. I saw them help poor people, visit the sick. My mama always baked a chicken. You had a problem at your house, somebody died or whatever, here'd come Miz Hunt with a chicken." He never had a time of doubt or a crisis of faith. When he went to N.C. State, he joined First Baptist Church in downtown Raleigh. He was there almost every Sunday. He got involved in the youth program. "I'd always come to Sunday school. I always found Sunday school to be a time to really learn and explore and try to figure things out. What does God want you to do? What's right? How do we do it in our lives?"

He came to wonder how, if God loved everyone equally, Christians could justify treating black people unequally. "It just won't square," he said later. "It's completely contradictory."

He and his brother tried to get their father to change his views, which weren't as progressive as their mother's. He wasn't a racist, but he wasn't for integration either. The boys argued with him about race relations. They gave him a copy of the book *Black Like Me* by John Howard Griffin. Mr. Hunt never mentioned the book, but the boys thought he moderated some.

At N.C. State, Jimmy Hunt quickly stood out as a serious young man. Although majoring in agriculture, he enrolled in a political science class taught by Dr. Abraham Holtzman. Holtzman was struck by Hunt the first day of class. The professor went home and told his wife he had a student who would be governor or senator one day. Years later, Holtzman remembered Hunt: "He was bright, accomplished, and sharp. He could immediately deal with an issue, understand all the implications. Most students were afraid to open their mouths, and when they did there wasn't much there."

That presence was one reason that, throughout his life, Hunt had the reputation of someone who had been running for governor since he was in college—or before.

His cousin Carl Henley maintained years later that Hunt announced when they were fourteen or fifteen that he would be governor someday. Quentin Lindsey, a professor of Hunt's at N.C. State who became a mentor and later his aide in the governor's office, recalled meeting Hunt's father when Jimmy was in high school. "I've got a son who'll be going to State," Lindsey recalled Mr. Hunt saying, "and he'll be governor one day."

Hunt always winced at stories like that. "Baloney," he said. His wife and brother agreed. They never heard him talk back then about running for political office.

But everybody agreed there was something about Hunt. People just knew he was going to be governor—or even president—someday. His interest in politics and his experience in parliamentary procedure and public speaking naturally led him into campus politics. He remembered hearing as a freshman that elections were coming up for class officers and the Student Senate. He decided to run as a freshman class representative to the Student Senate. He won. And he kept on winning. As a junior, he was elected vice president of the student body. Then the president-elect dropped out of school. Hunt became student body president, then ran for reelection and served a second term. Before he became North Carolina's first two-term governor, he was a two-term student body president.

Norris Tolson, one of his friends at State who served in his cabinet in the 1990s, said later, "I don't know whether this was real or not, but I remember people at N.C. State telling me, 'This guy has mapped out his political career as a student. He's going to be student body president, he's going to be Young Democrats Club president, he's going to get into statewide politics, and he's going to wind up being president of the

United States.' Whether that was true or not, that was the myth a lot of us understood as kids that knew him."

Paul Essex, another friend from State who later worked for Hunt, recalled when President Hunt spoke at freshman orientation: "His hand gestures and voice were those of a presidential candidate. I thought that at the time. When he was introduced, he raised his hands over his head and waved. He had a big voice and used it. It struck me, made an impression on me. He made a political statement just with his appearance."

It become a joke later: "How do you pick out Jim Hunt in his third-grade picture? He's the one in a coat and tie." Sometimes, he did wear a coat and tie on campus. "And a man's hat," added Phil Carlton, another friend at State.

Hunt dressed that way because he was always heading to a meeting with a dean or the chancellor or to a student government meeting. He usually presided, calling on the skills he had learned in D. B. Sheffield's parliamentary-procedure class and his years of running FFA meetings. Hunt and his friends in the Agriculture School built a political machine at State. They lined it up for Carlton to be elected senior class president when Hunt was student body president. They set it up for Eddie Knox, then Bob Cook, to succeed Hunt. Norris Tolson was still a high-school student in FFA when they recruited him. Sure enough, Tolson was later elected student body president.

Hunt and his friends weren't beer-drinking fraternity boys. A lot of them were married, for one thing. Hunt had met Carolyn Leonard, a farm girl from Iowa, in the spring of 1955, when they were high-school seniors. They both were at a national Grange Youth conference in Hamilton, Ohio. Hunt was president of the North Carolina Grange Youth. Carolyn was on the national Grange Youth committee. Hunt said later, "I spotted this girl with auburn hair who was just pretty as a picture, and I was pretty good at picking out pretty girls, so I knew I wanted to get to know her." He found a way to sit beside her at the last event of the conference.

When he got back home, he told his parents he'd met the girl he

Carolyn and Jim Hunt on their wedding day, August 20, 1958. They met at a Grange Youth conference as high-school seniors. Hunt hitchhiked to Iowa to see her through his early college years.
PHOTO FROM GOVERNOR HUNT'S PERSONAL COLLECTION

wanted to marry. They had a lot in common. Carolyn recalled, "We had very similar backgrounds, very similar. Both growing up in the country, working hard on our families' farms, beliefs, faith, all those things."

Hunt wrote her every day, and he broke up with the girl he had been going with. In college, he started hitchhiking to Iowa to see Carolyn every holiday. "I thumbed out Thanksgiving. I thumbed out Christmas. I thumbed out spring vacation. My family didn't see me all year. I went to Iowa every time."

People did a lot of hitchhiking then. They dressed neatly and held signs for where they were headed. Just to be safe, Hunt carried a switchblade. He never had to use it.

One trip, Hunt went without sleep nearly twenty-four hours. His last ride dropped him off about ten miles from the Leonards' house. He called, and Carolyn's father drove to pick him up. It was a bitterly cold Sunday morning, and the Leonards were heading for church. Hunt was tired but went along. They sat down together in the second row. The church was warm, and he went to sleep within about thirty seconds. "Carolyn was embarrassed to death, but I couldn't keep my eyes open to save my life."

Carolyn attended Iowa State Teachers College, now the University of Northern Iowa, for a year until her father was injured in a farming accident. She left school to help out on the farm and also took an office job at an insurance company. She and Hunt were engaged in the summer of 1957, and she moved to Raleigh. She got a room in a house on St. Marys Street and worked in the textile lab at N.C. State.

In the summer of 1958, they were both employed at the FFA camp at White Lake. Carolyn worked in the store, and Hunt was a counselor overseeing games and activities. When camp was over, Carolyn went back home. Hunt, his parents, and Carl Henley packed up the family's Ford Falcon and drove to Iowa. The couple got married and had a one-day honeymoon in Ames, Iowa, twenty miles away. Then they returned to the Leonards' house, loaded the presents on top of the car, and drove to North Carolina. "You do a lot for love," Hunt said years later.

Back at State, Hunt finished his two terms as student body president.

After graduating, he won a fellowship that enabled him to stay for graduate school, studying agricultural economics. He got more active in the College Democrats and the Young Democrats. And in that seminal year of 1960, he became involved in his first big-time political campaign.

Chapter 2

"Bert Bennett's Boy"

Many idealistic young Americans became excited about politics in 1960 because of John Kennedy. Hunt liked Kennedy, but he had another political hero closer to home: Terry Sanford. Sanford was running for governor that year. His campaign would propel Hunt into North Carolina's progressive political tradition.

Sanford was a paratrooper in World War II. He jumped into France after D-Day and fought in the Battle of the Bulge. Like a lot of men in the war, he came home with a bigger view of the world. Like them, he was impatient to change things. Sanford moved to Fayetteville and became a lawyer. He got active in local civic clubs. He became a Kerr Scott man. And he came under the influence of Frank Porter Graham.

"Dr. Frank" was the president of the University of North Carolina, a gentle man who was one of the South's leading liberals. He was a friend of Eleanor Roosevelt, organized labor, and blacks. At UNC, Sanford listened to Graham speak about how blacks and whites shared the same destiny. Growing up in Laurinburg, a small town near the South Carolina line, Sanford had never heard talk like that. North Carolina was still a solidly conservative state, its university in Chapel Hill a lonely outpost of liberalism.

In 1949, one of North Carolina's United States senators, J. Melville

Broughton, died in office. Governor Scott appointed Frank Graham to finish Broughton's term. The appointment touched off one of the ugliest and most infamous political campaigns in modern history, a battle that presaged decades of political warfare in North Carolina.

Graham ran for a full Senate term in 1950. His strongest challenger in the Democratic primary—the only election that mattered in those one-party days—was Raleigh lawyer Willis Smith. Smith was tall, courtly, and distinguished. He had been president of the American Bar Association, chairman of the Duke University Board of Trustees, and speaker of the North Carolina House of Representatives. He had the support of the business community—and under-the-table help from an energetic young radio newsman in Raleigh named Jesse Helms.

The first primary was close. Graham led but didn't quite get the 50 percent of the votes required to win. Smith thought about conceding the race and not calling for a runoff. But Helms went on WRAL, the local radio station. He called on Smith's supporters to rally at his house and urge him to fight on. They did, and Smith ran.

Smith's campaign leaders decided that their original strategy of painting Graham as too liberal—as a socialist or even a communist—wasn't working. They turned to the old Southern recipe of race baiting. They circulated fliers and ran ads that said, "White People Wake Up." They raised the specter of black boys sitting beside white girls in schools, black men working beside white men in factories, black men sitting beside white women at soda fountains.

The dirty tricks became legendary. Photographs were doctored to show Graham's wife dancing with a black soldier. Rural white voters got late-night phone calls in which black voices urged them to "help Dr. Graham help the black race." The callers purported to be with "the Harlem Committee to Elect Dr. Graham."

The Smith campaign's tactics worked. Graham lost the runoff. Jim Hunt was thirteen years old, and he never forgot that Election Day. He was with his parents at a family wedding reception when they got the news that Frank Graham had lost. Elsie Hunt broke into tears. Hunt said it was the first time he saw his mother cry.

WHITE PEOPLE

WAKE UP

BEFORE IT'S TOO LATE

YOU MAY NOT HAVE ANOTHER CHANCE

DO YOU WANT?

Negroes working beside you, your wife and daughters in your mills and factories?

Negroes eating beside you in all public eating places?

Negroes riding beside you, your wife and your daughters in buses, cabs and trains?

Negroes sleeping in the same hotels and rooming houses?

Negroes teaching and disciplining your children in school?

Negroes sitting with you and your family at all public meetings?

Negroes Going to white schools and white children going to Negro schools?

Negroes to occupy the same hospital rooms with you and your wife and daughters?

Negroes as your foremen and overseers in the mills?

Negroes using your toilet facilities?

Northern political labor leaders have recently ordered that all doors be opened to Negroes on union property. This will lead to whites and Negroes working and living together in the South as they do in the North. Do you want that?

FRANK GRAHAM FAVORS MINGLING OF THE RACES

HE ADMITS THAT HE FAVORS MIXING NEGROES AND WHITES — HE SAYS SO IN THE REPORT HE SIGNED. (For Proof of This, Read Page 167, Civil Rights Report.)

DO YOU FAVOR THIS — WANT SOME MORE OF IT?

IF YOU DO, VOTE FOR FRANK GRAHAM

BUT IF YOU DON'T

VOTE FOR AND HELP ELECT

WILLIS SMITH for SENATOR

HE WILL UPHOLD THE TRADITIONS OF THE SOUTH

KNOW THE TRUTH COMMITTEE

One of the racially charged fliers used by the Willis Smith campaign in 1950 against Frank Porter Graham. Hunt recalled his mother "bursting into tears" when Graham lost the United States Senate primary.

For years, rumors persisted that Helms played a part in the Smith campaign's photo doctoring and its race-baiting handbills. Helms always denied it. But Jim Hunt never believed him. Hunt said years later that the Smith people "were racist, peddling hate and fear." He was right, but they had won.

For the rest of the twentieth century, like some ancient feuding tribes, the descendants of the Graham forces and the Smith forces battled again and again for political supremacy in North Carolina. Jesse Helms and Jim Hunt would become the dominant figures in their rival clans.

In 1954, Kerr Scott exacted a measure of revenge when he won election to the United States Senate. His campaign manager was Terry Sanford. In 1958, Scott died in office. Luther Hodges, "the Businessman Governor," appointed a conservative, B. Everett Jordan, to replace Scott. That made Sanford and the Scott people mad.

Jim Hunt was editor of the *Agriculturalist* student magazine at N.C. State that year. He drafted an editorial blasting Governor Hodges for Jordan's appointment. Hunt said years later, "I thought it was a sellout." But the dean of the School of Agriculture, Dr. D. W. Colvard, told Hunt that the governor was helping the school in other ways. Hunt toned down his editorial. It was a lesson in how to get along in politics—and not burn bridges.

Sanford had already been planning to run for governor in 1960. Hodges's decision to appoint the conservative Jordan made him more determined.

The 1960 election was a turning point for North Carolina. In his book on the campaign, *The Triumph of Good Will*, John Drescher, later executive editor of the *News & Observer*, wrote that the state faced "a stark choice" between Sanford, a moderate on racial issues, and I. Beverly Lake, an avowed segregationist. "In choosing Sanford," Drescher wrote, "voters permanently changed the course of the state and, indirectly, the South."

Just as in 1950, race was an explosive issue. The first civil-rights sit-ins in the nation took place in Greensboro in 1960. Lake, who vehemently opposed school desegregation, was determined to make the election about race. Although he was a mild-mannered law professor, his politics were anything but mild. At his campaign rallies, the band played "Dixie," the crowd waved Confederate flags, and the emcee presented I. Beverly Lake by saying, "I don't know what the *I.* stands for, but it sure isn't *Integration*."

Sanford didn't care for Lake's approach, but he also knew that an outspoken supporter of integration could not be elected governor. He remembered what had happened to Frank Graham. He might have had the same beliefs as Graham, but he sure wasn't going to make the same mistakes. When Lake brought up integration, Sanford would say, "Professor Lake"—he always called him Professor Lake—"is injecting a false issue on integration and it is false because I am and he knows I am opposed to integration. The difference is I know how to handle it and he doesn't."

Of course, Sanford never quite said how he would "handle" integration. Instead, he turned to a set of code words, stock phrases, and stratagems he had been writing down in a spiral notebook for years. Like "prayerful consideration." When asked about race, he would say solemnly that the issue required "prayerful consideration."

Jim Hunt took a lesson from how Sanford handled the issue. "Terry had to be somewhat deceptive. If he hadn't, he'd never have won."

One of Sanford's redneck supporters once confronted the candidate: "Terry, where do you stand on this nigger issue?"

Sanford stared right back at the man and said, "You know exactly where I stand on that."

Relieved, the fellow said, "I thought so, but I wanted to be sure."

Sanford had spent years building his campaign organization across the state. He ran as a fresh face challenging the status quo. He campaigned for better education. He put Lake on the defensive: "We will not be led down the dark trail of fear." Sanford also had the benefit of a sympathetic press corps.

In the Democratic primary runoff, Sanford split the white vote with Lake. He got the great bulk of black votes, though there weren't many in those days before the Voting Rights Act. Sanford won the nomination with 56 percent of the vote—a margin of seventy-six thousand votes.

North Carolina was still a one-party state, so Sanford was virtually assured of election as governor in November. But the old paratrooper was never one to play it safe. Most Democrats in North Carolina and the South supported Lyndon Johnson of Texas for president. But Sanford took a liking to a fellow World War II vet, John Kennedy. In turn, Kennedy and his brother Robert, his campaign manager, had their eyes on Sanford. They were looking for a Southerner, just one Southerner, to break from the pack and endorse Kennedy. A Sanford endorsement would show that Kennedy wasn't just a Northeastern liberal, that a Catholic could win in the South.

After Sanford won the Democratic nomination, the Kennedys started courting him. Robert Kennedy flew down to Raleigh and met Sanford in the College Inn near N.C. State. Kennedy took off his shoes, and they talked for two hours. The meeting was supposed to be secret, but a hotel clerk tipped off reporters. At first, Sanford tried to deny the meeting. But that didn't work. He got embarrassed trying to hide it.

Bert Bennett, Sanford's campaign manager, said years later that John Kennedy and Sanford had a lot in common: "Young, smart, ambitious, loved politics. And in it for the right reasons." Plus, Kennedy looked like a winner. It wouldn't hurt Sanford and North Carolina to have a friend in the White House. Bennett and Sanford thought history was knocking on the door. Sanford told friends, "If you're going to make a fool of yourself, you might as well be a big fool." He not only endorsed Kennedy but made a seconding speech for him at the national convention in Los Angeles: "We need John Kennedy's leadership. John Kennedy is another Franklin D. Roosevelt."

The reaction back home was overwhelming—overwhelmingly negative. Thousands of telegrams poured in denouncing Sanford. So many arrived that his campaign aides wouldn't show them to him.

But Sanford's endorsement of Kennedy just made him more of a hero to young Democrats like Jim Hunt. Hunt and his friend Phil Carlton got involved in Sanford's campaign. Carlton was from Edgecombe County, next door to Wilson. He and Hunt knew each other in high school from when their schools played each other in basketball and when they had FFA public-speaking competitions. Carlton met Sanford through the Methodist Church. Sanford had a way all his life of attracting young people. He had an open, friendly manner. He looked a bit like Andy Griffith in his Sheriff Taylor days.

Carlton worked in Sanford's headquarters in the Carolina Hotel in downtown Raleigh. Hunt was put in charge of organizing college students. He went to campuses all over the state, recruiting students, organizing activities, urging students to vote for Sanford and to get others to do the same. Hunt went to Sanford's campaign kickoff rally in Fayetteville. "I remember being so impressed by the spirit of what he said. A new day, a commitment to change things, and a stress on education."

A couple of times, Hunt rode with Sanford to campaign stops. Once, they went to a tobacco warehouse in Rocky Mount, just north of Wilson. Sanford shook hands and spoke with the men there. After they left the warehouse, Sanford suddenly said, "Hold on. I called a fellow by the wrong name. I have to go back and call him by the right name." They drove back, and Sanford went in and spoke to the man again, getting his name right this time. That made an impression on Hunt.

Hunt worked hard for Sanford—and for Kennedy. Many North Carolina Democrats avoided Kennedy that year. But not Hunt and the students he organized. "We were the only group that would go out and canvass for Kennedy," Hunt said years later.

Sanford later figured that his endorsement of Kennedy took a big chunk of his victory margin. But he won anyway, getting just over 54 percent of the vote against Republican Robert Gavin in the November election. Sanford's winning margin was over 120,000 votes. He figured he would have won by a quarter-million if he hadn't endorsed Kennedy. And Kennedy carried North Carolina by 58,000 votes. The president said the College Democrats helped win the state for him, Hunt boasted.

During the campaign, Hunt made friends—and future political contacts—all over the state. He went to the meetings of Sanford's statewide campaign organization. And he met Bert Bennett.

Although he usually stayed behind the scenes, Bennett was a towering figure in North Carolina politics and in Jim Hunt's career. It was Bennett who spotted Hunt and Carlton in the 1960 campaign. He said later, "You could tell they would be involved twenty years down the road." It was Bennett who kept the Sanford organization together after Sanford left the governor's office in 1965. It was Bennett who decided that Hunt had what it took to be governor and that the old Sanford group should get behind him.

In 1975, when I was an *N&O* reporter, I interviewed Thad Eure, North Carolina's longtime elected secretary of state, in his big office in the Capitol. Eure liked to call himself "the oldest rat in the Democratic barn." He was plugged into the conservative wing of the Democratic Party. I asked him about Jim Hunt. "He's Bert Bennett's boy," Eure sniffed.

Bennett was a wealthy man from North Carolina's upper crust. He and his cousin Jimmy Glenn ran Quality Oil, a family-owned Shell distributor in Winston-Salem. Bennett was comfortably entrenched in the city's aristocracy. But he had progressive attitudes. He had been student body president at Carolina, where he met Sanford. Like Sanford, Bennett was a veteran. He was on an LST during D-Day. When Sanford needed a prominent businessman to support him in 1960, he recruited Bennett to manage his campaign.

Bennett had no use for Beverly Lake and the segregationists. He had eight children and saw racial issues through the eyes of a father: "How would you like to be a parent going down the road, and your child had to go to the bathroom, but you couldn't go to the bathroom?" he said years later. "It's just hard to believe what you'd see. The lynchings, the attitude, what they [African-Americans] were called. Well, that wasn't my nature, as far as race. No, I just had Democratic principles. Sanford

Jim Hunt with Graham Bennett, left, *and Bert Bennett after Hunt left the governor's office in 2001. Bert Bennett was Hunt's political mentor. Graham was the first of three of Bennett's sons to work for Hunt.*
Photo courtesy of Bert Bennett

and Hunt had the right attitude: human dignity, based on ethics and work and not color or background or money."

Bennett relished telling a story that reflected Sanford's personality—and his own. After Sanford won in 1960, he appointed Bennett state Democratic Party chairman. That meant going to the kinds of political dinners and speech-fests Bennett hated. As Bennett told it years later, "We'd won, and there was some damn speaking thing, you know. I had to go. I had to sit at the head table. And I listened to it, and I took a napkin, and I put a note on it, and I said, 'Terry, why do you stay in this business?' I knew his wife had called him, giving him hell, not being home, all that. So he quickly put it back to me, not showing it to anybody. He wrote, 'To keep the sons of bitches out.'"

Bennett was a tough, no-nonsense manager. He had cold blue eyes that could impale a person. He presided over campaign meetings with crisp efficiency. He thought about running for governor himself in 1964 to succeed Sanford, who was limited to one term. But Sanford had become unpopular. To pay for his education program, he had pushed a sales tax on food through the legislature. His opponents called it "Terry's Tax." Private polls showed Bennett couldn't win, close as he was to Sanford.

Hunt's friend Phil Carlton was planning to work full-time in Bennett's campaign. In 1963, Bennett asked Carlton to meet him in Winston-Salem. When Carlton arrived, Bennett told him, "I want to introduce you to somebody. I hope you like him because I'm not going to run for governor. He is. He wants you to work for him just like you were going to for me. So I'm going to introduce you and get out of the room." Then Bennett introduced Carlton to "this distinguished-looking gentleman" named Richardson Preyer.

Preyer was a federal judge appointed to the bench by Kennedy. The wealthy scion of the Greensboro family that owned the Vicks Chemical Company, he had a courtly bearing and a careful temperament. "They had Rich rehearsed," Carlton recalled of his meeting. "They always had him rehearsed, because he had no natural ability as a politician."

Sanford and Bennett tried to pretend Preyer wasn't Sanford's handpicked successor. They had what was supposed to be a secret meeting in Burlington one Sunday afternoon to rally Sanford's supporters behind Preyer. Sanford sneaked in wearing a hat and sunglasses. But somebody had tipped off the *News & Observer*, and a reporter followed Sanford's car to the meeting. "The great cover-up lasted two days," Carlton laughed later.

Nat Townsend, a Raleigh lawyer, was Preyer's campaign manager. But Phil Baddour, a college student from Goldsboro whom Hunt had recruited for the campaign, recalled going to a meeting at the headquarters in Raleigh. Bennett was presiding. "There was no question who was in charge," Baddour said. Eight years later, during Hunt's campaign for lieutenant governor, Baddour went to a similar meeting. Bennett was clearly in charge there, too.

Preyer led the first primary in 1964, just as Frank Graham had in 1950. But once again, Jesse Helms played an on-air role. By now, Helms was working for WRAL's television station. Over and over on primary night, he emphasized to viewers that Preyer was leading because of "the black bloc vote." Carlton remembered Preyer supporters calling headquarters and asking, "Do you see what they're doing to us on WRAL?"

I. Beverly Lake ran again but finished third this time, behind Preyer and Dan Moore. Moore was a judge from the mountains who, though conservative, did not have Lake's segregationist image. Moore got Lake's endorsement in the runoff. That doomed Preyer. Just as in 1950, the progressive Democrats suffered a bitter loss. And just as in 1950, it was all about race.

After the primary, Hunt flunked the state bar exam. The star scholar from Rock Ridge—a Phi Beta Phi honor student at State, the serious young man who had received a bachelor's degree in agricultural education and a master's in agricultural economics and then earned his law degree at Carolina—failed. He had spent too much time in the campaign and too little studying. "We were driving to the Carolina Hotel in Raleigh every night and working until eleven o'clock," recalled Jane Smith Patterson, another young Preyer worker. Years later, Hunt delighted in reassuring young people who had the same experience. "You know that failing the bar is a prerequisite for being governor of North Carolina," he would tell them. But it was a crushing disappointment at the time.

He quickly arrived at a backup plan. One of his old professors at State, Quentin Lindsey, was working with the Ford Foundation as an economic adviser to the kingdom of Nepal. He was trying to persuade farmers there to adopt modern methods. He needed help, and he thought about Jim Hunt: smart, hardworking, a farm boy himself with an outgoing personality that would enable him to get along with the Nepalese. Lindsey sent Hunt a letter in 1964 offering him a Ford Foundation post in Nepal.

Carolyn Hunt said later that she and her husband had talked about joining John Kennedy's Peace Corps. They were idealistic and believed in serving people. But the Peace Corps wasn't taking married couples with children. By now, the Hunts had two. Rebecca was born in Raleigh the last day of 1960—"just in time for the income-tax deduction," Hunt recalled—while he was in graduate school. James Baxter Hunt III was born in 1962 while Hunt was working for the Democratic National Committee in Washington. He was national college director, organizing campuses across the country, the way he had done for Sanford in 1960. Hunt worked at the DNC during the day and went to law school at George Washington University at night. He did a workshop on precinct organization in Massachusetts for the Senate campaign of young Edward Moore Kennedy in 1962. That same fall, he was supposed to be on Air Force One when President Kennedy flew to a political event in California. The event was canceled. It was the week of the Cuban Missile Crisis. Hunt later remembered wondering whether or not the world was going to be blown up—and whether or not there was any sense in going to class. Of course, he kept going to class.

Now, back in North Carolina, their future uncertain, the Hunts decided to pack up their young family for what Hunt cheerfully called "an adventure" in a Third World country halfway around the globe. Carolyn Hunt described the Nepal adventure years later: "For two years, we couldn't call home. We had no TV, just a short-wave radio. Electricity only a few hours every day. We had to make it on our own." But the experience "told us, when we were quite young and took two children and had a third one there, that we could make it on our own. You had to create your own family time. You didn't have movies, all those things. You didn't have the canned stuff you can rely on here. We had to shop for food in an open-air bazaar and cook meals from scratch."

Hunt with villagers in Nepal, where he and his family lived from 1964 to 1966. Hunt was a Ford Foundation economic adviser. The experience shaped his approach to economic development and the global economy.
Photo from Governor Hunt's personal collection

Carolyn taught second-graders at a school in Katmandu, the capital. She had gone back to college, taking night and summer courses while Hunt was finishing at State. She earned her degree in education at UNC–Chapel Hill, graduating the same day Hunt did from law school.

She had their third child, Rachel, at a missionary hospital in Katmandu. Rachel developed gastroenteritis and nearly died. It was mostly up to Carolyn to care for the children because Hunt spent much of his time "out in the boondocks" working with farmers and village leaders.

Hunt was part of a team of four economists advising the royal government in Katmandu on a five-year economic-development plan that included land reform, a system of land records, and the adoption of modern agricultural methods. If he had been sent to a country like India, Hunt said later, he might have been buried in a corner of the government bureaucracy. Instead, he and the Ford Foundation team worked with top government leaders, helping develop a plan for an entire nation.

He flew around the country in a DC-3, enjoying views of the Himalayas and sometimes Mount Everest. The plane would land on a grass strip after buzzing the cows to chase them off. If somebody knew he was coming, Hunt might get a ride to the village of Budhabare, nestled against the mountains. "Most of the time, the telegram didn't get through and there wasn't a Jeep there, so I walked in with my bedroll on my back, a pack with my water and filter and food and a mosquito net, all the things I had to have. You walked by yourself if there was nobody there to meet you. And I walked until I got to that village thirteen miles away."

Hunt saw worse poverty than he had ever witnessed at home—"people living in abject poverty, dumping human waste in a little ditch down the side of our street, washing clothes in sewers."

Hunt read the *Times of India*, the *Economist* magazine, and publications about Southeast Asia. "I learned to get a big view of a country," he said later. "What you have to do to develop a nation—the importance of educating people, providing infrastructure like roads, electricity, banks." His time in Nepal, he said, made him less ideological and more pragmatic. "I learned a basic thing" that shaped his approach when he became governor: "It isn't just a matter of dividing the pie. You can grow the pie. That's a very fundamental thing to know. Because a lot of people don't understand that and just want to fight and take it away from one person to give it to another. But my approach has always been that, if we're smart about it and have the right policies, we can find a way to grow the pie, and everybody can have more."

The experience in Nepal gave Hunt a global view and shaped the kind of governor he would become. "I learned that there was a big world out there. I'd been in it, and I'd read about it a lot. So I was very comfortable later on in trying to get jobs and investments from anywhere—and in learning how other countries did it. I always wanted to learn who's doing things better."

All the while, Hunt was preparing to return home. He kept up with politics. He had Phil Carlton clip "Under the Dome," the political column in the *News & Observer*, and mail him the articles. On January 1, 1966, the beginning of his second year in Nepal, he began studying to retake the bar exam. He established a strict routine. He went to his office from seven to nine every morning, six days a week, to pore over his law books. It was cold, and the room had only a small heater, so he wrapped up in a blanket.

When the Hunts got back home, he took the bar exam again. He passed this time.

Chapter 3

Young Democrat

After Hunt brought his family back to Wilson in 1966—and passed the bar exam—he started a typical small-town law practice. He searched land titles, settled estates, and handled separations and divorces. When troubled couples came in, "I had this view that my job was to try to get them back together." Sometimes, he succeeded. Problem was, he didn't get paid then. "That was pretty counterproductive work," Hunt laughed later. "But I still see couples today who were bent on divorce, and I got them back together."

He discovered that, for many young couples, marital troubles started over money. "You don't make enough, and you start fussing and fighting about what to do with the money and how to pay the bills."

He learned that clients sometimes lied to him. He was the court-appointed attorney for a woman accused of killing her husband with a hatchet. "She said she didn't do it, and I believed her." But she was lying. She skipped town.

Hunt represented another woman who killed her husband. The

man was an alcoholic who beat his wife and their children. When he came home roaring drunk, she and the kids would have to leave the house and sleep in the cornfield. "One night, he started beating her terribly," Hunt recalled. She got the shotgun, they wrestled, and the gun went off. He died. Hunt convinced the judge to find no probable cause to indict her. "The judge probably figured that, if she shot him, he deserved it, and let her off," Hunt said. The verdict left him with a respect for judges' and jurors' common sense.

The Hunts' fourth child, Elizabeth, was born in Wilson. Carolyn had her hands full running the home and raising the children. Hunt was a young man on the go. He was a joiner. He joined the Jaycees and the Sertoma Club. He joined the local bar association.

He got involved in the Young Democrats Clubs of North Carolina. The YDC was the minor leagues for up-and-coming politicos. The YDC was where they made contacts, became known, and got ready to run for office. Terry Sanford had been YDC president in the 1950s.

Hunt and his friend Allen Thomas, another lawyer in town, organized a YDC chapter in Wilson County. Hunt said later, "Politics had always been cut-and-dried in Wilson County, run in large measure by the conservative Democrats. But nobody was doing anything between campaigns. So I got all the active young people together, and we had monthly meetings, went to state meetings and conventions."

Hunt started moving around the state, speaking in the forty-plus counties that had Young Democrats Clubs. He knew a lot of the Young Democrats from when he was at State and Carolina and when he worked for Sanford and Preyer. He knew how to make friends—and count votes. In 1967, he was elected state YDC president. He led a delegation to the national YDC convention in Las Vegas. One member of the North Carolina group was an outspoken black student from North Carolina A&T State University in Greensboro: Jesse Jackson.

Meanwhile, the Democratic Party was being torn apart in the South. First came the civil-rights revolution. The Voting Rights Act, signed by Lyndon Johnson in 1965, brought newly enfranchised African-American voters into the Democratic Party. Conservative whites

Hunt at the beach with daughters Rachel (left) *and Elizabeth in 1975*
Photo from Governor Hunt's personal collection

began abandoning the party and becoming Republicans. Through 1966 and 1967, the Vietnam War split Democrats even more deeply.

Hunt was more liberal than most whites in his home county but more conservative than many Young Democrats. He thought the party needed moderates and conservatives: "I knew that, to win, you had to reach across lines, build bridges, get people to work together, so that we could have a broad-based majority."

Hunt saw what was happening just down the road in Rocky Mount, where a silky smooth young man named Jim Gardner was becoming the boy wonder of Republican politics. More than anyone else—more than Jesse Helms—Gardner led the Republican Party to political power in North Carolina, especially in the eastern part of the state, which had been hostile to Republicans since the Civil War.

A local boy who married the daughter of one of Rocky Mount's wealthiest families, Gardner was part of a group of businessmen who started the Hardee's hamburger chain. He wasn't the business brains, but he was a great salesman. He was young, good looking, and dynamic. Hardee's was a roaring success. Gardner was hailed as a business hero. He got involved in an American Basketball Association franchise that brought a professional team, the Carolina Cougars, to hoops-crazy North Carolina. And he went into politics.

Hunt remembered hearing Gardner speak to a local Jaycees club. Gardner railed against Washington. He wheeled out what Hunt thought were racial code words: welfare, forced integration, an all-powerful federal government. He denounced Democrats and their policies with a simple indictment: "That's just wrong." Hunt didn't like Gardner's politics, but he recognized that the rhetoric was powerful stuff.

In 1966, Gardner took on what looked like a foolhardy challenge to Harold Cooley, the longtime Democratic congressman from the area. Cooley had risen to the ultimate position of power for a Southern politician in those days. He was chairman of the House Agriculture Committee. Cooley presided over the tobacco and peanut support programs that made farming profitable for thousands of people in his rural district. But 1966, which brought the first off-year election since

Lyndon Johnson's 1964 landslide, was a good year for Republicans. Race trumped tobacco and peanuts. Gardner beat Cooley in a stunning upset.

Hunt saw clearly what could happen if North Carolina voters thought the Democratic Party was too liberal. He explained years later, "The goal was to win, not to just rail about issues. Young Democrats in many places would take far-out positions. But you win in politics by being on the right side of issues according to how people see things and then by pulling together people from various points of view, various factions within the party." If the party didn't win, it couldn't change things.

Hunt tried to steer a middle course amid the tensions tearing apart the South and the Democratic Party. It wasn't easy.

The night Martin Luther King, Jr., was assassinated in April 1968, Hunt got a call at home from a neighbor, a professor at Atlantic Christian College (now Barton College) in Wilson. Some whites in the community were planning to attend a memorial service for Dr. King at a black Baptist church downtown on Sunday. It was a way of showing black citizens that whites, too, opposed bigotry, racism, and violence. Would Hunt join them? He would. He went to the service. At the end, the minister announced that the service would conclude with a candlelight procession to the courthouse, about three blocks away. Hunt's antennae went up. He knew how some whites would feel about the procession. "Here we were," he recalled years later. "This service was to be concluded on the steps of the courthouse, and people were asked to go there in a procession." He walked quietly with the others down the street. The mood was solemn and mournful, he recalled. At the courthouse, a prayer was offered, and the service ended.

The procession would plague Hunt politically for years to come. Betty McCain from Wilson, one of his earliest and most enthusiastic supporters, recalled that "he really took a beating over that," then and in the future. At one of the first strategy meetings I attended when I joined the Hunt campaign in 1976, we talked about how the story had morphed into rumors that Hunt participated in a civil-rights march.

Whispers were even heard that he had marched with Dr. King. In Wilson, some racist whites never forgot. They grumbled that Hunt was too liberal, pro-black, a "nigger lover." Even members of their own church "talked ugly" about the Hunts for years, McCain said.

Hunt was at another searing event in 1968: the Democratic National Convention in Chicago. While protesters and police battled outside, Hunt was inside the hall in coat and tie. He was the sponsor of a resolution to make each state YDC president a member of the Democratic National Committee, which was then made up of one man and one woman from each state. He was allowed to address the convention about his resolution. He went around and signed up delegates in support. He studied how politics worked on the inside. "I was alert to learning who these people were in the different factions of the party. I made it my business to get to know them personally in Chicago." Since Carolyn was from Iowa, he made a special point of getting to know the Iowa Democrats. The Iowa caucuses weren't important in presidential races then, but the connection might have proved valuable in a presidential race later.

He kept going all hours, meeting people and lobbying for his resolution. It didn't pass, but he thought many North Carolinians were impressed by how he handled himself. Hunt was always watching, learning. "I was interested in all the people, the speakers, the chairman of the convention, how the delegations worked. I'd seen this kind of thing in state conventions and some of the national groups I'd been involved with, but it was a real learning experience."

He and other delegates inside the hall, though, couldn't experience what Americans were seeing on television—and how it was hurting Democrats. The scenes of rioting didn't go down well with the public. The protests weren't Hunt's style. He was older than most antiwar Democrats, having been born in 1937, a decade before the baby boomers. He was a boy during World War II. He remembered the blackouts. He had kept up with the battles on big maps. He believed that evil existed in the world and America had to confront it. "I was a hawk. I didn't have any sympathy for the demonstrators who were trying to force us out of Vietnam." Because he was married and had four children, he was never eligible for the military draft.

When he got back home after the convention, he spoke to civic groups and praised Chicago mayor Richard Daley for keeping order in the streets. "Probably the line in my speeches when I came home that got the most applause was when I applauded Mayor Daley."

Hunt didn't care for Gene McCarthy. He supported Hubert Humphrey. He liked Lyndon Johnson. "Johnson knew poor folks," Hunt felt. He admired Johnson's mastery of politics—his command of issues, his gut feeling for what people wanted, and his detailed knowledge of members of Congress, what they wanted and what their districts and states needed. Most of all, Hunt admired Johnson's ability to put together coalitions and get bills passed.

Hunt knew Democrats were in trouble in the 1968 election. After Martin Luther King was assassinated, riots broke out in cities across the country. Lyndon Johnson announced that he would not run for reelection. Robert Kennedy was assassinated. The nation seemed to be coming apart. The Democratic Party clearly was.

The Democratic candidate for governor in North Carolina was Bob Scott, Kerr Scott's son. Bob Scott gave the national ticket a wide berth. After all, he had a tough opponent in November. Jim Gardner had grown restless after just two years in Congress and was now the Republican candidate for governor. This might be the year Republicans broke through and won the governor's race in North Carolina.

Terry Sanford and Bert Bennett moved to Washington for three months to help Humphrey's campaign. Sanford was the national chairman of Citizens for Humphrey, and Bennett ran the operation. In the end, Humphrey came close. Bennett said years later, "I believe another week or two and we'd have won it."

Humphrey lost to Richard Nixon, who later fashioned his "Southern strategy" of winning over disaffected conservative Democrats. The race wasn't close in North Carolina. Nixon carried the state with just under 40 percent of the vote. Humphrey finished third with 29 percent, behind George Wallace, the segregationist governor of Alabama who

Hunt greeting Vice President Hubert Humphrey in 1967. Hunt was president of the North Carolina Young Democrats Clubs. He supported Humphrey for president in 1968 and spoke at the Democratic National Convention in Chicago.
Photo from Governor Hunt's personal collection

ran as a third-party candidate and won 31 percent. Bob Scott held on to win the governor's race over Jim Gardner by the narrow—for then—margin of 54 to 46 percent.

The aftermath of the 1968 Chicago convention—and Governor Scott—soon gave Hunt a political boost. The convention had been dominated by state delegations handpicked by party bosses. Now, liberal Democrats were demanding reforms. The national party decreed that state parties had to be more inclusive and more open to women, minorities, and young people. Scott appointed Hunt to chair a state party commission to come up with a reform plan. The task required a delicate balancing of old and young, liberals and conservatives, establishment and activists, blacks and whites, men and women, Sanford supporters and Lake supporters, Jesse Jackson people and George Wallace people.

Hunt held a series of statewide hearings during which he sat patiently for long hours listening to Democrats vent their grievances and offer their ideas. He treated every witness politely and respectfully. He and his commission members heard anybody who came out. Hunt remembered one day in Durham when the organizer of some black street protests testified. He was Ben Ruffin, who later traded in his Afro and dashiki for a trimmed look and a three-piece suit when he became Governor Hunt's minority-affairs assistant.

Hunt got to know every one of his sixty-plus fellow commission members—not just their names but "those little things you do, find out about somebody's work and family and all that." That was something he had learned from Bert Bennett. Bennett never started a conversation by talking about politics. He asked about work, family—something personal. It was a way of learning more about people and putting them at ease.

Jim Hunt welcomed former I. Beverly Lake supporters to his commission. "We didn't want anybody keeping anybody else out," he said. How did he overcome his differences with the Lake supporters on race? "By moving on. We didn't talk about race. The Lake people felt like they were kind of left out and ostracized in a sense. Some of the liberals despised them. I wanted them all back in the party. I went to them. I asked them to be part of it."

His commission proposed—and the party adopted—a series of reforms that included new state party vice chairmanships to be filled by a woman, a black, and a young person. The commission also supported lowering the voting age from twenty-one to eighteen.

Hunt made friends. He was building his own statewide organization, just like Sanford had. He kept card files on them all: the boys he had known back in FFA, the State students he met in campus politics, the law-school students, everybody he had met in the Sanford and Preyer campaigns, and everybody he had met since then.

He was ready to jump into elected politics himself. Hunt said later that, despite all the stories about his mapping out a political career as a teenager, "I didn't have a set plan. I didn't have a certain thing in mind." He had always followed politics. As an eleven-year-old in 1948, he kept up with Harry Truman's race for president. Later, "it dawned on me that I'd enjoy being deeply involved in politics, to make changes," he said. Carolyn Hunt recalled that it was in the late 1960s when he began to consider being a candidate.

Hunt turned to Bert Bennett. He recalled that in 1971, "I wrote Bert a long handwritten letter on a yellow legal pad, telling him about what I was thinking and the various positions I was considering."

I asked Bennett in 2007 if he remembered Hunt's letter. He did. What did it say? "Well, he was in heat, you know what I mean?" Bennett recalled. "He was just like Sanford in '60. Hunt, he was eaten up, eaten up with long-range plans in politics."

Phil Carlton, who felt he was closer to Bennett than Hunt was, recalled that Hunt asked him to set up a meeting of the three of them. They got together in Greenville for dinner one night in 1971. Bennett was making his annual inspection tour of his service stations and motels around the state. As Carlton recalled the meeting, Hunt told Bennett he wanted to run for office. Bennett wanted to be sure Carlton had no competing plans. Carlton didn't. From that day, Bennett—who made a fetish of working for only one candidate at a time—dedicated himself to Hunt.

Hunt was raring to run. But for what? The usual launching pad for young politicians was the legislature. But Hunt's law partner Russell Kirby was already in the North Carolina Senate, and Wilson County would hardly stand for two lawyers from the same firm in the legislature. Hunt and Bennett started looking at statewide offices. North Carolina has an elected Council of State that encompasses not just well-known offices like lieutenant governor and attorney general but also lesser-known ones like secretary of state, commissioner of agriculture, state auditor, treasurer, and superintendent of public instruction.

Hunt thought about running for commissioner of agriculture. His hero Kerr Scott had held that office. But now it belonged to a longtime incumbent, Jim Graham. Unlike governors, who were limited to one term, Council of State members could serve forever. Thad Eure had been secretary of state since 1936.

By coincidence, North Carolina had revised its Constitution in 1970. One provision made the office of lieutenant governor full-time, with a salary and a staff. Hunt and Bennett knew a statewide race was a big step for a first-time candidate, but they were nothing if not audacious.

Sitting in church in Wilson one Sunday early in 1971, Hunt made up his mind to run. Church was one of the few places where the talkative, hyperactive Hunt had to sit and listen. Or think. Years later, he remembered being in church that Sunday and considering his political future, especially the impact a campaign would have on his family's finances. "I said to myself, 'I've got these fees that are going to be coming in, estates that are going to be settled and so forth.' So I could project a year's income from my law practice with the fees I'd built up." He could feed his family for a year. But at the end of that year, he wouldn't have any money left. If he lost, he would have to start over. He probably would have to borrow money for a while.

Then "it struck me that sometimes you just have to take a leap of faith."

Chapter 4

Old Politics, New Politics

Hunt started his campaign for lieutenant governor early in 1971. He began moving around the state, meeting the leaders of the old Sanford-Preyer organization—the "keys." The network was organized like a military operation. Sanford and Bennett were at the top. Under them were regional keys responsible for five or six counties each. Then came the one hundred county keys. Each county was given a quota of money to raise for the campaign. The keys were responsible for meeting the quotas. They took Sanford around when he campaigned in the counties. In return, they were the go-to guys in their counties after Sanford won when anybody wanted something from the governor—a road or a state job or an appointment to a judgeship or state board.

"Bert was sending me to see all the Sanford keys around the state," Hunt said. Then Bennett would check in with the keys to learn what they thought. What he heard was encouraging. Bennett sent Hunt to see Clint Newton in Shelby. Newton arranged for Hunt to speak to the Rotary Club. Newton supported him from then on.

Hunt also went to Beverly Lake people and Dan Moore people. He traveled to Wilmington to meet John Burney, one of Lake's biggest supporters in 1960. He told Burney and others who hadn't supported Sanford that he understood their concerns that the party was becoming too liberal. He assured them he wanted it to have room for conservatives, too. Burney agreed to support him.

Then there were all the younger—and usually more liberal—contacts Hunt had made in FFA, at N.C. State, on college campuses around the state, in the Young Democrats, and on the party reform commission. Phil Baddour, the UNC student from Goldsboro whom Hunt had recruited for Preyer, recalled, "He was so dynamic, driven, popular, knowledgeable, you knew he'd be successful. He believed in things you cared about."

And there was Joe Grimsley. About the same age as Hunt, Grimsley had grown up in Stantonsburg in Wilson County. He and his brothers were all good ballplayers, in every sport. Grimsley, stocky and solid—he was later called "the Bulldozer"—went to UNC–Chapel Hill. Then he worked with the Peace Corps in Honduras and Washington, D.C. Hunt and Grimsley had known each other almost all their lives. Their fathers were friends. They had the same "go forward" philosophy of Kerr Scott. "We were rural people who knew what hard work was like," Hunt said. "We cared about other people, and we wanted to see progress made." One day in the early 1970s, Grimsley bumped into Hunt on a street in Washington. Hunt told him it was time "to come back home because we can do something to change the state." Grimsley sold his house in Oriental near the coast so he could work on the campaign full-time without pay.

Jane Smith Patterson, who lived in Greensboro, was another committed young volunteer. "All of us worked for nothing," she recalled. "We believed in him so much. We were a ragtag group."

Hunt needed a campaign manager. Bennett wasn't interested in living in Raleigh and doing it. Hunt later said that one of the hardest things to find in politics is a good campaign manager. He found one in Grimsley.

Grimsley knew how to make the different parts of a campaign run and mesh smoothly together. Hunt counted on him to keep the big

A flier from Hunt's first political campaign—the race for lieutenant governor in 1972. The coat-over-the-shoulder photo was meant to portray Hunt, then only thirty-five, as a young man on the go.

picture in mind—"what the state was like, where the voters were, what issues would be appealing to people, how to use communications and technology, and [how] to invite in a variety of people and not be threatened by them, but welcome them, welcome help and reach out for different kinds of people."

Hunt was to have a complicated and sometimes uncomfortable relationship with Grimsley over the years. Grimsley thought he was smarter than Hunt, and he didn't hide it. He talked openly about how "somebody needs to manage Jim." But Jim did not want to be managed, especially by Joe.

Tension also grew between Grimsley and Bennett. The two men were worlds apart. Grimsley thought Bennett was "old school." Bennett believed in statewide organizations built on personal relationships and patronage jobs in government; Grimsley believed in coalitions built around issues and groupings of women, teachers, labor, and liberals. Bennett was a businessman; Grimsley worked in government all his life. Grimsley believed in public opinion polling; Bennett took his own polls by calling his contacts across the state. Grimsley cared passionately about issues. Hunt said years later, "I never had a discussion in my life with Bert Bennett about issues." Grimsley believed campaigns were becoming more and more about television ads. Bennett saw that, but television ads cost money, and he never quite trusted the rising new class of political consultants—he always referred to them as "the so-called pros"—to spend the campaign's money responsibly.

Still, Hunt valued Grimsley. Grimsley attracted bright people with creative policy ideas. He understood how issues could cement the support of teachers, state employees, union members, women, and black voters. He knew how to make the complicated pieces of a statewide campaign run. But Hunt was never willing to trust Grimsley with the title of campaign manager. He made him "campaign director."

Bennett and his group raised the seed money to launch Hunt's campaign. And for two years, Hunt campaigned flat out, full-time for lieutenant governor. He said later, "I figured during that campaign that I drove a hundred thousand miles and I shook a quarter of a million hands. I would go to Kannapolis and go to the plant gates at Cannon Mills. I've been there many times. I'd be out there before the sun came up, and when the first shift came in I'd shake hands with them and hand them a card."

He boasted that he went to 102 counties. North Carolina has only 100 counties, but U.S. 64 was closed on one trip to the far western mountains, so he had to go through a pair of counties in Georgia.

Nobody saw Hunt's intensity more closely than Mike Davis, a recent Wake Forest University graduate who joined the campaign as a volunteer driver. Jane Smith Patterson recalled that, after a couple of late nights, a sleepy Hunt ran off the road, "so we got Mike to drive him."

Davis, though a dozen years younger and six inches taller than Hunt, could hardly keep up as Hunt charged down streets on the way to meet people. "We'd start at six in the morning and go to midnight every dad-gummed day of the week," Davis said. "The guy never stopped." Not a minute was wasted. If they had extra time, Hunt would look for a pay phone by the road. Davis would park and wait while Hunt checked in with Bennett or Grimsley. Like Sanford's run in 1960, Hunt's campaign portrayed the candidate as a young man on the go. His brochures had a picture of Hunt with his coat slung over his shoulder.

"Gosh almighty," Hunt said years later. "It's the hardest work in the world. Shake hands with a thousand people a day. And I don't just shake hands, I grip 'em. I'd hold their hand and hold their arm, get 'em almost in an embrace and talk to 'em, look 'em in the face and get a reaction from them, have a conversation with 'em."

Hunt traveled cheap and lived off the land. "Sometimes, I'd stay in people's homes. Most times, I'd stay in cheap motels." He and Davis usually shared a room.

Hunt came up with a gimmick to bind supporters to him: a little lapel pin shaped like North Carolina. He got the idea from the Jaycees. The campaign ordered thousands of the pins, which would become a trademark of Hunt's supporters throughout his career. Hunt and Davis carried "Jim Hunt pins" in their coat pockets, always ready to put them on new supporters. If he was caught short, Hunt would take off his own pin and stick it on a person's coat. Davis saw it as Hunt almost anointing his supporters, saying, "You're part of the team. You're important."

He started addressing bigger groups. Thanks to all that experience speaking in public—FFA, N.C. State, the Young Democrats—Hunt was good at it. Early in the campaign, he spoke to the state teachers' association in Wilson. He was comfortable with the group. His mother was a teacher. He had a degree in agricultural education and had done practice teaching himself. Hunt spoke about raising teacher salaries. "Damned if the teachers didn't like it," he remembered. "I came out on cloud nine."

His restless energy never flagged. Paul Essex, who had known Hunt at N.C. State, quit his job at the *News & Observer* to work without pay in the campaign. Essex recalled going with Hunt on a long day of campaigning in Charlotte. They started early with a breakfast and ended up staying overnight at a supporter's house. The host, Essex, and Hunt watched the news. Hunt sat in an easy chair. "After a few minutes, Hunt starts patting his hands on the armrests," Essex said. "Suddenly, he jumps up and goes to the phone and makes a call." Then he sat back down. "After a few minutes, he jumps up again and makes another call."

Then back down. Back and forth he went, again and again, until it was time for dinner.

The first time I met Hunt was during the 1972 campaign, at a greet-the-candidates event in Fuquay-Varina, just south of Raleigh. I had heard he was a comer in politics, so I was surprised to see a slight young man with his dark hair combed back in a pompadour that screamed *country*. To compensate for his age and his youthful appearance, Hunt adopted a serious, solemn air. He didn't look very impressive to me.

He had formidable opponents: Roy Sowers, a member of Governor Scott's cabinet; Allen Barbee, a member of the State House; Margaret Harper, the publisher of a small newspaper; and Reginald Frazier, a black lawyer.

Hunt recalled, "The opponent that we probably thought about the most early on was Roy Sowers." Sowers had been in Governor Scott's campaign and had the connections to raise money. But Hunt had money, too, thanks to Bennett and friends. And he had an organization that rivaled those of candidates for governor. Plus, Hunt was relentless. When Durham's powerful black political committee endorsed Frazier, the black candidate, Hunt put together his own coalition in the county. He got the conservatives, including the fundamentalist ministers who later became an important part of the Reagan-Helms coalition, by assuring them that he was committed to a moderate, big-tent party. He got his friends from the Young Democrats and progressive whites who were close to Duke University. He picked off a few black supporters. He carried Durham.

Hunt had the support of business people who knew Bennett. He and Grimsley also went after progressives. Hunt supported higher salaries for teachers and statewide public kindergarten for five-year-olds. He supported stricter controls on development on the coast and in the mountains. He called for good-government reforms for the legislature, like ethics rules, disclosures of financial interests, and electronic voting so all votes would be recorded publicly.

Hunt had it all: money, organization, issues, and, most of all, a fresh image. He led the first primary with 46 percent of the vote, getting nearly twice as many votes as Sowers, the second-place finisher. Sowers decided against calling a runoff.

The night of the primary, Hunt noticed that, while he carried most of the big counties, Margaret Harper had won Alamance County, which included Burlington. He made a few calls and found that Harper's campaign chair in the county was Maude Wood, who was active in the North Carolina Women's Clubs. The next morning, Hunt drove to Alamance and found Wood. He asked her to help him. From then on, she was one of Hunt's campaign chairs in the county.

Hunt was one of the first politicians in North Carolina to bring women into key positions in his campaigns and administrations. His longtime friend Betty McCain from Wilson had a statewide leadership role in all his campaigns. He later appointed her chair of the North Carolina Democratic Party and, in his last two administrations, secretary of the Department of Cultural Resources. And Jane Smith Patterson was a key aide through all four administrations.

While Hunt was winning the primary in 1972, his Democratic Party was coming apart. White voters in the South were deserting. Terry Sanford learned what was happening the hard way when he made an ill-fated run for president that year. His campaign came to a humiliating end after he lost North Carolina's presidential primary to George Wallace, Alabama's segregationist governor, by a hundred thousand votes.

Nationally, the Democratic Party was splitting into liberal and conservative wings. North Carolina Democrats were distancing themselves from George McGovern, the nominee for president. They didn't want McGovern in the state, they didn't want to talk about him, and they didn't want to be seen with him. Hunt didn't care for McGovern either. "McGovern was way too liberal for me," he said. "I didn't like his crowd. I thought they were hurting the party."

It all meant trouble for the Democratic candidate for governor, Hargrove "Skipper" Bowles. Bowles had a sparkling, energetic personality. After working his way through Carolina, he married well and soon owned one of the largest grocery distributors in the state. He lived across from the Greensboro Country Club and moved easily in the state's business and social stratosphere. He served in Governor Sanford's cabinet as director of the Department of Conservation and Development, a plum post that put him in charge of the state's economic-development programs. His department also oversaw the state parks system. Bowles and Sanford quietly ordered all the parks desegregated.

Bowles introduced North Carolina to a new kind of politics. He spent big money on polling and television ads and hired top talent like Bob Squier, one of the country's first political-media consultants. Bowles's opponent, Lieutenant Governor Pat Taylor, was from the county-courthouse crowd and the rural grassroots-organization approach. Bowles's high-flying, high-spending campaign won the primary. But instead of healing divisions after their win, Bowles's people widened them. One of his key supporters was famously quoted as vowing that, when Bowles became governor and it came time to split up the patronage, the Bowles people would get "the white meat" and the Taylor people "the dark meat."

The Bowles campaign was confident. His people saw little reason to campaign with Hunt. Hunt recalled, "There was a little rivalry between our organization and Bowles's. There was a little feeling, I think, because Bert got in there behind me and put his total effort into me and our campaign."

Bennett said later, "I had a theory that you could mess with one race and no more. I voted for Skipper, but I did not sit at the table, didn't get involved with his inner circle."

The Bowles campaign's confidence waned as Election Day neared. Ever since Sanford endorsed JFK in 1960, Republicans had been steadily gaining in governors' races. Jim Gardner, who had come close in 1968, ran again in 1972. But he lost a tight Republican primary to a longtime legislator from the mountains, Jim Holshouser.

Holshouser was a slight, soft-spoken man. He was a moderate who supported statewide kindergartens and higher teacher pay. He had a Mr. Clean image at a time when newspapers were reporting questionable financial activities among Governor Scott and some of his supporters. Pressed by Pat Stith of the *News & Observer* to answer questions about his personal finances, Scott sent Stith a handwritten letter: "I am aware that you are having pressure brought on you by your editor to dig into this, but you can tell him to go to hell as far as the subject of my personal affairs is concerned."

Holshouser also was riding a Republican tide. President Nixon swept to reelection over McGovern, winning Southern states big. He walloped McGovern in North Carolina by a 69 to 29 percent margin.

Years later, Holshouser recalled that he sensed things were going his way near the end: "I told Hunt ten days, two weeks before the election, 'I think it's going to be you and me.'"

Bowles sensed it, too. Bowles/Hunt stickers started appearing at his rallies. Bowles called with a request: How about if he and Hunt campaigned together in the final days? Previously, the Bowles campaign's attitude toward Hunt had been, as one veteran of the Hunt campaign put it, "We might be able to bring him in on our coattails." Now, the Hunt campaign took quiet satisfaction in telling the Bowles folks they'd try to work in some joint appearances. They did.

But Holshouser's feeling was right. He and Hunt won. Holshouser's margin over Bowles was 51 to 48 percent. Hunt won by 57 to 43 percent.

Hunt was now the highest-ranking elected Democrat in North Carolina. Holshouser was the first Republican elected governor in the twentieth century. And North Carolina elected its first Republican United States senator in the century: Jesse Helms.

Hunt might have been the top elected Democrat, the titular head of the party, and a front runner for governor in 1976, but Lieutenant Governor Whippersnapper didn't exactly get a warm welcome from the Democrats who ran the Senate—"the heavies," Hunt called them.

The Senate Democrats were for the most part older and more

conservative than Hunt. They were spooked by the Republican gains in 1972. The Republican contingent in the Senate was larger than ever before: fifteen of fifty senators.

Hunt later recalled of the Senate Democrats, "They didn't really appreciate this young upstart coming in here, thirty-five or thirty-six years of age, never having been in the Senate for a day." The first thing they tried to do was take away his office space in the Legislative Building. More important, they tried to strip him of his authority to appoint Senate committees and refer bills. With those powers, North Carolina's lieutenant governor was almost as powerful as the governor, who could not run for a second term and—alone among all the states' governors—could not veto legislation. The Senate heavies argued that the newly full-time office now was more a part of the executive branch than the legislative. The lieutenant governor had no business running the Senate anymore, they said. It was nothing personal about Hunt, they insisted. It was all about the institution of the Senate.

But Hunt was tougher than he looked. "Politics is a rough business," he said in 2007, "but it's also about making friends." And building a team. "The people in there were not my team. I had to build a team, and I did it by making a friend here, appointing somebody there, making a speech yonder, and personally being nice to people, getting them to where they gradually came to trust me and work with me."

Hunt was not going to win votes schmoozing with senators over drinks. He was a teetotaler. Most evenings during the session, he drove the forty-five miles back to his farm in Rock Ridge to be with his family. But he was always ready to do a favor for a senator. Speak to his civic club? Sure. Give the keynote address at a county Democratic convention? Put it on the schedule. He was glad to spend his weekends and nights going to senators' districts. Hunt was tireless. When others were drinking, he was driving to another stop.

He had allies in the Senate. The strongest was veteran senator Ralph Scott, Kerr Scott's brother and Bob Scott's uncle. Hunt's old law partner Russell Kirby was a senator. So was Eddie Knox, his old friend from college and FFA. Hunt got to work making friends with Kenneth

Royall, Jr., an intimidating bull of a man whose father had been secretary of the army under Harry Truman. Hunt found that Royall wanted to be on the inside, part of the leadership team. He courted Royall, sought his advice, and turned him into a solid member of his team from then on.

Hunt had another weapon in the fight to keep his powers: the statewide organization that had elected him and had a vested interest in his success. As he would do later throughout his terms as governor, Hunt called on his keys around the state to put pressure on the legislators. "It was a combination of our people out in the field calling and telling them not to do it and me fighting and not being willing to give up one single thing in terms of the powers of the office. And making friends with them and gradually them coming to understand that I could be a team player, I respected them, appreciated their abilities and interests, and wanted to work with them."

He won the fight to keep his powers.

But Hunt found it hard to work with some people, like Jim Ramsey, the speaker of the House during Hunt's first two years in Raleigh. "Jim Ramsey never had an agenda," Hunt said. "I knew how to trade. But you can't trade with a fellow who doesn't have anything he wants."

Hunt's problems with Ramsey were nothing like those he had—his last two years as lieutenant governor and for years to come—with Ramsey's successor as speaker, James C. "Jimmy" Green. Green and Hunt never got along. They were opposites politically and personally. Green was an old-style conservative, a tough, chain-smoking former marine. He was from Bladen County in southeastern North Carolina and owned a string of tobacco warehouses, several of which later burned amid suspicious circumstances. "He wanted to run things his way," Hunt said of Green. "He didn't want to share power, and he sure as hell didn't want to share it with this young upstart. Probably thought I was a very liberal person, and he probably couldn't believe I was there."

As a reporter, I once asked Green off the record what he thought of Hunt. He didn't say a word. He just held his finger up in the air. The silent gesture meant that he thought Hunt wavered with the political winds. It was a portent of the flip-flopper image that later hurt Hunt.

Hunt sometimes got along better with Holshouser, the Republican governor, than with Green and conservative Democrats in the legislature. Hunt and Holshouser had a good relationship—not close but friendly. As the state's leading Democrat, Hunt sometimes took public shots at the governor. "I teased him later that, about once a month, he would stand up and give me hell," Holshouser said. But "we never had a falling-out. It was remarkable, really, given the situation" of a governor and lieutenant governor from different parties. One reason was that Hunt and Holshouser supported some of the same programs.

Hunt helped Holshouser fend off legislative efforts to reduce the governor's powers over spending and agency operations. Years later, Holshouser remembered Hunt for it: "When the chips were down, he was always there." Of course, Holshouser noted that Hunt had a selfish interest, since he might be governor himself one day.

Hunt claims he deliberately didn't think about the governor's race at first. "The first two years of my lieutenant governorship, I tried very hard, very consciously, to not think about the governor's race," he said later. His public mantra, then and always, was, "I didn't want to be distracted from what I was doing. And I always felt like, and I still do, that if you don't do your job well, you don't need to worry about your next race. You aren't going to be in it."

But everybody expected him to run for governor. He was making speeches to Democratic groups all over the state. One aide recalled, "There was an air of, 'I'm going to do this, but I don't want anybody to think I'm going to do this.'"

Hunt took on some tough fights. One was for building a medical school at East Carolina University in Greenville, not far from his home. ECU had an aggressive, politically astute chancellor, Leo Jenkins, who was pushing for a medical school. The president of the university system, Bill Friday, opposed it. So did most of the state's big newspapers, which didn't think North Carolina needed another medical school, since UNC–Chapel Hill already had one. They didn't like the legislature dictating a decision like that to the university system.

Strong opposition to the medical school came from some of Hunt's own supporters, especially in Charlotte. The opposition reflected the regional tensions in North Carolina politics. Hunt remembered that one of his biggest supporters and contributors in Charlotte, radio broadcaster Stan Kaplan, told him, "You'll never carry Mecklenburg County again."

Hunt said years later, "That really stuck in my craw." He had never forgotten waiting three hours to see a doctor. "I knew that was wrong. We had to make a big change, and this looked like the best thing we could do to get doctors out in poor areas, rural areas with poor people, and have more doctors." The ECU medical school would focus on primary-care physicians and family doctors.

It proved a bitter battle. Hunt recalled, "That was one where they lined up and they took names, and, boy, the UNC people fought us tooth and nail. I really worked the Senate on that thing." He lined up votes. He made sure the medical school appropriation got through the Senate. And in the end, the ECU forces won. They beat the UNC establishment in Chapel Hill and the big-city editors. The medical school was built. Over the years, the school transformed Greenville. It fostered a regional hospital system and a fast-growing hub for medical offices. The bad feelings faded. Hunt and Bill Friday grew close. The newspaper editors got over it. And Hunt recalled with a smile that he carried Mecklenburg every time he ran—"by huge margins," he added.

When the legislature was in session, Hunt spent much of his time on his feet at the rostrum, presiding over the Senate. He was smooth and decisive. After all, he had spent hundreds of hours learning parliamentary procedure in FFA and overseeing student government meetings at N.C. State and meetings of the Democratic Party reform Commission. He didn't hesitate to exercise his power.

One day, the Senate was debating the controversial Coastal Area Management Act, which would give the state more control over development along the beaches in seventeen coastal counties. CAMA was strongly supported by environmentalists and hotly opposed by conservatives, who said it would erode private-property rights and hurt the coastal economy. Hunt, a supporter of the bill, was presiding during the contentious debate.

Leading the fight against CAMA was the dean of the Senate, Senator Julian Allsbrook of Halifax County. The stubborn, strong-minded Allsbrook believed his seniority deserved respect from other senators—and from the presiding officer. He rose repeatedly to offer amendments to water down the bill. Each time, after lengthy debate and close votes, his amendments lost. Finally, Hunt and the bill's supporters decided to end the debate. The next time Allsbrook rose to be recognized for an amendment, Hunt ignored him. Instead, he recognized a supporter of the bill, who moved for a final vote. Allsbrook fumed, but the vote carried. He never forgave Hunt.

As always, though, Hunt had something for the conservatives. He worked hard to get close to the state's sheriffs, elected officials who had considerable political power in those days. He heard about a national program, Neighborhood Watch, that trained community residents to keep an eye out for crime. The Neighborhood Watch program gave Hunt a chance to visit communities, meet with sheriffs, and talk about fighting crime. The press coverage was always good.

He came up with one idea that appalled his liberal supporters, as well as staffers like Joe Grimsley and Paul Essex. It was a statewide conference on sex and violence on television. Hunt's friends in Raleigh, Chapel Hill, and Charlotte were mortified. They thought Hunt sounded like a small-minded moralist. But as his son, who went by the name Baxter, noted years later, "He was very religious. And personally conservative socially. He had the old-fashioned values of rural North Carolina."

He was not exactly tuned into the cultural *zeitgeist*. One aide recalled going on an overnight trip with Hunt. They were eating dinner off trays in front of the television when rock-and-roll legend Chuck Berry came on. "Who is Chuck Berry?" Hunt demanded.

As lieutenant governor, just as when he was in college, Hunt had an air of youthful seriousness. The capital press corps routinely made fun of him. He had an exuberant way of greeting people that struck some as insincere. He called nearly every man "good buddy." I perfected a pretty good imitation of him.

Stephanie Bass, then a radio reporter and later a Hunt aide, recalled, "It was a time when people were trying hard to be cool and hip, and he was decidedly uncool and unhip." We reporters were a cynical bunch, especially in the days of Watergate and Vietnam. Our heroes were Bob Woodward and Carl Bernstein at the *Washington Post* for uncovering Watergate and unseating Richard Nixon, as well as the *New York Times* for printing the Pentagon Papers. We distrusted all politicians, including Hunt. We believed the stories that had him running for governor since he was a boy.

One thing worried some of Hunt's friends. He was being talked about as a candidate for governor in 1976. Some people even thought he might become president. They thought this small matter might be a problem, but they talked about it only behind his back. It was his hair. He still wore the kind of slicked-back pompadour popular in the 1950s. After much anguish and debate, several supporters prevailed on Paul Essex to bring the matter up with Hunt. They told Essex, "You've got to do something."

Essex screwed up his courage and went in to talk to Hunt about his hair. More than thirty years later, he remembered what happened. "I went through the whole litany: 'You're headed for national greatness, but you need to change your appearance.'" Hunt was stone-faced while Essex talked on. "He just sat there and stared at me. He didn't acknowledge it or talk about it." Essex left not knowing if he had made any impression—or still had a job.

One day a few weeks later, Hunt came into the office. His hair had been cut in a new style. He never said a word about it, but clearly he would do whatever it took. And Essex kept his job.

Chapter 5

Happy Days

I went to work at the Jim Hunt for Governor campaign on January 1, 1976. In my role as campaign press secretary, my work ranged from dealing with reporters to writing Hunt's speeches. From my first day, I got an introduction to the different and sometimes dueling political worlds that revolved around Jim Hunt.

Next door to the press office was the campaign scheduler, Graham Bennett, Bert's son. Just out of Carolina, he was getting an apprenticeship in politics. Graham looked and sounded just like his father, with the same clipped, staccato way of talking. He had inherited his father's instinct for politics and for handling people. The old Sanford contacts around the state liked being able to call Bert's son. And Bert had a set of eyes and ears inside the campaign.

Weldon Denny, the campaign's director of organization and an old Bob Scott man, told me proudly, "This is the best organization North Carolina politics has ever seen." Somebody was assigned to every group. Claude Ferrell, recently retired from the North Carolina Association of Educators, was in charge of organizing teachers. The aging John Larkins, one of the first African-Americans ever hired in state government, organized black voters. Lynwood Smith of High Point, a furniture executive who had served in the State Senate, was finance chairman and liaison with manufacturing executives. The campaign had "Farmers for Hunt," "Women for Hunt," "Students for Hunt." Every county had a Hunt campaign chair. And a teacher chair and a farmer chair, on and on. We spent half our time in the press offices announcing various chairs and committees.

On the other side of our office was Joe Grimsley, who was building a modern political campaign with high-level professional consultants. The pollster was Peter Hart from Washington. Hart would become one of the country's best-known pollsters. Working with him was Michael Barone, later a Fox News commentator and editor of *The Almanac of American Politics*. The media consultant was David Sawyer, a sophisticated New Yorker who had made documentary films before getting into politics. Before his untimely death at age fifty-nine, Sawyer became one of the best-known media consultants. His firm exported American-style political consulting around the world.

Hunt had still not formally announced he was running, but there was no doubt. He was never one for the maybe-I'm-running, maybe-I'm-not dance. "My approach always was to be the first one out of the box. And be very clear about what I was going to do. Others could say they were thinking about it if they wanted to. We always made up our mind early and told people what we were going to do and asked for their vote."

Early on, we kept hearing that Skipper Bowles might run again for governor. He sent a letter to his old supporters suggesting that. He asked for their help against "candidates who have been seeking support for several months, one for several years." That would be Hunt. But Hunt and Bert Bennett had already lined up much of Bowles's old team, and Bowles passed on another race. Still, some of his supporters were not entirely happy with Hunt and cast around for another candidate.

They settled on George Wood, a former state senator and wealthy farmer from Camden County in the northeastern corner of the state. Although a conventionally conservative member of the legislature,

Wood wore more liberal colors in the campaign. He made much of his support for the good-government proposals—like establishing a statewide initiative and referendum process—that were the rage in the reformist seventies.

To counter Wood, I made my first plunge into the dark art of negative politics. As a state senator, Wood sponsored bills that loosened standards for the housing that he and other farmers had to provide for migrant laborers. We dug out the bills, and I gave them to a reporter. Wood was hard-pressed to explain them to the liberals he was courting.

Another opponent was Tom Strickland, a quiet state senator from Goldsboro. Though very conservative, Strickland always had been friendly to Hunt. They had worked together on crime legislation. A deeply religious man, Strickland was close to the fundamentalist ministers from small country churches. Hunt, surprised to hear Strickland was running, asked him about it. Hunt said later, "Tom told me that God told him to run for governor. I thought to myself, 'Well, God didn't tell me to run, but if He told you, I can understand you running.'"

Hunt and Bennett were more concerned about wealthy Charlotte businessman Ed O'Herron, an executive in the Eckerd drugstore chain who reported a net worth of more than $20 million. "We heard he was going to drop a ton of money into the race," Hunt recalled.

But Hunt had prepared for that eventuality. In the wake of Watergate, North Carolina and other states were swept up in a wave of campaign-finance reforms. As lieutenant governor, Hunt helped pass several. One just happened to limit the money a candidate could spend on media advertising. The ceiling was a formula tied to the number of registered voters. So, in 1976, no candidate could spend more than $360,000 in a primary—and the same amount in the general election—on broadcast advertising. The limits neutralized O'Herron's and Wood's money and also helped Hunt, who enjoyed the visibility and publicity of statewide office. For Hunt in that case, good government was definitely good politics. Years later, the courts would strike down such restrictions on campaign spending.

Hunt raised plenty of money himself with the help of Bert Bennett and his network. Hunt boasted that he had a "broad-based people's campaign" that brought in donations from more than twenty thousand individuals. But newspapers noted that about three hundred contributors had given 40 percent of the $1.5 million he raised. The big donors were from the businesses that traditionally funded gubernatorial campaigns—construction, highway contracting, trucking, oil and gas, and real estate. At the start of the campaign, Bennett and some of his friends made loans to the campaign—$3000 to $6000 in some cases. Less than two weeks after the election, the campaign repaid the loans.

The youthful Hunt was concerned about getting support from businessmen. Some of them were contemptuous of his background: no business experience, small-time law firm, full-time politician. Many thought he was too liberal, especially on taxes. Hunt knew how the food tax had hurt Terry Sanford. That was not going to happen to him.

The primary that year was in August, so we delayed a formal announcement until April. On the big day, we went all out. We decked out the headquarters. We brought in a special podium and put a television-friendly background screen behind where Hunt and his family would stand. We ordered refreshments for supporters and well-wishers.

The announcement statement was carefully crafted with help from Hart and Sawyer. The night before, several of us on the staff huddled with Hunt to prepare him for reporters' questions. These pre-briefings would consume hours of my time for years to come. We developed a routine. We would fire questions at Hunt that he might get from reporters. Then we would bat around possible answers. Hunt would take copious notes in his bold handwriting, filling page after page of a legal pad. He would carefully study his notes and take them with him to the rostrum.

We knew Hunt would be asked about raising taxes. But during our prep session, he was uncharacteristically terse on the issue. Grimsley and Arnold Zogry, an economist hired to work on issues, pressed him, but Hunt would say only, "I can handle that one."

After Hunt read his statement the next day, he and reporters quickly got into a tense exchange about—sure enough—taxes. Reporters asked him if his education proposals, like a statewide reading program in the early grades, would require a tax increase. No, Hunt said. The reporters pressed him. Suppose it turned out that a tax increase was needed. Would he support one then? He wouldn't need to raise taxes, Hunt repeated. Back and forth they volleyed. Finally, one reporter demanded a yes-or-no answer: Would he rule out raising taxes? Yes, Hunt declared, he would rule it out: "I'm not going to be pushing for raising taxes in North Carolina."

Reporters and even some of Hunt's progressive supporters thought he took the position purely out of political expediency. On top of that, Hunt had tied his hands. Late in his first term, he would decide that a gas-tax increase was needed to pay for road maintenance. But he had to put off raising the tax until after he was reelected in 1980. By then, Ronald Reagan was president, the political climate had changed, and a strong antitax sentiment flourished among voters.

Years later, Hunt told me the back story of his no-tax-hike pledge. Early in the campaign, he had met in Winston-Salem with John Medlin, president of Wachovia Bank, then a big statewide bank but nothing like the behemoth it would become. Hunt said, "I remember being in John Medlin's office, and John Medlin talked to me, almost kind of explained to me, that in the best of worlds the way to get more money for programs is to grow the economy, rather than raising taxes. It really made sense to me. I was in a learning experience. I was learning how things work, how the economy works, how business works, how schools work, you know. That's the job of a leader, it's to learn, keep learning, learn all the time. And I learned from that. I've never forgotten that. And so I am sure that that was in my mind when I said I would not raise taxes. It doesn't mean we won't do more things. We're going to grow this economy, and we'll have the money to do more things."

Did he deliberately overrule Grimsley and Zogry? "I'm sure I did. I don't recall directly us talking about it, and I'm sure they would take the traditional liberal approach" on raising taxes. Hunt was not going to be a traditional liberal. But he was torn. His liberal instinct was to spend more money on education. His conservative instinct was to avoid being labeled a tax raiser. It was the tightrope he always walked.

Hunt put a lot of work into his issues, in that and every campaign. He truly cared about them. As a college student, he had kept files of newspaper clippings, organized by issue. Years later when asked about campaign strategy, Hunt always responded by talking about issues. "My primary concern was the things I wanted to get done, the things I wanted to do as governor, have North Carolina do. These grew out of things I'd learned in my life and things I'd done when I was lieutenant governor."

As lieutenant governor, he had been a member of the State Board of Education. There, he recalled later, "I had found out how many children were not learning to read. Third-grade teachers told me how many kids they had who were nonreaders. I had found that we didn't have any testing system statewide to see how kids were doing and thus were not remediating those kids." Those two themes—improving instruction in the early years and finding ways to measure if students were learning—remained a focus of Hunt's education programs from then on.

In 1976, he proposed a Primary Reading Program that he had developed on the State Board of Education. The program put a "reading aide" alongside the teacher in every classroom in the first, second, and third grades. The goal was to have every child learn to read by third grade.

Hunt and Grimsley put a lot of time and effort into developing issues like the Primary Reading Program. Grimsley was good at recruiting people—inside state government and from various interest groups—to generate policy ideas. Then we tested the ideas in Peter Hart's polls.

The state's citizens were angry about rising electric rates, so Hunt proposed creating a public staff in the North Carolina Utilities Commission to represent consumers. For conservatives concerned about crime, Hunt railed against judges who were soft on criminals. He called for fixed sentencing that allowed no discretion for judges.

That idea drove liberals crazy. Even worse was the ad David Sawyer made. Hunt stood by an open jail-cell door. He talked about locking up dangerous criminals. Then he slammed the cell door. *Wham!*

It echoed through the cellblock. Many of Hunt's supporters, especially blacks, cringed. But Wallace voters and conservative Democrats got the message. Hunt reassured African-Americans and liberals that he would appoint judges who were fair, and that a number of those judges would be black.

We spent weeks preparing lengthy, detailed position papers on issues. We pulled together interest-group leaders and policy experts to develop the details. We held press conferences all over the state to roll out Hunt's proposals. For all that, the process didn't always work like a political-science textbook. Ed O'Herron made a big splash by saying he would move the state's industry-recruiting office into the governor's office. The country was just coming out of a bad recession, and North Carolina's unemployment rate was among the highest of any state. The state's traditional manufacturing industries—textiles, furniture, and cigarettes—were beginning what turned out to be a decades-long decline. Jobs were a big issue, and O'Herron had one-upped us.

We struggled for a response. One day, we were batting around ideas with David Sawyer. It was always a big deal when the media producer from Manhattan came to town. Now, Sawyer was standing at an easel, pushing us for an idea he could use in an ad about jobs.

"We could propose the same thing O'Herron's doing," somebody offered.

"That's real leadership," Sawyer shot back.

"We could change the name of the department," somebody else said. It was still the Department of Conservation and Development that Skipper Bowles had headed.

Sawyer's sarcasm was withering: "A name change! That's exciting. What else have you got?"

Finally, a timid voice—I can't remember whose—offered, "Well, there's a Department of Commerce now."

Sawyer perked up. "What's in it?"

"Not much. It's just a holding department for agencies like the utilities commission and the milk commission."

Sawyer came to life. "That's perfect." He ripped the old sheet of paper off the easel and started writing on a new one. "We'll take the Department of Commerce. It's nothing now. We'll revitalize it. We'll put industry hunting there. We'll make it the lead agency for getting jobs. For the first time, economic development will have its own cabinet department."

Hunt proposed it, the legislature enacted it, and the Department of Commerce became North Carolina's premier economic-development agency for decades to come, thanks to a Manhattan ad man.

Sawyer turned Hunt's issue ideas—the reading program, the Department of Commerce, electricity-rate reform, the cell door slamming—into beautiful commercials. He did the filming himself, some of it at Hunt's farm. Hunt recalled later, "You had pretty big equipment back in those days, and David would strap on to me this thing, I guess it was the battery for a microphone, a great big metal thing on my back. We were out there around my house filming, I had this metal thing strapped onto my back, and I backed into an electric fence. Shocked the heck out of me."

Hunt had cut his teeth on old-style organizational politics. But he understood the growing power of television. As always, he saw both sides. He told me later, "Bert was an organization man, you were a media man, and I was kind of both. I believed in both. I still do."

Winning campaigns needed four elements, Hunt thought: "You've got to have the candidate, you've got to have the issues, you've got to have the organization, and you've got to have the money, which can get you convincing media. You've got to have those four things. We had them all."

And we had gimmicks. In those days when person-to-person, county-by-county politics still mattered, the state Democratic convention was a big event. Getting the support of party activists around the state was important in the primary. So all the candidates spoke at the convention and tried to make a big show of support. That year, the convention was held in the middle of summer in Dorton Arena at the North Carolina State Fairgrounds. The arena had no air conditioning. Campaign aide David Erdman from Charlotte came up with an idea that Mike Davis, now the assistant press secretary, and I thought was ridiculous. Erdman wanted to make cardboard fans that read, "I'm a Jim Hunt Fan," and hand them out to people at the convention. Silly, we scoffed. A waste of money. But Joe Grimsley gave Erdman the go-ahead.

The day of the convention was stifling. The place was packed when Hunt walked in. And every single person was waving a Jim Hunt fan to ward off the heat. It was a sea of Jim Hunt fans. Davis and I never again dismissed any idea as too silly.

Most of all, our campaign had a tireless candidate whose earnestness appealed to people. He could make connections, he said later, because people believed he really wanted to do something for them: "People believed that, sensed that, bought into that."

Hunt went everywhere. And everywhere, he made local connections. He would start his speech by talking about a friend who was there, maybe someone he knew in college or FFA. Often, he used a distant family connection.

His driver, a farm boy from Wilson County named Walt Williamson, heard Hunt make the local connections over and over. On one stop, in the state's far western mountains, Williamson and a Raleigh reporter listened as Hunt spoke. Several generations back, it seemed, one of his forebears had known someone distantly related to a face he recognized in the crowd. Williamson leaned over to the reporter and said, "Hunt's from all one hundred counties, you know."

The 1976 campaign had another thing going for it that would become rare for Democrats in years to come: a national tide. Republicans were still reeling from Watergate and Nixon's resignation. Hunt said years later, "You'd had all the tragedy of Watergate, and people were upset about it and embarrassed about it. But by 1976, there was kind of a new spirit."

That spirit was captured by Jimmy Carter. Carter was something new: an outsider not from Washington. He was fresh, and he talked about government being as good as the American people. He promised never to lie. Best of all for Hunt, Carter was a Southerner and a governor. He was more moderate than many Democrats in Washington and had balanced budgets in Georgia. He had been in the navy. He was a devout man not afraid to talk about religion.

After a speech by Carter in Raleigh in March, the *News & Observer* wrote, "Jimmy Carter demonstrated here Friday a willingness to talk about his personal religious feelings in a way no other presidential candidate has." Carter said that in 1967 he had undergone a "profound religious experience that changed my life dramatically." He said, "I formed a close, intimate personal relationship with God through Christ that has given me a great deal of peace, equanimity." He added that he prayed before making important decisions. "I spent more time on my knees the four years I was governor in the seclusion of a little private room off the governor's office than I did in all the rest of my life."

Just like John Kennedy in 1960, Carter looked like a winner. We tied Hunt to him as closely as we could. When Carter came to North Carolina, we got a picture of him with Hunt. We featured the shot prominently in a campaign flier. Our opponents cried foul, but we kept moving.

That year, North Carolina held its presidential primary in March, long before the state primaries in August. Four years earlier, George Wallace had beaten Terry Sanford in the primary. In 1976, Carter beat Wallace by 54 to 35 percent. We saw that as a sign that the New South was rising.

But in the Republican presidential primary, the Old South triumphed. Ronald Reagan was challenging President Gerald Ford for the nomination. Ford had won all the early primaries. Reagan was on the ropes. Some of his supporters even wanted him to drop the fight. North Carolina looked like it could be the end for him. Governor Holshouser and much of the party establishment supported Ford. Holshouser and six other Republican governors called on Reagan to end his challenge to the president. But Reagan, campaigning in Charlotte, shot back, "I'm going to follow the will of the people, not the politicians."

Reagan had determination. And in North Carolina, he had Tom Ellis. Ellis was Jesse Helms's Bert Bennett. He had directed

Helms's election to the Senate in 1972. To pay off the campaign debt, Ellis organized a permanent fundraising and political operation called the Congressional Club.

Ellis, a Raleigh lawyer and conservative activist, was a genuine political genius. He had an instinct for emerging campaign technologies like polling, television advertising, and direct-mail fundraising. When the Reagan ship came to North Carolina, Ellis seized the helm. Over the objection of the more moderate advisers then running the campaign, Ellis wanted Reagan to give the Republican conservatives some red meat. The issue was a treaty the Ford administration supported to give Panama control of the Panama Canal.

Ellis bought thirty minutes of statewide television time and broadcast a speech Reagan had given in Florida denouncing the canal "give-away." The speech was a big hit, and money poured in.

Ellis also knew how to play the race card. He and Helms had "cut their teeth on politics" in the 1950 Willis Smith campaign against Frank Porter Graham, wrote Rob Christensen in *The Paradox of Tar Heel Politics*. "They learned to defeat progressives by using racial appeals to split off white farmers and mill workers." Now, in 1976, Ellis had fliers printed noting that President Ford was considering Senator Edward Brooke of Massachusetts—a black man—for his running mate. The fliers featured a big picture of Brooke.

Reagan upset Ford in the North Carolina primary, winning by 6 percentage points. The stunning defeat for Ford, Holshouser, and the party moderates energized the national conservative movement and kept Reagan alive politically. Ford held on to win the nomination in 1976, but the North Carolina primary led directly to Reagan's nomination and election as president in 1980. All thanks to Tom Ellis.

That was of little concern to our campaign in 1976. We had our own primary and—like Frank Graham's and Rich Preyer's campaigns—we worried about getting 50 percent of the vote and avoiding a runoff. Fear of runoffs was deep in our DNA.

The night of the primary, our campaign staff gathered in a Raleigh restaurant before heading over to the hotel where Hunt's supporters

Joe Grimsley announces vote totals on primary night in August 1976 during Hunt's first race for governor. Behind Grimsley are Betty McCain, a longtime Hunt friend, and Eddie Knox. Knox would become embittered after losing the 1984 Democratic primary for governor.
Photo by Advent Communications, Inc.

had gathered to watch the returns. We were nervous, giddy, and exhausted. Eddie Knox—Hunt's old friend from college, now a co-chair of his campaign, along with Betty McCain—gave us a little pep talk. "In a few hours," he said, "we'll either be crying or we'll all be hugging each other."

We were hugging. Hunt won over 53 percent of the vote and avoided a risky runoff.

He kept the momentum through the fall. His opponent, David Flaherty, a former furniture executive who served as secretary of the Department of Human Resources in Holshouser's cabinet, was able to mount little challenge. The Republican Party was still reeling from Watergate and President Nixon's resignation in 1974, as well as the aftereffects of the recession and the nation's first experience with long

Hunt the night he was first elected governor, November 2, 1976. From left are Dennis Rogers of the News & Observer, *Joel McCleary with the Carter for President campaign, the author, and Mike Davis.*
PHOTO FROM THE AUTHOR'S COLLECTION

lines at gas stations. The Ford-Reagan battle had split Republicans. Still, Hunt campaigned relentlessly, and Joe Grimsley drove us hard.

Just a week before the election, the *News & Observer* ran a poll across the top of the front page that said Hunt had a lead of 52 to 26 percent. Flaherty canceled most of his public appearances and threw all his money and hopes into a last-gasp televised address warning that "the big money, big machine, big horses are about to deliver" the governorship to Hunt. The broadcast had little impact.

Traveling with Hunt on a campaign plane in the final days, Ferrel Guillory, political reporter for the *News & Observer,* overheard the candidate whistling "Happy Days Are Here Again," the old FDR Democratic victory song. "It was a soft, serene whistle, not really meant for others to hear," Guillory wrote. "But it expressed the sure self-confidence with which the Democratic candidate for governor approaches Tuesday's election."

On election night, we celebrated as Hunt swamped Flaherty with 65 percent of the vote. The victory was part of a national Democratic wave. Carter, who was narrowly elected president, carried North Carolina. An exuberant Hunt shouted in his election-night speech, "Happy days are here again!"

Chapter 6

"Mr. Total Initiative"

Jim Hunt could be a long-winded orator. But his first inaugural address was one of the shortest speeches he ever gave—just six minutes. The brevity was welcome, for the ceremony was held outdoors on a windy, icy-cold Saturday in January.

Hunt echoed John Kennedy's call to service—"I hold the office of Governor; you hold the office of citizen"—and the populist-progressive tradition of Kerr Scott and Terry Sanford—"I want to declare here, today, to all those who seek a better life—to the child struggling to learn in school, to the working parents planning their future and their children's future, to the young people trying to find a place in society, to the farmer in his fields, to the millworker, to the elderly, to the sick, to the disabled, to the handicapped—that you have a friend in the Governor's Office."

From his first days in office, Hunt set a tone he would follow for four terms: aggressive, hyperactive, and—always—a balance of old and new politics.

The afternoon of his swearing-in, Hunt spent over five hours greeting thousands of friends and supporters from across the state at the Executive Mansion. Democrats had suffered through four years of a

Hunt delivering his first Inaugural Address after being sworn in as governor on January 8, 1977. The speech was only six minutes long—welcome brevity on a freezing-cold day.
Photo by Charlie Jones

Republican governor. Now, they wanted political payback—and state jobs. In poor communities, especially down east and in the western mountains, a Department of Transportation motor grader job was the best in town. It meant a steady paycheck, health insurance, and a retirement plan.

The pressures of the old politics competed with the pressures of the new. Hunt had promised a new tone in state government. On Monday morning after his inauguration, he signed an executive order establishing an ethics code for his cabinet departments and invoked the post-Watergate spirit of reform: "One of this administration's most sincere compacts is to strive to restore public faith and confidence in the honesty of public officials."

He had promised new faces in state government. He appointed the first African-American cabinet secretary, naming Howard Lee, the

Jim and Carolyn Hunt with their children at the 1977 Inaugural Ball. From left are Baxter, Rebecca, Rachel, and Elizabeth.
PHOTO BY CHARLIE JONES

first black mayor of Chapel Hill, as secretary of the Department of Natural Resources and Community Development. Harold Webb became the first African-American director of the North Carolina Office of State Personnel. Webb had been a teacher, a principal, and deputy state schools superintendent. He was also a key member of a tight-knit group of black political leaders in Raleigh. Hunt appointed women to his cabinet. Sarah Morrow, director of the Guilford County Health Department in Greensboro, became secretary of the Department of Human Resources, while Sarah Hodgkins from Southern Pines was named secretary of the Department of Cultural Resources.

Hunt tried to set a new tone in the Department of Transportation, long a bastion of politics and patronage. Lauch Faircloth, a crusty, conservative millionaire who had headed the highway department under Bob Scott, wanted the job again. He didn't get it. Faircloth had been one of Governor Scott's key fundraisers, and rumors swirled about a federal investigation into possible wrongdoing. That would hardly fit with Hunt's emphasis on ethics. So he appointed Tom Bradshaw, an energetic thirty-eight-year-old former mayor of Raleigh who had a clean image, to head DOT. Hunt named Faircloth secretary of the Department of Commerce as a consolation prize.

Always, Hunt balanced his liberal and conservative sides. He named Joe Grimsley secretary of the Department of Administration, a position Grimsley considered "first among equals" in the cabinet. But Hunt had other plans. He appointed Banks Talley, former dean of student affairs at N.C. State, whom Hunt knew from his college days, as his executive assistant. Talley didn't have a political background but had learned something about sharp elbows in academia. He wrote in a journal that he kept while he worked for Hunt, "I felt the Gov. and I had an 'unspoken' understanding that Joe G. was part of my agenda of serving in the Gov. office." In other words, he was to keep Grimsley in his place.

Grimsley wasn't happy when Hunt appointed Talley. Grimsley told friends, "He's not part of our team. He doesn't know what we're trying to do." So Grimsley—"the Bulldozer"—charged ahead. Soon, cabinet secretaries complained that he was interfering in their departments. Plus, "Hunt was afraid Joe would do something to jeopardize his political career," one aide said. "Even if Hunt or a powerful legislator told Grimsley not to do something, he would just find another way to do it." Talley and Grimsley would engage in a series of running battles throughout that first year.

Talley had the political sense to ingratiate himself with Bert Bennett, frequently calling and meeting with Hunt's mentor. Together, they solved Hunt's first internal crisis.

Weldon Denny, the old Bob Scott man who worked in Hunt's 1976 campaign, had been put in charge of handling the flood of patronage requests from Hunt's keys around the state. But no one was getting hired. And the keys were mad about it.

Bennett heard the complaints. So did his son Graham, who was in charge of appointments to state boards and commissions, working out of a hideaway office behind Hunt's in the Capitol. And Hunt was getting an earful. In fact, the constant complaints wore him down. He said later, "Everybody that came in had talked to Weldon. He'd give them this sweet talk and listen to them. They all wanted jobs. And he promised jobs for everybody, or they thought he had." The demands were "just piling up. Nothing was happening."

Late one afternoon a couple of months after taking office, Hunt left the Capitol, weary from enduring a string of calls from angry keys. He recalled, "I literally remember going back to the mansion one day and climbing those back steps to the second floor and thinking to myself, 'Can you resign this job?' I don't think I really meant it, but the thought did cross my mind."

Talley credited Bert Bennett with finding the solution. That solution was the man Hunt would later say saved him as governor: Joe Pell.

Pell was a businessman from Pilot Mountain, just north of Winston-Salem, who had made a lot of money in tobacco and nursing homes. He had been chairman of the Surry County School Board for thirty years. He was tough and canny.

Hunt and Bennett thought Pell would never take the job. He was in his early sixties, an age when most men thought about retirement. But Hunt tried the hard sell, telling Pell how much he needed him in Raleigh. Pell agreed. He replaced Denny, who moved to the Department of Agriculture. For the next eight years, Pell and his wife, Tut, lived in a hotel room in Raleigh during the week, then drove back to Pilot Mountain on weekends.

Every morning, Pell was in his office—across the hall from Hunt's in the Capitol—before seven. He stayed until late in the evening, taking endless phone calls from keys across the state, holding hands, cracking heads, solving problems, soothing hurt feelings.

Bennett shook his head years later as he marveled at Pell's devotion to Hunt: "Living in a hotel, that's no life. Leave Pilot Mountain and the businesses he was in." He added, "Pell deserves a lot of credit. People liked him. Maturity. Could afford it, could take the time off. And he was a good politician. He liked it." When Pell talked, Bennett said, "people knew he was talking for the governor. And they didn't cross Joe."

Pell became known as Hunt's patronage chief. He had the delicate job of handling keys' requests for jobs in state government for Hunt supporters.

Once, a county key was pressuring Pell to find a job for a local boy. Pell asked, "Is he qualified?"

The key replied, "Hell, Joe, if he was qualified, we wouldn't need you in Raleigh."

Pell was a master of people. One day, I was in his office when he took a call from a state senator named Arthur Williamson. Williamson was famous for boasting about the money he made and the clout he commanded. That day, he was in a rage. Someone in his county had been hired for a state highway job without his knowing about it. It was an insult, he fumed to Pell. How dare Pell do this without checking with him first?

Governor Hunt eats a hot dog in downtown Raleigh in March 1978 while listening to Joe Pell. Pell ran Hunt's legendarily efficient patronage operation. Hunt would later say Pell was the man who saved his administration.

Photo courtesy of the *News & Observer*

Pell let Williamson go on for several minutes. Finally, he cut in: "Arthur, this is all my fault. I told my staff not to call you about this. I told them, 'Now, listen here. Arthur Williamson is an important man. He is a very busy man. He doesn't have time for little stuff. I don't want you bothering him with anything unless it is absolutely top-level. Top-level, I said.'"

Williamson went silent. Then he lit up: "That's absolutely right, Joe. Just top-level stuff. That's me. I knew you would understand." He hung up happy, and Pell winked at me.

With Pell's help, Hunt began to put his staff in order. At the end of his first year, he installed one more piece. When Banks Talley returned to N.C. State, Hunt made John A. Williams, Jr., his new executive assistant.

Williams was a Raleigh businessman and accountant whom Hunt had appointed as his budget director at the beginning of the administration. Williams had been state Democratic Party treasurer when Bob Scott was governor. Like Pell, he was in his early sixties, wealthy, and independent. He understood politics and business. He would turn out to be more than a match for Grimsley, in part because Hunt let Williams remain budget director. The budget is where the power always is in government.

Talley wrote in his journal, "Joe Pell, Bert Bennett and I have been successful in persuading the Gov. to move JAW [John A. Williams] to his office. It means a stronger role for the Gov. in budget and it means a *strong person* to handle Joe G. in relation to Cabinet, budget and Gov. office." Talley exulted, "A victory on departure."

Williams and Pell were more conservative than Grimsley and other members of Hunt's staff. That grated on some aides. But Hunt was comfortable with them. He trusted their judgment and loyalty. He had confidence that he, not they, would set the ultimate direction of his administration. And he needed Pell and Williams to help him get his program through the legislature.

It was an ambitious program right out of the 1976 campaign commercials. Hunt wanted his Primary Reading Program and his testing

While visiting a school during his first administration, Hunt takes a swing at the plate. He was constantly in motion as governor—traveling the state, speaking, and especially visiting public schools.
Photo by Lucy Vance

program in the schools. He wanted to make the Department of Commerce the lead economic-development agency. He wanted a public staff to advocate for consumers before the North Carolina Utilities Commission.

He had a big crime-fighting agenda his first year—so big that, two weeks after the traditional State of the State Address to the legislature, he went back to deliver a special address on crime. He proposed the creation of a Department of Crime Control and Public Safety, a law to speed up criminal trials, tougher penalties for violent crimes, and a massive prison-building budget.

Hunt would continue to give a separate legislative address on crime throughout his administrations. In 1979, he would return to the legislature with another list of crime-fighting proposals—tougher sentencing laws, victims-advocate proposals, and, for juvenile offenders, a combination of stricter punishment and expanded prevention programs. Many of the proposals were developed by Hunt's old friend Phil

Hunt shows his competitive side as player-coach for "Hunt's Heroes" in a March 1982 basketball game against a team fielded by then-Attorney General Rufus Edmisten. Behind Hunt is Jack Cozort, then his legal counsel and later a judge. Hunt's team lost.
Photo courtesy of the *News & Observer*

Carlton, who had been a district court judge for nearly ten years before Hunt appointed him the first secretary of the Department of Crime Control and Public Safety. Hunt would later appoint Carlton to the court of appeals and then the state supreme court.

In 1977 and 1979, the legislature passed virtually everything Hunt wanted. In 1977, he also got a $300 million highway bond issue, an echo of the Kerr Scott initiative that paved the road by the Hunt farm.

Hunt developed a formula for working the legislature. When big votes were coming up, he and Joe Pell would mobilize Hunt's keys across the state. Call your legislators, the keys were urged. Tell them to vote for Hunt's bills. Often, the keys were also the legislators' biggest contributors and fundraisers. When the keys called, the legislators listened.

When the legislature was in Raleigh, Hunt met with a team of his legislative supporters every morning. He set aside hours on his schedule every day to talk to legislators in the Capitol or at the mansion. He called them all hours of the day and night. He was so persistent that one legislator pleaded with a Hunt aide, "Tell the governor I'll vote for his bill. Tell him to please not call me anymore."

Hunt also deployed Pell and Williams. Both men knew how to deal, how to trade, and, when necessary, how to intimidate. Hunt didn't have veto power, but he had "green stamps"—jobs, roads, appointments to state boards, and the other favors a governor could give.

Pell knew who in the legislature had voted for Hunt's program and who had not. He remembered that when legislators called to get something for a supporter or a daughter or a nephew. "The mule that pulls the plow gets the corn," Pell would say. "No plow, no corn."

Williams could always find money in the budget for the pet projects of legislators and county keys who helped Hunt. If they weren't supportive, Williams would slam the door with pleasure. "The legislators were scared of him," recalled Zeb Alley, who served later as Hunt's legislative liaison. Williams had a way of getting into the small groups of four or five key legislators who always resolved the final budget at the end of the session.

When things got tough, Hunt sent Pell to the legislature, too. If legislators saw both Pell and Williams walking the halls, they knew something important was up. Few of them were willing to challenge Hunt's twin titans.

My job as press secretary was to help Hunt use another power: his power to communicate with the public. Having seen relations between past governors and the press corps up close, I didn't think Hunt's predecessors had used their bully pulpit effectively enough. We resolved to be more aggressive.

We began holding weekly news conferences. We would announce a new piece of legislation, a new appointment, or a new initiative in a cabinet department. Then Hunt would take questions. Reporters would ask about problems and controversies in state government. Hunt quickly learned that even tough questions could work in his favor. He found out about problems early. Sometimes, these were problems his own appointees had kept from him. The weekly discipline kept him sharp and on top of issues.

Hunt had been a newspaper reader all his life. He paid close attention to what was written about him. He could rail—and cuss with gusto—at a bad story. But he rarely lashed out personally at reporters. He and I developed a good relationship despite the obvious differences between us. Like many of Hunt's young staffers, I was an unapologetic liberal. I had taken part in antiwar protests. I wore my hair long and rarely sported a tie. Once, the commander of the North Carolina Highway Patrol spotted me outside Hunt's office and grumbled, "He'd never make it in my outfit." He was right, of course.

One of Hunt's strengths was that he was always open to people of different ages, backgrounds, and viewpoints. Jack Cozort, his legal counsel, said later, "He had John A. Williams, Joe Pell, plus all us young idealists. He liked to be challenged by ideas. He never minded you disagreeing with him."

Hunt trusted my instincts about reporters and gave me a wide berth in my job. He agreed to be accessible to the media, and we generally enjoyed good coverage.

He was rarely satisfied, though. One day, he made up his mind that some story—I can't recall exactly what—should be on the front page of the *Winston-Salem Journal*. We pulled out all the stops. I promised the editor whatever access he ever needed if he would just help me out. It worked. The next day, the story was right there under a multi-column headline across the bottom of the front page. I triumphantly took the paper in to show Hunt. He examined it for a few minutes, then said, "That's great, Gary. But I sure wish it was above the fold."

Hunt needed all the tools—the media, his keys, his personal lobbying, Pell and Williams—because the governor's office was so weak. A governor then could serve only one four-year term. North Carolina was

Hunt with John A. Williams, Jr., who served as budget director and executive assistant during the first two terms. Williams and Joe Pell were Hunt's all-powerful senior aides. Williams was especially effective in lobbying the legislature.
Photo courtesy of the *News & Observer*

the only state in the nation where the governor had no veto power.

Hunt was determined to change the balance. He decided to tackle succession first. He later said, "I figured out I'd rather have more time than the power of the veto." Another term would mean four more years to carry through programs and build on new initiatives, rather than being limited to the start-and-stop pattern of a new governor.

He figured out why governors before him could never get succession passed: "All the governors before had said, 'Do this for the state, but don't have it apply to me. I'm not asking for it for myself.' " That sounded noble, Hunt thought. But making succession apply to him "gave my people a reason to work for it and fight for it. And boy, did they do it." After all, four more years for Hunt meant four more years that his keys had a friend in the governor's office.

Hunt needed his team to work hard because succession faced a formidable obstacle in the Senate. The lieutenant governor—and presiding officer of the Senate—was now Jimmy Green, the former House speaker who had bedeviled Lieutenant Governor Hunt. Green was planning to run for governor himself in 1980. He wanted no part of succession for Jim Hunt.

So Hunt went around Green—to the friends he had made presiding over the Senate for four years. One by one, he got their commitments. He went to the chairman of the Judiciary Committee, Senator Luther Britt, who was from Robeson County, right beside Green's home county of Bladen. The succession bill would have to go through Britt's committee. Hunt got his support.

By the time Green found out about the succession bill, Hunt had lined up two-thirds of the senators as sponsors. He had his organization all across the state mobilized. He had the editorial pages behind him, though some expressed concern that Hunt wanted to apply succession to himself. The House, led by a progressive speaker, Carl Stewart of Gastonia, supported the bill. Pell and Williams walked the halls, taking names and twisting arms. Green, who had always dismissed Hunt as a weakling, got run over by the succession steamroller.

Hunt lined up a bipartisan group—former governor Holshouser, Democrats and Republicans, businessmen and reformers—to support the succession amendment in the ensuing November referendum. At the last minute, conservative Republicans mounted a campaign against it, running "Stop the Power Train" ads. Jesse Helms's Congressional Club got involved. The club's executive director, Carter Wrenn, said later he always thought the amendment would have lost if he had not been late getting out a last-minute mailing against it.

The vote was 52 to 48 percent, closer than we expected. But Hunt was no longer a lame duck.

He was off to a fast start. With Pell and Williams in the governor's office, Hunt said later, "I had put the house in order." He was enjoying the job and setting a grueling pace. He relished traveling around the state, giving speeches, and cutting ribbons for new roads and businesses. He was a hurricane of energy. William D. Snider, the veteran editor of the *Greensboro Daily News*, wrote, "As one who has seen Tar

Heel governors in action for over three decades, I must confess that Governor Jim Hunt beats them all for sheer drive and enthusiasm."

Every day, Hunt rose early, worked nonstop, and stayed up late. He recalled later, "I lay awake at night figuring out how to do it." People who worked for him were likely to get a call anytime from early in the morning to late at night. Normally, he forced himself to wait until seven in the morning to start calling. When my phone at home rang promptly at seven, I knew who it was. The state troopers at the mansion even had the numbers for restaurants and bars where I hung out at night with co-workers and reporters. They would track me down when he wanted me at nine or ten o'clock at night—or later. There was no escaping him.

At one cabinet meeting, Phil Carlton leaned over to a colleague and said, "Most governors have one or two things they want to do. Jim wants to do everything." Grimsley called Hunt "Mr. Total Initiative."

All the legislative and executive activity didn't exhaust Hunt's energy. He decided to set an example to encourage volunteerism, especially in the schools. He started a routine of working as a volunteer in public schools near the mansion in Raleigh. He would spend an hour or so every week practicing what he preached: tutoring students in reading, working with children who had discipline problems. He would keep volunteering throughout his sixteen years in office.

What Hunt sacrificed was time with his family. Years later, he admitted to one aide that he was an absentee father: "I went day and night, and I didn't see my children nearly as much as I wanted to." His children ranged in age from eight to seventeen when they were lifted from their farm in Rock Ridge and plopped into the Executive Mansion—and the downtown Raleigh schools. Asked later how the family managed, Hunt's answer was simple: "Thank God for Carolyn Hunt."

When the family first moved into the mansion, the staff planned to cook them breakfast and send it upstairs. "That lasted two days," Hunt recalled. Carolyn decided it would be better if she cooked breakfast upstairs herself, in a little kitchenette off the family quarters. She was a full-time mother, helping with homework, doing the shopping, handling the multitude of crises inherent in raising four children. On top of that, she volunteered in the schools herself and hosted all the social events that Hunt loaded onto the mansion schedule. She oversaw open houses at the mansion for ten or twelve days every Christmas, so the public could view the elaborate decorations.

Betty McCain, one of the Hunts' closest friends, said years later, "She works just as hard as he does."

Hunt was always sensitive to rumors that his wife hated politics. "She didn't hate it," he said later. "She kept trying to pull me to give time enough to the children and the family. But my God, if she hadn't believed in it, we'd have never done it, and she helped me do it. And without her doing what she did, I couldn't have done it and shouldn't have done it."

Chapter 7

Weathervane

Joe Grimsley once described Hunt as "politically progressive, but morally conservative." The combination led to inevitable tensions, particularly because governors, like presidents, don't have the luxury of picking and choosing all the issues they face. Crises erupt. Outside events intrude.

Almost as soon as Hunt became governor, the case of the Wilmington Ten landed on his desk—and dragged him and North Carolina into international controversy.

Wilmington, a port city in southeastern North Carolina, had a bitter racial history going back to white-supremacist riots in 1898. In 1971, racial violence had exploded again. When local officials refused to let a black high school hold a commemorative program for Dr. Martin Luther King, blacks launched sit-ins and boycotts. Rock throwing, shootings, and firebombings followed.

One organizer of the protests was Ben Chavis, a young minister from Oxford, near the Virginia line, who later became a nationally known civil-rights leader and head of the NAACP. After the violence in Wilmington, Chavis and nine other activists were arrested, tried, and convicted of conspiring to burn a store and encouraging shooting at firemen and police officers. They were given harsh prison sentences ranging from twenty to twenty-five years. They became known as the Wilmington Ten, and their cause was taken up by civil-rights groups and Amnesty International. CBS's *60 Minutes* did a story casting doubt on their guilt. Congressmen from around the country called on Hunt to release the "political prisoners."

Hunt put his legal counsel, Jack Cozort, to work researching the case. Cozort was from Drexel, a small town in the foothills of western North Carolina. He later recalled, "There were more people in my first biology class at college than in my hometown." Like Hunt, he had been a student leader at N.C. State. Also like Hunt, he was a diligent workaholic. Cozort pored over trial records. He interviewed law-enforcement officers, prosecutors, and defense attorneys involved in the case. He compiled a vast research file.

Hunt read all the material. He met with people on both sides. He talked with Chavis's mother. The meetings often were emotional and angry. But Hunt always kept his cool, asking questions, taking notes, listening patiently.

He waited until the Wilmington Ten's legal appeals ran out in January 1978. Under mounting pressure and a glaring media spotlight, Hunt announced his decision on January 23 in a speech televised statewide from the library of the Executive Mansion. For days, Hunt, Cozort, and I had labored over the draft speech. It was long because television stations across the state had given Hunt thirty minutes of prime viewing time. David Sawyer, our media consultant from the 1976 campaign, rescued the speech. He flew to Raleigh to help prepare Hunt for what we considered a make-or-break performance. He watched Hunt rehearse the speech. Way too long, Sawyer decided. Too wordy. Too legalistic.

Just hours before Hunt was to speak, Sawyer came up with a simple solution: Cut the speech to the bare bones. Have Hunt say what he had to say and stop. Let the stations fill the time. Frantically, Sawyer and I cut the speech to just over ten minutes. The cuts angered the TV stations but also made the speech better—shorter, stronger, and more succinct.

Hunt told North Carolinians, "I have concluded that there was a fair trial, the jury made the right decision and the appellate courts reviewed it properly and ruled correctly. I have confidence in what our courts and judges have done. Accordingly, I cannot and will not pardon these defendants."

But he did believe the sentences were too severe. He ordered the prison terms reduced, though he made clear his order "does not mean that the defendants are free to walk out of prison." They would have to wait for parole.

Blacks and supporters of the Wilmington Ten exploded in anger. "A step backward," said their attorney, James Ferguson of Charlotte, one of the state's leading civil-rights lawyers. Elizabeth Chavis, Ben Chavis's mother, said, "He will never serve as governor again. The governor has lost a chance to prove himself morally worthy of his position. This was a political decision." The *News & Observer* wrote in an editorial, "Unfortunately, the governor did not move far enough in the right direction. . . . [Hunt,] it seems, sought to please both sides and wound up pleasing neither."

But the decision did please whites and conservatives. L. M. Cromartie, who had been mayor of Wilmington in 1971, said, "The governor tempered justice with mercy." State Senator Ralph Scott, Hunt's old ally, said, "It was one of those difficult decisions to make, but I think it was as fair as could be." After surveying Hunt's (mostly white) keys, Joe Pell told me, "He's never been more popular." What about Hunt's black supporters? Pell was blunt: "Where do they have to go?" He was confident that, over time, the anger among African-Americans would diminish.

Hunt's decision mirrored the competing impulses within him—and the balance he always sought. One aide involved in the case asked years later, "What's wrong with doing something that's acceptable to both sides?" Hunt said he did not try to satisfy both sides but instead based his decision on the facts. In truth, he searched for a middle ground—not only in public opinion but within himself. Hunt believed that blacks often were treated unjustly by the criminal justice system, but he also felt crime was a serious problem that required tough action.

Liberals, then and later, dismissed Hunt's tough-on-crime stance as a political ploy. But he always maintained that his feelings went deeper: "Crime hurts people. It's wrong and it hurts people. And it hurts people who are disadvantaged and who are poor and live in poor communities more than anybody else."

Critics especially questioned Hunt's support for the death penalty. He had not always felt that way. Growing up and in college, Hunt recalled, he was "somebody who was pretty progressive in my thinking, maybe a little liberal, maybe questioned the death penalty." The fundamental question, Hunt concluded, was, "Do you have greater safety, fewer lives lost, less hurt if you have capital punishment than if you don't have it? In other words, is it a deterrent? I thought a lot about it then and later on as governor. And I concluded that it was a deterrent."

Vengeance could not be a justification for capital punishment, he said. "You cannot morally justify that, in my opinion. You can morally justify taking a life only as a way to save other lives, innocent lives."

Like his father pulling out a clipping when he argued about government farm programs, Hunt had a newspaper article that supported his position. The story was about an inmate in California who was convicted of murder during a time when that state did not have the death penalty. Asked if the death penalty would have deterred him, the inmate said, "You're darned right. I'd have taken a life many a time if it hadn't been for that. I didn't want to die." Hunt carried the clipping in his wallet for years. Not until nearly twenty years later, toward the end of his fourth term, would he commute a death sentence and prevent an execution.

Just as the Wilmington Ten decision represented Hunt's conservative side that first year, his support for the Equal Rights Amendment to the United States Constitution represented his liberal side. The effort to guarantee equal rights for women had sailed along for years with bipartisan support. The amendment needed to pass in just one more state to be ratified. Its supporters looked to North Carolina—and Jim Hunt.

But conservatives were mobilizing against the ERA. They had a powerful ally in North Carolina: former United States senator Sam Ervin. By now eighty years old, Ervin had served in the Senate from 1954 to 1974, retiring after his star turn in 1973 and 1974 as chairman of the Senate's special Watergate Committee. In that role, he had won national acclaim as a lovable and principled "Uncle Sam," something of a latter-day founding father who stood up against Richard Nixon and all the president's men.

But Ervin also had another side. He was always an implacable foe of civil-rights laws. Now, he was thundering against the ERA. His status as a constitutional scholar gave intellectual weight to the amendment's opponents. So did the opposition of North Carolina's chief justice, Susie Sharp. Although Governor Kerr Scott had appointed her the first woman judge in the state back in 1949 and Terry Sanford made her the first female justice of the North Carolina Supreme Court in 1962, she opposed the ERA for women.

The State House easily passed the amendment. The Senate was the obstacle. Hunt's count showed he was just one vote short. He met with every senator he thought he could persuade. A handful of holdouts, most from conservative rural districts, were his targets. But the legislators were intimidated by the loud and growing chorus of opposition led by Ervin, Sharp, and pastors from small fundamentalist churches back home.

Hunt's last hope was Senator R. C. Soles, a longtime legislator from rural Columbus County in the southeastern part of the state. Soles said he wanted to help Hunt. He would go home over the weekend and think about it. But when he came back, he told Hunt he couldn't do it. His mother had told him to vote against the ERA, he said.

Hunt mused years later, "How can you ask a man to go against his mother?"

Later, Hunt found a bright side to the defeat. The legislators who said no to him on the ERA felt they had to say yes the next time he asked for something. Like succession.

But supporters of the ERA—both then and in 1983, when Hunt

tried and failed again to pass the amendment—accused the governor of not doing all he could. After all, they fumed, he won plenty of other tough fights in the legislature. Why couldn't he pass the ERA?

Hunt said later of his critics, "They thought we could work magic, I guess. The fact that we'd been so successful made a lot of people think that anything we wanted to do we could get done. Many of them were urban people who didn't understand what rural North Carolina is like out there."

Hunt understood how conservative North Carolina could be, especially when it came to race. And he was determined to change that.

He brought Ben Ruffin, the black activist from Durham who had testified before Hunt's party-reform commission, into the governor's office as special assistant on minority affairs. He appointed Richard C. Erwin of Winston-Salem as the first black judge on the North Carolina Court of Appeals. He appointed Clifton E. Johnson as the first black superior-court judge.

Jim Phillips, who later became a prominent attorney and chairman of the University of North Carolina Board of Governors, landed a job out of college working as Hunt's assistant on appointments to state boards and commissions. Phillips said years later that he realized Hunt "was remaking the state's power structure by appointing African-Americans to judgeships, boards, and commissions and to state government for the first time."

Howard Lee, whom Hunt had appointed as the first black cabinet secretary, said in 2008, "He was the first governor to bring women and minorities, especially blacks, into central roles in government. He was willing to take risks. It was risky. Appointing me was a hell of a risk. There was still a tinge of racism in the state, including among a lot of Hunt's supporters. Some even told him he shouldn't appoint me. He was a very political, astute individual. But very courageous. He doesn't get enough credit for that."

Always, race was an issue. On top of the Wilmington Ten case, Hunt was thrust into a battle when the federal government in Washington—a Democratic administration, no less—cast the University of

Hunt at the swearing-in of his first cabinet on January 10, 1977. From left are Joe Grimsley, Sarah Morrow, Howard Lee, Sarah Hodgkins, Tom Bradshaw, and Lauch Faircloth.
Photo by Charlie Jones

North Carolina system, the bastion of liberalism and racial enlightenment, as an illegal outpost of discrimination.

Several of the university's sixteen campuses had nearly all-black student bodies. In the early 1970s, the United States Department of Health, Education, and Welfare began questioning whether or not that arrangement amounted to separate—and unequal—systems of higher education. The pressure increased dramatically in 1977 when President Carter appointed Joe Califano secretary of HEW. Califano, a longtime liberal warrior who had been one of President Lyndon Johnson's aides, was determined to eliminate what he believed were vast—and illegal—disparities between the university's black and white institutions.

Bill Friday, the longtime president of the university, was stung by the charge of racial discrimination. He didn't like the criticism and didn't welcome interference from Washington. He especially didn't like being accused of unfairness to African-Americans. After all, he was a protégé of Frank Porter Graham.

Hunt saw both sides of the debate. He said later, "We did have a system that was too much segregated, for historical reasons, and we needed to change that." The black institutions were short-changed when it came to money and programs. Their buildings and academic offerings were inferior to those at the predominantly white campuses. But Hunt added, "When you're governor of the state, you can't either let, or appear to let, the federal government overrun you. People don't respect you." He and Friday felt pressure from university alumni who resented Califano and HEW.

The dispute raged for years. Hunt and Friday urged the legislature to appropriate money to improve facilities and programs at the historically black institutions. Hunt tried unsuccessfully to mediate between the university and HEW. The issue was hurting the image of the university—and the state, he thought. But the situation did not ease until 1979, when Carter, under growing political pressure and with his popularity plummeting, dumped Califano.

Before Califano left—as if he hadn't already done enough to antagonize North Carolina and make Hunt politically uncomfortable—he launched a loud and aggressive crusade against tobacco, the crop on which Tar Heel farmers—and indeed entire communities, universities, and the state's economy—had relied for so long. As a boy, Hunt had harvested tobacco on his parents' farm. In graduate school, he wrote his master's thesis on the tobacco price-support program. His paper won a prize from the American Farm Economics Association as one of the three best in the country. Tobacco was sacred in North Carolina politics. A must-stop on every politician's schedule in late summer was auction day at a tobacco warehouse.

Since 1964, the nation's surgeon generals had labeled smoking a health danger. But the federal government had never taken strong action. Now, Califano did. Washington seemed determined to make tobacco—and the state that grew so much of it—a pariah.

Tobacco farmers, encouraged by the R. J. Reynolds and Philip Mor-

Hunt grew up on a tobacco and dairy farm and was comfortable making the obligatory campaign stops at tobacco warehouses. He appears here with Thad Sharp, Jr., and Sharp's son Pender at the Liberty Warehouse in Wilson in August 1984.
Photo courtesy of the *News & Observer*

ris cigarette companies, erupted in rage. Farmers' trucks sported bumper stickers reading, "Califano Is Dangerous To My Health." Jesse Helms and fellow Republicans gleefully pilloried Califano and Carter. Even loyal Democrats like Agriculture Commissioner Jim Graham blasted Califano. Graham, a crusty farmer from Rowan County who had been commissioner since 1964 and would keep the job until 2001, mounted a sign in his office: "Thank You For Smoking."

Hunt understood the health risks. He never smoked himself; his father had discouraged it. Still, he felt Califano was wrong: "I thought they were really trying to put us out of business with tobacco."

He also feared Califano would put Democrats out of business politically in North Carolina. Helms was up for reelection to the Senate in 1978, and Califano was a godsend for his campaign. Califano was the kind of liberal Washington bureaucrat Helms had always demonized.

Helms was still viewed as a one-term fluke of the 1972 Republican landslide. Democrats' best hope for unseating him seemed to be Luther Hodges, Jr., a successful banker in Charlotte and son of the "Businessman Governor" of the 1950s. But in accordance with Bert Bennett's rule, Hunt told his political team to stay out of the Democratic primary.

We were stunned when Hodges was upset by John Ingram. Ingram was a maverick state representative from Randolph County who had been elected commissioner of insurance in 1972. In that office, he earned a populist reputation by regularly attacking the insurance industry. Ingram's 1978 campaign was amateurish and scared the business community. That fall, Hunt tried to strike an uncomfortable balance between keeping his distance from Ingram and doing what was expected of the party's titular leader. Ingram, who raised little money, lost to Helms.

Hunt never turned against Jimmy Carter even though the president let Califano cause so much trouble in North Carolina. Years later, Hunt talked about the line he walked on tobacco and desegregation of the university system: "You've got to stand up for what you think is right. You've got to be loyal to your people and your institutions. But you've got to also be open to people pointing out where you aren't doing things fairly, you aren't doing things adequately. You've got to be open to people from outside pointing out problems and pushing to get changes made. But there's a right and wrong way to do it, and you have a responsibility to stick up for your state and your people, but not to be close-minded about whether or not change ought to be made."

Amid the social tremors of the times, Hunt's instinct was always to search for stable middle ground. He was cautious and careful, constantly calculating how far he could go politically. Because of where he came from, he understood people who resisted change. Because of where he wanted the state to go, he saw the need for it. His ability to see—and talk to—both sides was a political asset. But he increasingly acquired a reputation as too cautious, as a governor always with a finger to the political wind.

He would later pay dearly for that reputation.

Chapter 8

Education Governor, CEO Governor

Joe Califano's crusade against tobacco foreshadowed an economic revolution in North Carolina. Change had begun arriving in the 1950s as national companies moved their plants to the South, where the weather was warm, wages were low, and unions weren't welcome. North Carolina was in a perfect location, halfway between Florida and the Northeast. The state had a business-friendly climate.

It also had a handful of visionaries who thought the state could attract research-based companies. They had the audacious idea of establishing a research park between Raleigh, Durham, and Chapel Hill, drawing on the area's three major universities: N.C. State, Duke, and UNC. At first, the idea looked like pie in the sky. Until IBM put a facility there, the land set aside for the Research Triangle Park sat empty for years.

Then Terry Sanford's gamble on John Kennedy in 1960 paid off. Sanford wanted the new National Institute of Environmental Health to be located in the Research Triangle Park. The institute's bureaucrats wanted it in Washington. Kennedy's friends wanted it in Boston. But

Kennedy remembered Sanford's support in 1960. The president put the institute in North Carolina. The park began a boom that was to transform the region—and the state.

In the 1970s, Hunt said later, "I saw what was happening to our traditional industries." Textile and furniture companies were shedding jobs and beginning to move overseas. For a time early in the decade, North Carolina had the highest unemployment rate in the nation. "I certainly was watching agriculture change, because I was in it. We saw the forces arrayed against tobacco."

Hunt grew up and lived on a farm. He was trained as an economist. He had worked as an economic adviser in Nepal. He knew about poverty. "I came from a poor section, and I knew a lot of poor folks," he said years later. "I was anxious to get good jobs and transform the economy so we would have more good, high-paying jobs that had a future."

Hunt believed that a governor's job was to "have a vision for the future and sell it." His vision was beginning to focus on new technologies. He said later, "Coming through N.C. State was kind of important for me because I learned about science. I learned about the scientific method and developed a real interest in scientific and technical things."

Most of all, Hunt came to believe the future would belong to the well-educated. "All the new industries required people who were brighter, more creative and innovative," he said in 2008. "So the schools had to be better." In giving his second State of the State Address in 1979, he put the challenge this way: "Are we ready for the 1980s?"

Wayne McDevitt, who filled a series of jobs throughout Hunt's four administrations and later served on the State Board of Education, said later of those days, "It used to be okay to drop out of school at sixteen, because you could go to work on the farm or in the mill. He positioned North Carolina to be ready for the wave. He connected the dots before others did. He educated all of us."

Educated is the right word. Hunt had a lot of teacher in him. And when he got wound up at the podium, he had a lot of preacher in him, too. He saw it as his job to educate North Carolinians—and to convert them. He said later, "The governor, like the president, is supposed to educate people, tell them what they need to know, to help get them educated about the issues that affect them."

Hunt began emphasizing the connection between education and the economy. He heard that message from corporate executives he was recruiting to North Carolina. They needed an educated work force. They needed more than strong bodies; they needed brains.

He recalled touring a new telecommunications plant in Greensboro with the company's executives. After Hunt cut the ribbon, the plant manager introduced him to an employee who had developed a device that won the firm a big contract with a Japanese telephone company. Hunt said, "I figured that this is a brilliant Ph.D. from N.C. State." Instead, the man turned out to be a graduate of Guilford Technical Community College. Hunt got the lesson: "He was bright. And the point simply is that we have to focus on developing innovation and creativity all the way through the schools—in community colleges, on the plant floor, in higher education, of course. Everybody's got to be more creative, the whole work force."

That meant reforming and modernizing the public schools, Hunt believed. He had confidence that he knew what the schools needed to do. He had teaching in his blood and had done a few months of practice teaching while studying agricultural education at N.C. State. As lieutenant governor and a member of the State Board of Education, he had spent four years learning about and going to schools. Hunt said later, "I found kids who were not performing. They were not learning to read." That's how he came up with the Primary Reading Program that put a reading aide in every first-, second-, and third-grade classroom in the state. Suddenly, "my school had twice as many teachers," recalled one elementary-school teacher.

Teachers loved Hunt. The North Carolina Association of Educators endorsed him in 1976. But teachers didn't like all of his ideas, especially about testing. North Carolina's students were not learning what they should, Hunt thought, because schools had no systematic way to measure their progress. "The only way we measured before was how much money we spent," he said later. He became one of the nation's first advocates for standards and accountability. He proposed standardized annual tests for students, as well as a minimum competency test to assure that high-school graduates achieved a basic level of education.

Many teachers resisted standardized tests. They thought the tests might be used to evaluate them. African-Americans feared the tests would discriminate against or stigmatize black students. But Hunt believed the state had to determine whether or not students were learning. He pushed the testing program through the 1977 legislature.

In 1979, Hunt's education program raised teacher salaries and reduced class sizes. He got more money for students who needed special help. He established an institute to train principals and a second location for the summer Governor's School for gifted students. He pushed the State Board of Education to raise the core requirements for high-school graduation, especially in English, the sciences, and mathematics. He got money to fund dropout-prevention programs. He formed a committee of business executives to work on improving math and science instruction. He appointed Betty Owen, a teacher and consultant in Charlotte who had worked in the 1976 campaign there, as his education adviser, which allowed him to boast that he was the first governor in America with an adviser focused solely on education issues.

From the perspective of three subsequent decades of education reform, Hunt's early program "was pretty crude," said Ferrel Guillory, who was watching Hunt and writing editorials at the *News & Observer* in the 1970s. "But it was the best we knew then. He got us started."

Hunt also started North Carolina on a new pursuit of high-technology jobs. The roots of North Carolina's old economy were dying, and Hunt was planting seeds for the future. He said later, "We saw the world changing. We knew that we had to change. We spotted where the jobs of the future were going to be, and we went after them."

He plunged into the industry-recruiting game with characteristic energy. Hunt was a natural salesman. He recruited CEOs the same way he lobbied legislators—by bombarding them with calls, letters, and visits. Did they need to look at potential plant sites? Hunt would dispatch the state airplane or helicopter. Need job training? Hunt was on the phone to community college presidents. Want information about roads, water and sewer, land costs, taxes? Hunt would see they got it.

He drove the Department of Commerce's industrial recruiters like he drove campaign aides. The recruiters couldn't give him too many calls to make, too many companies to visit, or too many executives to host at the mansion or the Capitol. He went to London three times to recruit the pharmaceutical giant Glaxo. He went to Europe. He went to Japan. He went all over the United States. He wore out two sets of security men—one shift in the morning and another in the afternoon and night.

He liked to keep score: how many companies announced they were coming to North Carolina, how much money they planned to invest in plants and equipment, how many jobs they would bring. Every time there was an announcement of a new industry, Hunt wanted to be on the program. Every time a ribbon was cut, he was there with the scissors. Every quarter, he wanted a report on how North Carolina was doing, and he wanted it public. He trumpeted the numbers in his press conferences and speeches. For his 1979 speech to the legislature, he had his staff build an electronic board so he could show how many companies his administration had recruited and how many communities were getting new plants and jobs.

Hunt wasn't selling just North Carolina. He was selling himself. Many businessmen in the state—and they were nearly all men then—were suspicious of Hunt. He was a politician. He was young and had a liberal reputation. He had never worked in business. He had been a lawyer for only a few years, and they had no use for lawyers anyway.

Some old-line businessmen also didn't like Hunt's emphasis on new jobs, new industries, and a more educated work force. Many of the tough, conservative men who owned textile mills and furniture factories wanted strong-bodied, hardworking employees. A mill worker didn't need much education. Some owners thought too much education was dangerous. It could lead to unions, uppity employees, and demands for higher wages.

Early in Hunt's term, the Raleigh Chamber of Commerce "hit the ceiling" when he recruited a unionized company to the area, recalled Ferrel Guillory. But "Hunt stared the chamber down. He said, 'We're going to put wage levels first. We need higher wages.' That was an indication of his mind-set. The old instinct was to be antiunion or at least suspicious of the union. He said, 'We've got to change, and I have to ride it and foster it.'"

Much the same thing happened in Cabarrus County when Hunt recruited a Philip Morris cigarette plant there. Cannon Mills, the giant textile company based in Cabarrus near Charlotte, was not pleased. Cannon was strongly antiunion, and Philip Morris was a unionized company that paid high wages—as much as $100,000 a year for some line workers. Hunt recalled, "I went all out. South Carolina and other states were trying to get Philip Morris." It was the kind of campaign Hunt loved. Cabarrus County residents organized a big rally for Philip Morris. Thousands of people came. Hunt remembered, "People brought up bushel baskets full of petitions signed by people who wanted Philip Morris to come." Philip Morris came.

Hunt's horizons grew wider. He led trade missions not only to Europe, the traditional hunting ground for governors, but also to Asia. In Tokyo in 1978, Hunt had coffee with the United States ambassador, Mike Mansfield, a former senator from Montana. Mansfield told him, "The Japanese can smell the future." Hunt would return to Asia nearly a dozen times as governor and continue to visit long after he left office. In 1979, as China was beginning to escape the shadow of Mao Zedong and reach out to the rest of the world, Hunt led a trade mission there, becoming one of America's first governors to do so.

He began looking at emerging technologies. He heard about something called microelectronics—making the chips that drove computers. He wrote a note to Quentin Lindsey, his old college professor and the man who had recruited him to Nepal, who was now science and technology adviser in the governor's office. Lindsey recalled that the note said something like, "It seems that microelectronics is a growing field, and we need an organization that can push this. Let's get one like that."

Lindsey talked to professors and administrators at the state's universities, and they came up with the idea of establishing the North Carolina Microelectronics Center in the Research Triangle. The center would provide research and support to government, universities, and industries. The idea quickly caught the interest of companies like General Electric. Hunt convinced the legislature to put up money to establish the center. Soon, North Carolina began to earn a reputation around the country as a center for the fast-growing high-technology industry.

Hunt made recruiting trips to California's Silicon Valley, the center of the computer world. "What an audacious thing to do," Burley Mitchell, one of his cabinet secretaries, said decades later. "Asking them to come to North Carolina? Some of them didn't think we wore shoes."

Recalling his trips to Silicon Valley, Europe, and Asia, Hunt said later, "That's when I really got my eyes opened. We learned what the jobs of the future were going to be. They were going to be information technology, a big area. We learned they were going to be in life sciences, pharmaceuticals, biotechnology, all of that."

Hunt soon became known as one of what were called "Atari Democrats," after the then-hot video-game and home-computer company. The name referred to young, moderate party leaders interested in high-tech industries.

In 1981, as his second term began, Hunt persuaded the legislature to establish the North Carolina Biotechnology Center. The state eventually became home to a booming biotechnology and pharmaceutical sector. Lindsey said in 2008, "I've often thought that in terms of effect on society, the biotechnology center probably was the greatest thing we did in the long run." By 2010, North Carolina was the third-biggest state in the country in biotechnology.

Lindsey had another assignment from Hunt, one he got his first day on the job. Hunt summoned him to dinner at the mansion with John Ehle and Eli Evans, two old friends of Terry Sanford's who had helped him start the North Carolina School of the Arts. Now, Ehle and Evans had the idea of establishing a residential high school for students gifted in science and mathematics.

Hunt in a familiar setting: working on his speech while flying to an event
PHOTO FROM GOVERNOR HUNT'S PERSONAL COLLECTION

Hunt embraced the idea. He asked the legislature for the money, but it was no easy sell. Editorial writers questioned if the school would be elitist. The superintendent of public instruction, Craig Phillips, who was independently elected, didn't like the idea of the school being outside the control of his department. But business leaders loved it, Hunt recalled.

The school lost its first vote in the legislature. But as Lindsey recalled, "Jim got his organization going that night, and we turned that around the next day." Hunt asked his keys to call legislators. He arranged to fly a legislator back to Raleigh from western North Carolina for a vote. He won the fight. The old-school political organization saved a new-economy idea. The North Carolina School of Science and Mathematics, which was located in Durham and welcomed its first class in 1982, eventually became one of Hunt's lasting accomplishments. After leaving office, he delighted in meeting graduates of the school, especially those who lived in the James B. Hunt Jr. Dormitory.

The science and mathematics school showed that Hunt was willing to go outside the traditional state agencies when he wanted new initiatives. When he ran into resistance, he was willing to fight an ingrained business culture that for decades hadn't seen much need for education past high school. He was also willing to fight teachers and the education establishment. He wasn't afraid to use the powers of office, the power of his personality, and, most of all, the power of persuasion—and education.

He wasn't afraid of new ideas. "He's like a sponge," Lindsey recalled in 2008. "He soaks up knowledge and ideas wherever he goes and meets new and different people."

Hunt said later, "I think people who are intellectually curious—and who are not insecure in that they might appear not to know everything—like to hear ideas from a variety of sources. And by the way, one of the best ways you can learn anything is to get the hell out of your office and go out there where the people are."

Hunt was more than a salesman for North Carolina. He became the state's face to the nation and the world. He gave North Carolina the image of a state that put a high value on brains and innovation.

He said later, "Time was when they said about North Carolina, 'Well, you've got good universities, but your public schools are lousy.'" That reputation changed, especially in areas like the Triangle. The *New York Times* hailed the North Carolina School of Science and Mathematics. *Time* magazine wrote about Hunt's education reforms. The biotechnology center and the microelectronics center brought attention to the state.

Hunt had confidence in what he was doing. Burley Mitchell said later, "Nothing's too big for him. He had total confidence in himself and in the state. Few people would have tried to do what he did."

Hunt also had confidence he could get the public's support: "I've always been a big enough fool to think I could sell people on something if it's a good enough idea. I have always believed I could get people to see the importance of education and helping children and helping workers develop the skills they needed to do good jobs. And I always believed I could sell that to the great majority of the people. I always worked to do it, and I seldom failed."

He had another sales job he wanted to do: selling himself to North

The author, right, *and Lauch Faircloth with Hunt at the Great Wall of China in November 1979. Faircloth would later switch to the Republican Party and defeat his old friend Terry Sanford for the United States Senate in 1992.*
PHOTO FROM THE AUTHOR'S COLLECTION

Carolina's business executives. While he viewed some as narrow-minded and reactionary, he also admired businessmen. Bert Bennett was a successful businessman. So were Joe Pell and John A. Williams. So were many of the men who had raised the money and organized his campaign across the state. So were many of the legislators he worked with. Hunt respected them and wanted their respect.

He began courting them, just like he had the Sanford and Moore and Lake keys when he ran for lieutenant governor. Early in Hunt's administration, Paul Sticht, the president of R. J. Reynolds Tobacco Company, suggested that the governor create a special group of corporate executives to advise him. Hunt jumped at the idea. He called it the North Carolina Council on Business Management and Development. Membership was limited to big companies headquartered in the state—utilities like Duke Power and Carolina Power & Light (later Progress Energy), manufacturers like R. J. Reynolds, banks like Wachovia and North Carolina National Bank (later Bank of America). Four times a year, the executives met with Hunt at different places around the state. They started with a reception and dinner Friday night, then followed that with a private discussion of issues.

Sometimes, Hunt recalled, the business leaders sharply differed with him. Once, John Belk of Charlotte, who headed the Belk department-store chain, railed against Hunt's decision to permit state employees a dues "checkoff" for their statewide association. That was a step toward a public-employee union, Belk argued. Hunt disagreed—and didn't back down.

Saturday morning, the council of businessmen had a breakfast and then a formal business session. "I'd have my budget officer report on the state budget," Hunt said later. "Generally, the secretary of commerce reported on the state's economy. My education adviser would always be there, sometimes other people we'd invite in for special things. But we'd talk about the status of the state, where we were, what was going on, what we wanted to do."

The executives found Hunt to be smart, knowledgeable, and determined to win them over. He listened to them. He flattered them.

He cajoled them to support his programs. From that beginning, he built a relationship with the business community that few North Carolina politicians could match. Twenty years later, in his third and fourth terms, he could pick up the phone and mobilize CEOs from the state's biggest companies to lobby legislators for his initiatives.

Asked later about his approach, Hunt said, "I had a pretty good idea of what we needed to do, but I knew I had to have help. I had to get a broad partnership to do it. Some people in politics think, 'I've got my enemies, I'm not going to deal with them.' Well, I had those people in business who probably hadn't supported me. But we brought them in, I met with them on a regular basis, I listened to them, I learned from them, and I responded to their needs when I could. They had an open line."

Hunt liked to tell about a call he got from Bob Graham, the governor of Florida and later a United States senator. Graham suggested an interstate banking law that would let banks in the South open branch offices in other states. "I said, 'Bob, that's an interesting idea. Let me talk to some of my folks and I'll be back in touch with you.' " Hunt called his new friends, the presidents of North Carolina's biggest banks. They told him, "That's exactly what we want," he recalled. Eventually, the North Carolina institutions gobbled up Florida's banks and made Charlotte second only to New York among the nation's banking centers. "That was the last thing in the world Bob Graham had in mind," Hunt laughed.

He also wanted to reassure the business community he was no wild-eyed liberal when it came to taxes and spending. With banker John Medlin's prompting, Hunt had ruled out any tax increases in his 1976 campaign. In 1979, an antitax movement broke out in California and spread across the nation. Hunt became a zealous advocate of fiscal restraint. While his legislative address that year called for more education spending, Hunt also proposed a series of tax cuts. "We must be both frugal and compassionate," he said. "We must govern with our heads as well as our hearts." The *News & Observer* said in an editorial that Hunt's "heart seemed to pull him one way while his political head tugged another way. Hunt proclaimed grand goals, but took only limited steps toward them."

The speech captured the essence of Hunt. He wanted to bring everybody into his tent. Years later, he said that instinct went back to the way he grew up in rural North Carolina. With the big exception of racial segregation, "everybody was kind of equal," he said. "We didn't have any people who lorded it over us, or had power over us or anything like that. We all went to church together, went to school together. I wasn't a part of a situation where there were social betters and people who were not as good and you couldn't dare to get above your raising or anything of that sort."

That was his approach to campus politics at N.C. State. "I'd get the engineers, the agriculture people, and the education people, and the athletes. It's always been my approach, to organize every group you could find, put them all together. And that is the way to be politically successful. Some people want to divide folks up and separate them and set them against each other. That may work in the short term, but in the long term you don't get things done."

It was all about getting things done. It was about education, not just for its own sake but for North Carolina's economic future. It was about getting ready for a dramatic economic transformation.

Would that transformation have come without Hunt? "Probably, but not as fast," said Tom Lambeth, who had been a young aide to Terry Sanford and later became executive director of the Z. Smith Reynolds Foundation.

Lambeth was right. Few statewide political leaders at the time were as passionate as Hunt about the importance of preparing for a new economy. Always in times of wrenching change, it is easier for politicians to promise to protect the status quo, even when that is a doomed strategy. Throughout North Carolina in the late 1970s, people were wedded to the old economic structure. The natural human tendency was to fear change—and even deny that it was needed. Hunt not only preached that North Carolina could meet the challenge, he relentlessly encouraged people to embrace the opportunities that change presented.

Decades later, I asked Hunt what he thought would have happened if a political opponent—say, Jesse Helms—had been governor. He said, "You would not have had the funding for education. And I can't prove this, but I think they would not have had the enthusiasm for new ideas. I think they would have been very socially conservative, would have wanted things to be socially stagnant. They would not have been turned on by new ideas and pursued them vigorously in their own reading and their own learning. Would not have welcomed a great variety and diversity of people."

He added, "They would have done some things, of course. But they would have been ultraconservative and not wanted change and surely not have made education the top priority."

Hunt said he realized how much things had changed and the state had grown when, after leaving office in 2001, he was invited to cut the ribbon at a company he had recruited from Germany. Searching for the site in the now-massive Research Triangle Park, "I got lost," he said. "I drove around half an hour before I found the place."

Part II
Fall

Governor Hunt on election night 1980 with his mother, Elsie Brame Hunt, and father, James B. Hunt. Hunt was a combination of his father's tough stubbornness and his mother's kinder nature. At left is Hunt's son, Baxter.

PHOTO BY COLBERT HOWELL

Chapter 9

Against the Wind

For Hunt, 1980 was a triumphant year. It was when he became the first North Carolina governor in modern history elected to a second term. But it was also the year that foreshadowed his downfall. It brought the full force of a political tsunami that had been building since 1964, when Lyndon Johnson signed the Civil Rights Act, Southern whites began voting Republican, and voters across the nation started turning against big-government liberalism. The real winners in 1980 would turn out to be Ronald Reagan and Jesse Helms.

At the beginning of the year, though, we were more worried about a Democrat: Bob Scott.

Scott, who had been governor from 1969 to 1973, was the heir to North Carolina's premier political dynasty. He was the son of Jim Hunt's boyhood hero, Kerr Scott. Ralph Scott, Kerr's brother and Bob's uncle, was one of Hunt's strongest allies in the North Carolina Senate. Bob Scott helped launch Hunt's career by appointing him chairman of the state Democratic Party reform commission after the 1968 national convention.

The Hunts at the 1981 Inaugural Ball. Both the 1977 and 1981 balls were alcohol-free. By 1993, the famously straight-laced Hunt loosened up and allowed wine to be served at mansion events.
Photo from Governor Hunt's personal collection

But the ties frayed in Hunt's first term. Scott was only forty-three when he left the governor's office. He was a farmer, not a lawyer, so he couldn't pursue the normal post-official career of other governors. He struggled to land a suitable job. In 1979, he found one he wanted: the state's community college system needed a new president.

Scott went to see Hunt. He told the governor he was interested in the job. Hunt was guarded. He said later, "My recollection clearly is that I told him he's a qualified candidate, but that we had to go through the process of letting the board make the decision. And if Bob Scott was the best person, I figured he'd come through the process, the selection process."

That's not how Scott interpreted the meeting. He thought he had been promised the job, Hunt gathered later—"which is absolutely not true." Scott should have known how to read their conversation, Hunt believed. "When you talk to somebody and they say, 'I think you'd make a good one, but you've got to go through the process,' you don't take it and say, 'Well, that means I can have it.' Good gosh almighty. He's a politician."

Instead of Scott, the community college board picked Larry Blake from Oregon. Blake had a national reputation in community college circles but little instinct for how to operate in North Carolina. His selection was a mistake, Hunt decided later. But the damage was done with Scott. He thought Hunt had betrayed him.

Scott started making speeches and giving interviews around the state criticizing Hunt. The governor was not progressive enough, not bold enough, Scott said. Scott prided himself on having fought some tough battles when he was governor. He had put the first state tax on tobacco. He had fought to consolidate the state university system. He said Hunt was not providing the same courageous leadership.

Scott got attention in the press. He also received encouragement from other Democrats who were dissatisfied with Hunt, often because they—like Scott—hadn't gotten what they wanted from the administration. Some of Scott's old aides were eager to be back in power.

But politics had changed since Scott last ran in 1968. Most of his

Hunt and Bob Scott on primary night in May 1980. Hunt soundly defeated Scott and went on to be reelected in November. Scott, governor from 1969 to 1973, ran against Hunt after he was denied a bid to be president of the state's community college system.

PHOTO COURTESY OF THE *NEWS & OBSERVER*

old supporters were with Hunt now. They had good jobs and appointments. They had a direct line to Joe Pell in the Capitol. They had no interest in taking a gamble on Scott.

Hunt's poll ratings were high. Everyone knew about his intense pursuit of high-technology companies. He had pushed nearly all of his program through the legislature. His administration had avoided major scandals.

The Hunt campaign had plenty of money, and we organized an aggressive primary campaign. Scott had made enemies—and some mistakes—as governor. We used the tobacco tax against him in eastern North Carolina. We played on the press's suspicion that Scott was running out of personal pique rather than principle. Joe Grimsley left the

Department of Administration to once again direct Hunt's campaign. He organized a phalanx of groups for Hunt—teachers, women, labor, business people, African-Americans, farmers. David Sawyer made ads celebrating North Carolina's progress. One ad had Hunt holding up a computer chip, a symbol of the state's then-booming economy and the governor's relentless optimism about the future.

It wasn't close. We routed Scott. Hunt won over 70 percent of the vote and carried every county. Campaign staffers mounted a one-hundred-county map of the state and presented it to Grimsley. Hunt took special satisfaction that he carried even Scott's home county of Alamance.

The political weather that fall was more threatening. Jimmy Carter had stumbled badly in the White House. The economy was in the doldrums; both inflation and unemployment were high. The Iran hostage crisis was dragging on. Carter gave a speech that, though he never used the word, became known as the "Malaise Speech." His poll ratings jumped, then plummeted when he followed up by firing his entire

Carolyn and Jim Hunt at a campaign event in Wilson with President Carter and then-Congressman Charles Whitley in August 1978
Photo by Charles I. Buchanan, *Kinston Free Press*

cabinet. Ted Kennedy challenged Carter in the Democratic primaries.

Hunt said later of Carter, "I thought the world of him personally, and still do. But I thought that a lot of the people in the White House with him didn't work with Congress very effectively and that he didn't necessarily handle his politics particularly well."

As the 1980 presidential election neared, "I figured the Republican candidate was going to run strongly," Hunt recalled. As for Carter, "I knew that he was not going over too well, but I thought he would get reelected because I thought he was in the mainstream of America. And he would have if it hadn't been for Iran, maybe if it hadn't been for Teddy Kennedy challenging him."

That year, Ronald Reagan reenergized the Republican Party. He rode the nation's conservative, antitax mood. And Jesse Helms and his Congressional Club were in the vanguard of the conservative movement.

The Congressional Club was started after 1972 to retire Helms's campaign debt. Its first fundraisers were the chicken-and-a-speech dinners that were a mainstay of politics. But during Helms's reelection campaign in 1978, the club's godfather, Tom Ellis, discovered the power of direct-mail fundraising. The club identified thousands of conservatives across the nation who would send checks for a hundred dollars, fifty dollars, or less—and send them month after month—if they received the right kind of letter. Ellis's operation, overseen by Carter Wrenn, mastered pushing the right emotional buttons to maximize the take. The club's offices in North Raleigh had one floor filled with mainframe computers to maintain lists and spew out letters.

Its status as a money machine made the club a political powerhouse in its own right, separate from and more powerful than the state Republican Party. In 1980, as in 1976, Helms and Ellis threw everything they had behind Reagan's presidential campaign. And Ellis decided he wanted to elect another conservative United States senator in North Carolina—and a conservative governor. He began looking for candidates.

One prospect was the son and namesake of I. Beverly Lake, Terry

Sanford's opponent in 1960 and Ellis's colleague in the fight against school desegregation in the 1950s. Beverly Lake, Jr., was a state senator from Raleigh and a conservative Democrat. He had cosponsored some of Governor Hunt's tough anticrime bills. He had a name, and he had ambition.

Lake also had a mustache. Ellis told him it had to go. He shaved. Lake had a penchant for wearing loud sports jackets. Ellis sent him to Nowell's, one of Raleigh's finest men's stores, to buy some dark suits. Ellis told him to change his registration to Republican, then asked him whether he wanted to run for governor or senator. Lake said governor. Ellis, Wrenn, and their growing team of seasoned operatives at the Congressional Club began running Lake's campaign against Hunt.

But like Bob Scott, Lake had trouble getting traction. Many Helms supporters, especially conservative farmers in eastern North Carolina,

Hunt with Terry Sanford in January 1981 at the second inauguration. The first political campaign Hunt worked on was Sanford's race for governor in 1960. Hunt organized college students for Sanford and John F. Kennedy.
Photo by Charlie Jones

supported Hunt for governor. The hot national issues—like the Panama Canal—did not translate to the governor's race. The governor's office was about jobs, education, and crime.

Lake also lacked any particular fire in his belly. His staffers later told of having to go to Lake's house in the morning and wake him up. By the time he got started, Hunt had been campaigning for hours.

Ellis thought he spotted a vulnerability. The *News & Observer* had raised questions about contracts that Howard Lee, Hunt's secretary of the Department of Natural Resources and Community Development, signed with Wilbur Hobby, who headed the state AFL-CIO. Ellis could just see the pictures. Hobby looked like a caricature of a union boss, bald and overweight. And Lee was black.

Ellis set a trap. Lake and Hunt had one televised debate in the campaign. Knowing the history of Ellis-run campaigns, we carefully negotiated the rules. No props or visual aids would be allowed. We didn't want any surprises.

The night of the debate was the first time I saw Ellis and Wrenn. They accompanied Lake into the room. Wrenn was pushing a young man in a wheelchair. He was Bob Harris, who later became legendary as the Congressional Club's opposition researcher. Harris suffered from spinal muscular atrophy, which over time robbed him of the ability to move any part of his body, though his mind was unaffected. Eventually, Wrenn said, Harris became "pure brain." Lacking the distractions that occupied most people, he devoted his life to political research. He had delved into the Lee-Hobby contracts. That night, he was carrying several large covered boards in his wheelchair. They looked to be posters intended for display during the debate.

Stephanie Bass, the Hunt campaign's press secretary, immediately alerted Wade Hargrove, the attorney for the debate's sponsor, the North Carolina Broadcasters Association. Hargrove had worked out ground rules with both campaigns. Bass reminded him that visual aids were prohibited. Hargrove, a Republican himself, confirmed that she was right. Bass made sure Hargrove reminded the debate moderator, Wally Ausley, of the rule.

Ausley was an affable radio personality. He did play-by-play broadcasts for N.C. State football and basketball games and had a neighborly talk show. In the pre–Rush Limbaugh days, the federal Fairness Doctrine kept most political controversy off the airwaves. Ausley had no idea he was about to be hurled into a new world of political communications.

As the broadcast began, Lake unveiled his posters—large, unflattering pictures of Hunt, Hobby, and Lee. Hunt immediately objected. He asked Ausley to make Lake take the posters down. Ausley deferred to Hargrove, who confirmed that Hunt was correct. The posters were taken down. Deprived of the visuals, Lake had little luck making an issue of the Lee-Hobby deals.

When the debate ended, Ellis erupted right there in front of us all. He had a legendary temper and turned it full force on Hargrove. Ellis swore revenge. And he would exact it. After Reagan was elected president, Hargrove hoped for an appointment to the Federal Communications Commission. He was one of the nation's best-regarded communications lawyers and had been a Republican during the long years the party was in the minority in North Carolina. But Ellis vetoed his appointment. Hargrove never served on the FCC.

While Lake's campaign sputtered through the fall, Ellis had better luck in the Senate race. The incumbent Democrat, Robert Morgan, had conservative roots. After managing the campaign of Beverly Lake, Sr., in 1960, he had been elected attorney general in 1968, unseating an incumbent. In office, Morgan took on utility companies over electric rates and won a reputation as a consumer advocate. He distanced himself from Lake's segregationist views. In 1974, in the wake of Watergate, Morgan rode a Democratic wave into the Senate. But his staff operation there was sloppy, especially compared to Helms's legendarily efficient constituent service.

In 1978, Morgan had refrained from campaigning against Helms, expecting Helms to extend the same courtesy in 1980. Instead, the Congressional Club hit Morgan with a televised two-by-four. Using Helms's name on fundraising letters, the club drew millions of dollars from across the country for the Senate race. Most of the money went to ads attacking Morgan, especially on the issue that had carried North Carolina for Ronald Reagan in 1976: the Panama Canal.

North Carolina television sets were flooded with something new in politics: negative commercials. The ads hammered Morgan as a liberal and attacked him on the canal. One purportedly showed an aircraft carrier going through the canal, though in reality it was too narrow to accommodate such a vessel.

What the ads almost never showed was Morgan's opponent, John East. East was an obscure professor of political science at East Carolina University. He had been a perennial Republican candidate—and a perennial loser—until Ellis recruited him in 1980. East stayed out of sight. Few voters knew he was confined to a wheelchair because of an earlier bout of polio.

All that mattered was the drumbeat of ads against Morgan—and the growing Republican tide in North Carolina. Carter's winning coalition from 1976 was breaking up. Then, he had won thousands of votes from evangelical Christians. Now, the emerging religious right led by Jerry Falwell was lining up for Republicans.

Through the fall campaign, Hunt gave speeches for Carter and other Democratic candidates. But as always, he focused on his own election. He said later, "We were at the height of our political effectiveness. We had a team out there, we had a damn good one in '76, but it was a better one in '80, because everybody who helped us in '76 helped us again, and we got a lot of new ones in. So we just had a powerful team. We had a record. When you're up for reelection, you run on your record. You run on your promises your first time. After that, you run on your record."

There were stumbles. During the campaign, allegations erupted that a state employee named Mather Slaughter was sending political intelligence reports to the state Democratic Party. A brouhaha erupted in the media. But Hunt kept his distance, and the damage was limited.

Hunt's public persona, as always, was relentlessly positive. After four years in office, "we were engaged in trying to make major changes and improvements in education and getting North Carolina moving on a new economic course, toward new technologies and high technology, the kinds of jobs of the future that we needed to have," Hunt said. "We ran to continue and increase the progress that I thought we were making and to carry out the ideas that we had been working on in North Carolina."

He continued, "Our campaigns were always about issues. We weren't running just to win. We were running to set an agenda, to get a mandate to do certain things. That's the way we always campaigned. And that's why in large measure we were successful. When we ran on this stuff, we put it all on television, telling people what we were going to do if we won. They voted for us, we did have a mandate, a classic kind of mandate from the people to do it. And the legislature knew it."

On election night, our campaign was confident as staff and supporters from across the state gathered in Raleigh for a victory celebration. Hunt won big, garnering 62 percent of the vote. But the party fizzled when it became clear Carter was losing—in North Carolina and nationally. As the night wore on, the crowd was stunned to see Morgan and East locked in a close race. The next day, statewide results showed that Morgan had lost.

Hunt didn't expect Morgan's defeat. Hunt later said of him, "I didn't think he was in trouble. He'd had a good record as attorney general. He had been, I thought, a good senator. He was solid in the mainstream of North Carolina, with special connections to conservative voters in the state because of his background with Beverly Lake [Sr.] A populist, a real populist. I knew that Reagan was going to run strongly, but I didn't realize that Robert Morgan was going to be in trouble. So I was shocked when he lost to somebody who was a total unknown."

Most shocking was the effectiveness of the TV assault against Morgan. Hunt said, "That was one of the races where it really was stunning how effective negative ads could be on an issue."

For Hunt, "it was kind of a reality check, what was happening politically in the nation. But I was not discouraged about our prospects in North Carolina." His reelection told him that the state's citizens thought his administration was on the right track.

Soon, he got a wakeup call. The day Reagan was inaugurated in January 1981, Hunt recalled, he was sitting at the Capitol in Washington with the nation's other governors. Reagan proclaimed, "Government is not the solution to our problems. Government is the problem."

When Hunt heard that, he understood what he was up against, because he knew he was going to have to raise taxes. He had tied his hands for his first term when he made his no-tax-increase pledge in 1976. Now, he had decided privately that a gasoline-tax increase was needed to pay for road maintenance. He knew he would have to steer a course in Raleigh different from Reagan's in Washington.

Two weeks before Reagan's inauguration, Hunt had taken his oath for the second time. Although he had opposed Ted Kennedy's challenge to Jimmy Carter, Hunt borrowed a theme—and a line—from Kennedy's speech to the 1980 Democratic National Convention: "This is *not* a time to abandon the work of compassion. This is *not* a time to turn back from progress. Across the nation the winds of retreat are blowing, but North Carolina must sail against the wind."

Chapter 10

Rough Seas

The gas tax preoccupied Hunt and his inner circle before, during, and after the 1980 campaign. The issue was raised first by his business council. The members had commissioned a private study that said the state's secondary roads were deteriorating rapidly. More money was needed for repairs.

Throughout the 1980 campaign, Hunt bobbed and weaved on the issue. He didn't make a no-tax pledge like he had in 1976. He ducked behind a "blue-ribbon commission" he appointed to conduct a highly visible public study of the state's transportation needs. He named former governor Dan Moore chairman. Moore, a conservative, was close to the business community. The commission gave Hunt cover to say he had not decided what to do. But "I knew what the situation was," Hunt said later. "I knew what was going to be required."

The state's major highways weren't the problem. "The federal government put a lot of money in there," he said. Instead, the issue was the kind of roads Hunt, his neighbors in Rock Ridge, and rural people across the state lived on. "They were beginning to break apart. If a secondary road gets too broken, you'll lose the roadbed. You'll have to go out like you're starting from scratch to pave a road." As Hunt saw it, "I had no choice. If I was going to be responsible and have the economy continue to grow, people be able to travel efficiently, we had to fix the roads."

Hunt barely mentioned the issue when he gave his State of the State Address to the legislature in January 1981. He talked about economic development, the microelectronics center, and reducing class sizes. He boasted about the state's success in recruiting new industries. To inoculate himself against what was coming, he touted various cuts in spending and efficiency steps his agencies were taking.

He never used the words *gas tax*. Only toward the end of the speech did he say, "We cannot let our roads and highways and bridges fall into ruin and disrepair." He added, "I will not make any recommendation on this issue until the spring. I will be working until then to determine how much of our current revenues we can save."

Hunt knew it would be a tough fight. A newspaper survey in January showed forty-six of the fifty senators opposed to raising the gas tax. They weren't interested in challenging the Reagan-led antitax mood of the public. Hunt said, "I knew it couldn't go through without the governor putting his muscle behind it, with all that we had, particularly in light of the national picture, because we were flat running against the tide."

Hunt knew how he was going to sell the tax increase: it was necessary for economic development. He had talked for years about how the state needed better education and skills training for the economy to grow. Now, he said, it needed something else: "You have to have the economic infrastructure—roads, highways, airports, bridges."

He unveiled his plan on April 27 in a televised statewide speech. He always believed that if he could talk directly to North Carolinians, he could convince them. The next day, he addressed the legislature: "If we fail to act responsibly this year to protect our investment in our roads and highways, we have failed in our responsibility, and North Carolinians will pay the price for years to come. They will pay the price in lost industry, lost jobs, lost income, lost opportunities."

As in all political fights, the gas-tax battle brought out the competitiveness and determination Hunt inherited from his father. He said later, "The question was, When it's that damned tough, do you go for it and use all your chits, do what's right and responsible, or do you lay back and hope that times will get better, when it'll be easier to do it? I went for it."

He went for it with everything he had. He lined up his friends in the legislature. He had his transportation officials make speeches about the issue. He mobilized his keys around the state. Whenever a major vote was in committee or on the floor, he dispatched both Joe Pell and John A. Williams to the Legislative Building. "And then I worked it. I worked it personally, day and night, those early-morning calls, late-night calls, visits in the mansion, visits in the Capitol, going making speeches, everything that you could possibly do. Pulled out all the stops."

As if the going wasn't tough enough, the Department of Transportation became enmeshed in one of its periodic scandals. It turned out that, since the 1920s, the private companies that built roads in North Carolina had been colluding on bids for state projects. Every company got some business. But the taxpayers didn't receive the benefits of competition.

Investigations subsequently found that one-third of all highway contracts between July 1975 and December 1979 had been rigged. More than thirty highway contractors were later convicted of bid rigging in federal court. Some went to jail, and all were barred from doing business with the state. Allegations, never proven, suggested that DOT employees had made the state's estimates of road costs available to contractors before the bidding process.

The scandal made Hunt's sales job even harder.

Then Jesse Helms's Congressional Club jumped in. From the moment Hunt won a second term, the political world was anticipating a Hunt-Helms battle in 1984. Now, the club saw a chance to wound Hunt. It organized a "Committee Against the Gas Tax." It began running ads opposing the "thirty-three percent gas tax increase"—from nine to twelve cents a gallon. Ads attacked "cronyism" in the

Department of Transportation and accused Hunt of tolerating bid rigging. Hunt publicly condemned the ads as "lies."

The battle raged for two months. Hunt organized his own committee to support the legislation, which he dubbed the "Good Roads Bill." The fight polarized citizens along party lines, which helped Hunt line up Democrats. He maintained later that he never promised a legislator anything for a vote. But he, Pell, and Williams made it clear that "I had just been elected to my second term," Hunt recalled. "I had some damn power, and we'd never had a second-term governor before. And I wanted to be clear about how strongly I felt about it and that we were counting the votes and we were counting our friends. If you want the governor's help, you'd better vote for that bill, and if you didn't, you were not a friend and you couldn't expect to get any help in return. In other words, we were counting votes and we were counting friends. That was it. You didn't vote against us on that bill. If you did, you needn't come back and see us."

Zeb Alley, Hunt's liaison to the legislature, recalled how the governor lobbied for votes. "Every morning, he had two or three legislators to breakfast. The mansion served them with these awful sausage biscuits." Hunt turned his persuasive powers on the legislators. If that didn't work, he turned to Pell and Williams. "Pell was smooth," Alley said, "but John A. could get down and dirty."

Alley recalled one legislator who had been close to Hunt since his Young Democrats days. When Hunt asked for his vote, the legislator said he had already promised his constituents he would vote against the higher tax, and that he couldn't change his position now. Hunt said he understood. So did Williams. A few days later, an appropriation for the community college in the legislator's district disappeared from the budget.

"Word of that got around quick" among legislators, Alley said, "and they started falling like dominoes." In the end, he laughed, "the community colleges did about as well as the highways." Hunt won his battle. The gas-tax bill passed with relative ease, by seventy to forty-eight in the House and by thirty-two to sixteen in the Senate.

But there were casualties. One was Hunt's secretary of transportation, Tom Bradshaw, once the boy wonder of Raleigh business and politics. Raised in a public housing project, Bradshaw became a successful real-estate developer. He was just thirty-two years old when he was elected mayor of Raleigh. He had a brash, energetic style. Like Hunt, he was a born salesman. Hunt had assigned Bradshaw to get money from the federal government to finish Interstate 40 from Raleigh to Wilmington. Bradshaw virtually lived on the plane to Washington and wore out the carpet to the feds. He got the money, and I-40 was built to the coast. Hunt liked Bradshaw because he was honest and ethical. Hunt didn't want any new highway scandals. Bradshaw took that mission seriously—so seriously that he angered legislators who wanted favors and were accustomed to getting them. By the time of the gas-tax fight, the administration was in no position to refuse legislators' requests. Some of Hunt's strongest supporters in the Senate and House made it clear: In exchange for the tax increase, Hunt had to let Bradshaw go. In his place, Hunt put William Roberson of Washington, North Carolina, a former legislator who got along well with his old colleagues.

Hunt also had to replace Howard Lee, who had become a lightning rod over the AFL-CIO contracts. Hunt offered him the job of secretary of correction. But Lee, fearing the consequences if a prison riot broke out under an African-American department head, left the administration. In later years, Lee was elected to the State Senate, where he became a powerful member. He also became chairman of the State Board of Education and oversaw the school reforms that Hunt had launched.

Hunt was struggling to hold together his coalition of progressives and conservatives. The rise of Reagan and the conservative movement—combined with a national recession that hurt state tax revenues—pushed Hunt toward a fiscally conservative course. But his progressive supporters pressured him to keep the promise he had made in his inaugural address to resist the tide of the times.

The tension was never more dramatic than when Hunt froze teachers' salaries in 1982. He believed he had no choice. It was freeze salaries or cut teachers' jobs. A national recession was raging. Unemployment was high. Tax revenues were down. He had already raised the gas tax, and he didn't think the legislature would swallow another politically risky tax increase.

The North Carolina Association of Educators, the main teachers' lobby, saw it differently. Hunt had raised taxes for highways. Didn't the schools need money, too? The NCAE had endorsed him in 1976 and 1980. Now, the teachers' leaders felt betrayed and angry. They staged a march on the Executive Mansion. That hit Hunt hard. One of the protesters was Karen Garr, a Raleigh teacher who became a member of Hunt's staff when he returned to the governor's office in 1993. She recalled that Hunt, trying to make amends, invited the protesting teachers inside the mansion for lemonade and ice cream. He had only one taker. John I. Wilson, the NCAE leader, gave a fiery speech: "Not one of us should go to his lemonade table. He should come to the negotiating table." The hard feelings would linger—and hurt Hunt when he ran against Helms.

In our political strategy sessions, we struggled with how Hunt should position himself regarding President Reagan. Having been a vocal advocate of a federal balanced budget when Carter was president, Hunt praised Reagan for proposing cuts in spending. But he thought Reagan was cutting taxes too much and too recklessly. Hunt oscillated between praise and criticism of Reagan.

When Reagan first became president, Hunt said, "I thought he was just a typical conservative against government, against doing anything, against any taxes." He later developed a grudging respect. "What it took me a good while to appreciate about Reagan was the fact that for him it was always 'Morning in America.' He might be proposing things that were ultraconservative, but he did it with a smile. He was optimistic, he thought it would work. He really had this optimistic spirit about him, and that's the most important thing a political leader can have, is to be an optimist, believe in people, to believe . . . if we do the right things, the future will be good. He had it, and that's why people followed him."

But Hunt was never impressed by Reagan's performance. "During the four years that I overlapped with him, every time we'd go to the

Hunt and Jesse Helms smile for the cameras at a 1981 event in support of a campaign to save the Cape Hatteras Lighthouse.
Photo courtesy of the *News & Observer*

White House, the governors would go in to meet him, and he'd come in to what was to be a two-hour meeting and spend thirty minutes with his little cards, and not really engage in any Q&A with governors, which other presidents have done. So I didn't value him as a real knowledgeable leader who knew all the ins and outs of the issues and could explain it. He was always scripted. I did respect the way he could deliver a speech and be optimistic, stay on message, and stick to his guns. But I thought he was very wrong in terms of his policies. Still do."

While Hunt struggled with budget issues, his national political profile grew. An old friend from College Democrat days in the 1960s,

Charles Manatt of California, had become national party chairman. Manatt named Hunt to chair a study commission on presidential nominations—a process the Democratic Party seemed compelled to go through every four years, especially after losing a presidential race. The appointment put Hunt squarely in the middle of the dueling forces for Ted Kennedy, Walter Mondale, and John Glenn, all of whom were positioning for 1984. Hunt had to herd a disorganized and disputatious collection of Democratic big names and big egos—from volatile pollster Pat Caddell to profane apparatchik Harold Ickes to smooth operator Ron Brown.

Through 1981 and 1982, Hunt chaired meetings of the commission with his usual combination of courtesy and firmness. He pulled together the warring groups in late-night sessions and gave everybody their say. He appointed as staff director the scholarly David Price from Duke University, then executive director of the North Carolina Democratic Party and later a member of Congress. With the help of old North Carolina friends Jane Smith Patterson and Betty McCain on the commission, Hunt emerged unscathed and even forged a consensus.

The commission voted to shorten the primary season, though the candidates never cooperated by shortening their campaigns. It also created superdelegates—elected officials and party leaders who would be automatically seated as delegates at the national conventions. The idea was to ensure a continuity of leaders who had the party's long-term interests in mind. Also, Hunt hoped, the superdelegates would make sure the party nominated a winner. As it turned out, they assured the 1984 nomination for Walter Mondale, who then proceeded to lose forty-nine states to President Reagan. The superdelegates would not play a key role again until 2008, when they coalesced around Barack Obama against Hillary Clinton.

Hunt won praise from all factions of the commission, which had not only seventy members but also an advisory commission of political consultants and operatives. He swam with the sharks without getting eaten. Senator Patrick Leahy of Vermont, a commission member, said of Hunt, "I've had a lot of people from the Kennedy camp, the Mondale camp, the Glenn camp come up and say he did an extraordinary job. He was handling everybody from environmentalists to feminists to labor people."

As he chaired the commission, Hunt was hailed by Democrats across the country as a challenger to the hated Helms. The national press corps followed him closely. We collected names of people who promised to raise money.

A few of us—Hunt's younger staffers—wanted to explore the new world of direct-mail fundraising. We told Joe Pell we needed fifty thousand dollars to finance the first test mailing. Pell called it "going to Vegas." He asked us, "You want to put down fifty thousand dollars at the gambling table and see if it pays off, right?" That was correct. It helped that the idea was supported by John Bennett, Bert's son, who was on the governor's staff and was interested in fundraising. Hunt, Pell, and Bert Bennett made the bet. It paid off. By the end of the 1984 campaign, more money was rolling in through the mail than we ever expected—so much we couldn't spend it.

We organized our own version of the Congressional Club and called it the North Carolina Campaign Fund. Richardson Preyer was named chairman. Elected to Congress after losing the gubernatorial primary in 1964, Preyer was another victim of the Republican assault in 1980. Now, his name lent credibility to our effort. John Bennett used the North Carolina Campaign Fund to organize fundraising dinners and meetings around the country. By 1983, the fund was running into complications with federal campaign laws, so we shut it down. Still, Bennett had built a national fundraising list of thirty-eight thousand names.

Stung by the 1980 elections, Hunt was determined to stem the Republican tide. He told us he viewed 1982 as a warmup for 1984. He appointed Wayne McDevitt to run the party's coordinated campaign. McDevitt, just thirty years old, was from Madison County in the mountains. After getting his start in politics as a teenage volunteer for Hunt in 1972, he had worked in the governor's western North Carolina office and in the Department of Natural Resources and Community Development.

As it turned out, 1982 was a good year for Democrats. The nation was still mired in the same recession that caused budget problems for Hunt in Raleigh. Republicans and President Reagan took the brunt of the blame, and Democrats won resounding victories. One Democratic congressman in North Carolina, Ike Andrews, won reelection even after being arrested for drunk driving just before the election.

Despite his troubles with teachers at home, Hunt's national reputation as a pioneer in education was growing. He even found himself in sync with the Reagan administration on the issue. It was the same theme Hunt had taken up in his first term: the link between education and economic growth.

In 1983, Reagan's secretary of education, Terrell Bell, touched off a national debate by releasing a report titled, "A Nation at Risk." It warned that America's schools were failing to meet the need for a competitive work force: "The educational foundations of our society are presently being eroded by a rising tide of mediocrity that threatens our very future as a nation and as a people. If an unfriendly foreign power had attempted to impose on America the mediocre educational performance that exists today, we might well have viewed it as an act of war."

Hunt was ahead of the curve. In 1982, he had become chairman of the Education Commission of the States. He appointed one of his blue-ribbon commissions to study education and economic growth. It released a report in July 1983 that Hunt said—in an implicit comparison to "A Nation at Risk"—"does not bemoan what is wrong with education in American, but proclaims what can be made right." He said, "It is our strong conviction that America must rededicate its schools to the principles of accountability, rigor, hard work, discipline, performance, high standards and high expectations."

The commission recommended that every state's governor appoint a similar commission to come up with its own action plan. Hunt named a fifty-member North Carolina commission composed of business executives, educators, legislators, school-board members, labor leaders, parents, students, and citizens. He co-chaired the group with C. D. "Dick" Spangler, a billionaire Charlotte businessman who was chairman of the State Board of Education and later president of the University of North Carolina system, and Bland W. Worley, a Winston-Salem banker.

The commission proposed a sweeping set of recommendations in April 1984. Its action plan included partnerships among schools, businesses, parents, and community groups; clear standards for school curricula and student performance; improved pay, recruitment, training, and career incentives for teachers; better training, pay, and career status for school administrators; upgraded buildings and equipment; and programs targeted at gifted students, women, minorities, rural schools, dropout prevention, and skill training.

Hunt presented the recommendations in a speech to the legislature in June 1984. He told a story about his first days in college: "I found that my high school education had not prepared me as well as my new friends from Raleigh and Greensboro and Charlotte were prepared. I found out that I was behind, not because I had not worked hard, not because my parents did not care about education—but because of where I was from. I promised myself then and there that if I could ever do anything to see that kids from the country, or kids from the wrong side of town, or kids from poor families, could have a better chance—an equal chance—for a better education, I would do it."

The legislature approved what was then the largest educational program in North Carolina history. Called the Basic Education Program, it included $281 million to reduce class sizes, upgrade teaching, provide books and equipment, and raise quality statewide. The legislature also passed a 15 percent pay raise for teachers. Hunt proposed—and the legislature started—a "career growth" plan that would pay teachers more as they developed their skills. He proposed college scholarships for students who became teachers, giving birth to the North Carolina Teaching Fellows Program, which later provided thousands of scholarships to budding educators. He started the North Carolina Center for the Advancement of Teaching, located at Western Carolina University in Cullowhee.

Wanting to influence the state's future on an even more ambitious scale, Hunt established the Commission on the Year 2000 and appointed Bill Friday to chair it. The commission issued its 270-plus-page report in March 1983, covering virtually every aspect of the state's future: education, economic development, health care, housing, tax policy, technology, highway funding, energy, environmental protection, policy making, equal opportunity, crime, and the arts. It focused especially on persistent poverty, ignorance, and disease among the state's poor and rural populations. When Hunt left office, Governor Jim Martin and the legislature failed to follow up. "It died," Friday noted. But of Hunt, Friday later said, "More than twenty years ago, this man was saying to the state, 'Think about your future. Use the resources you've got. Let's get on with looking ahead. Let's don't get caught being negligent where it really is important.'" The commission said something important about Hunt, according to Friday: "He was never without a vision. He was always relating something that he wanted to move ahead."

Hunt's drive and enthusiasm never flagged. The editors of his official state papers examined his calendars and determined that, in his second term, Hunt gave an average of 370 speeches a year. He had his priorities: the gas tax, education, the economy, and the Senate race. But Jane Smith Patterson, who became secretary of administration in his second term, said Hunt let his appointees pursue their own passions. Hers was the new world of the "information highway" and what would become the Internet. Joe Grimsley, who succeeded Howard Lee at the Department of Natural Resources and Community Development, pioneered an "Outdoors North Carolina" agenda. Hunt enthusiastically plunged into plans by the Department of Cultural Resources and coastal Dare County to stage an elaborate observance of the four hundredth anniversary of the landing of the first English explorers to America at Roanoke Island—the fabled Lost Colony. He and Carolyn took a North Carolina delegation to Plymouth, England, where the settlers had set out to sea. They later hosted Princess Anne at a ceremony in Manteo.

Not everything went smoothly. In 1982, Hunt finished a four-year struggle with one of the state's worst environmental—and political—messes. In 1978, a truckdriver had dumped thousands of gallons of chemical PCBs along more than two hundred miles of roadsides in several counties near Raleigh. Scientists convinced Hunt that the dirt containing the chemicals had to be dug up and buried safely. The state found land for a burial site in Warren County, a poor, rural, heavily black county near the Virginia line. After years of conflicting studies—and public protests that had to be quelled by state troopers—the state finally buried the material at the site.

Through it all, Hunt remained popular statewide. He took pride in noting years later that, at the Southern Governors' Conference in the summer of 1983, a Republican governor took him aside and told him that his party had done polls all over the country, "and I was the most popular Democratic governor in America."

Hunt could have quit there, his legacy that of a successful two-term governor who had passed most of his agenda and set the state's course for years to come. After the bitter 1984 campaign, I was always amused to hear from people who claimed they had told us Hunt should not run against Helms, that he should wait for the easier race against John East in 1986. Helms's biographer, William Link, even quoted a political consultant who supposedly told me at a governors' conference in Atlantic City that Hunt shouldn't run. One problem: I've never been in Atlantic City. And I don't recall the conversation. For that matter, those of us who worked for Hunt would laugh later that we didn't recall anybody telling us before 1984 that Hunt shouldn't run.

Or maybe we just didn't want to hear it.

We—and Hunt—were spoiling for a showdown with Helms.

Chapter 11

"Where Do You Stand, Jim?"

As 1984 neared, Democrats around the country—as well as some Republicans and newspaper reporters—eagerly anticipated Helms's demise. Richard Whittle, who had been a reporter for the *News & Observer* from 1975 to 1980, wrote an October 1983 article in the *Washington Post* headlined, "Jesse Helms Has a Problem; He's Destined to Lose in '84." Whittle examined Hunt's and Helms's past election performances, analyzed the campaign outlook, and concluded, "Barring an act of God, Helms can't win."

We were confident—so confident that I made one of the dumbest statements in my thirty years in politics, telling the *Post*, "We'd have to be stupid to lose this one." I learned later that, after the election, Helms staffers took pleasure in hauling out my quote.

We had reason to be confident. Polls showed Hunt as much as 20 points ahead. He had led Democrats to big wins in North Carolina in 1982. He seemed to have survived the gas-tax fight and the teachers' salary protests. His poll numbers were high. He had successfully chaired the commission on presidential nominations. He had a growing reputation across the country. We were building a national fundraising organization. We dreamed of Hunt's vanquishing Helms and then being elected president.

The staff viewed the coming contest as good against evil, progress against reaction, the New South against the Old South. Joe Grimsley told a reporter, "This is the closest opportunity this generation will have for the progressive New South to replace the racist, reactive Old South. It's a truly transitional event." Hunt's father echoed Grimsley in an interview: "I call myself a progressive. Helms is a throwback to the slavery days. He's a throwback to the Old South. We're the New South."

The Helms campaign saw the polls, too. Carter Wrenn recalled that Arthur Finkelstein, the campaign's New York–based pollster, conducted a survey showing Helms 25 points behind Hunt in late 1982. Tom Ellis hadn't shown Helms a poll since 1972. That year, Helms had gone into what Wrenn called a "blue funk" after a poll indicated he was 30 points behind. From then on, Ellis had forbidden Wrenn from talking to Helms about polls.

Now, Ellis thought he needed to shock the senator. Helms enjoyed being in the Senate, but he had never liked campaigning. Ellis wanted him to know he would have to fight to win in 1984. Around the end of the year, Ellis brought Helms to the Congressional Club's offices in North Raleigh. Finkelstein went over the poll and even suggested Helms might want to think about retiring from the Senate. Helms said that, in fact, he had promised his wife, Dot, he would not run again.

Wrenn thought that was just a ploy to goad Ellis, who indeed took the bait. Ellis told Helms he had a responsibility to run, a responsibility to the conservative cause. Then Finkelstein asked Helms a question: If he could wave a magic wand and go back to the Senate for six years, would he do it? Helms allowed that, yes, he liked serving in the Senate. Ellis jumped in: Give the campaign a year to see if it could change those numbers, he told Helms, then decide if he would run again. Satisfied that he had put the burden onto Ellis, Helms agreed, giving Ellis the go-ahead to do whatever it took to win.

On Hunt's side, money was a big factor. Previously, the Bert Bennett network—augmented by Hunt's new business friends and

Joe Pell's efficient patronage operation—had always raised the money Hunt needed. But we were in a new age in politics. In Helms's 1978 reelection race, he had raised and spent more than $7 million, far more than Hunt had ever raised. We had seen what happened to Robert Morgan in 1980. We didn't believe we could match the Congressional Club's fundraising. It had been at it longer than we had. It had a huge national fundraising list. It had the power of incumbency. It had access to Republican money nationally.

Joe Pell especially worried about the money. Over and over, he warned us, "Can you imagine anything worse than getting to October 1984 and running out of money?" If that happened, Hunt would be helpless before a television onslaught in the final weeks of the campaign.

We expected the race to get closer. We knew we would never keep a 20-point lead. We knew many citizens had cast votes for Hunt *and* Helms—as in 1972, when both men were on the ballot. Both had done well among conservative rural and small-town voters. But those voters had never before chosen between the two men.

Heeding Pell's warning, we made a crucial decision early: We would husband our money for the end. Our first priority was to set aside what we would need in September and October 1984. In the summer of 1983, Hunt and Pell assigned Mike Davis to begin setting up the campaign. Davis said Pell's admonition was drilled into his brain: "Your job is to make sure that on Labor Day of next year, we've got enough money."

Tom Ellis had a different mind-set. He was more aggressive about spending money—and more bullish about his ability to raise it. Carter Wrenn recalled that, during campaigns, Ellis had accountants review fundraising prospects. The accountants would project how much debt the Helms campaign could take on—and pay back, even if Helms lost. Helms hated debt, but Ellis and Wrenn thought it was essential. Our campaign—supposedly a collection of big-spending, debt-happy Democratic liberals—was terrified by the prospect of saddling Hunt with a campaign debt.

For all our concern with money, Hunt never hesitated about challenging Helms. "He was a blot on the state," Hunt said years later in talking about the campaign. "He was the last old-time racist to hold a high position in politics in North Carolina." Although Helms offended Hunt's sense of right and wrong, the governor was sensitive to sounding like he hated Helms. "I don't hate him," he said years later. "He was just so wrong for North Carolina, so misrepresenting what the people of this state and the history of this state are about. So at odds with our best selves."

Another factor was also in play. If he beat Helms, Hunt would become a national hero in the Democratic Party. He would be hailed in Washington as a dragon slayer. He would be a logical candidate for president. Hunt, ever guarded, didn't talk about the White House. He didn't need to. We all had it in our minds. As close as he was to Betty McCain, they never discussed a presidential race, she said. But she told me in 2007, "I think if we had won in '84, he would have been president instead of Clinton. That's my life's greatest regret. I guess you and I will go to our graves diagnosing what we did wrong."

Hunt prepared just as he had in his three previous races. Mike Davis found a spacious headquarters building a couple of blocks down Hillsborough Street from the Capitol. He wondered how we would ever fill it. As it turned out, we didn't have enough room. Months into the campaign, Davis had to find extra space down the street.

As always, Hunt was determined to master the issues. He knew more than Helms—or almost any other senator—about economic development and education. But he wanted to be ready for questions on the federal budget, especially taxes and balancing the budget. He was worried about Helms's experience in foreign affairs and was determined to know just as much. He wanted to be conversant about national security and military affairs. He studied papers and was briefed by experts from all over the country. Years later, Hunt laughed about his discipline: "Sometimes, I wish I had all that time back. I thought I needed to know as much as Helms on those issues. Then I found out he was just opposed to them all."

As we prepared, Tom Ellis struck. In April 1983—more than

eighteen months before the election—the Helms campaign started running ads. The first were mostly in small-town and rural daily and weekly newspapers. One featured a big picture of Hunt's meeting in March 1982 with civil-rights leader Jesse Jackson, who was planning a run for president in 1984. The ad quoted a news story from 1981: "Gov. James B. Hunt, Jr., wants the State Board of Elections to boost minority voter registration in North Carolina." The ad ended, "Ask Yourself. Is This A Proper Use Of Taxpayer Funds?" Other ads linked Hunt with Senator Ted Kennedy, one of Helms's favorite targets over the years, and with Georgia state senator Julian Bond, a civil-rights leader one ad said was head of the "BlacPAC." It concluded, "Ask Yourself: Why do BlacPAC and Kennedy PAC want to elect Jim Hunt to the U.S. Senate?"

Then came radio ads. They ran about three times a day on average on the seventy-two stations of the North Carolina News Network. One North Carolina reporter calculated in June 1983—nearly a year and a half before the election—that, "coupled with the twelve-week run of ads in the one hundred and fifty newspapers, Helms's messages have gone out no less than fourteen thousand times since April 1." Despite Helms's frequent claims that he knew nothing about the ads, Mark Stephens, his campaign treasurer, "says Helms reviews most of the ads before publication or broadcast," the *Charlotte Observer* reported.

Joe Pell started getting worried calls from Hunt's keys, especially in rural areas where racial prejudice ran high. Pell reassured them that we were in the campaign for the long haul, that we couldn't shoot our wad now, that we'd need the money in the final weeks and months.

At first, the ads didn't seem to damage Hunt too badly. He had been governor for eight years. He was in the news constantly, and most North Carolinians had a positive attitude about him. They liked his record on jobs and schools. He was tough on crime. He had pushed for one tax increase, but that did not look so big in retrospect. Besides, he had made the teachers and state employees mad by freezing their salaries during the recession. That showed guts—and a tight-fisted fiscal approach. Clearly, voters saw Hunt as more moderate than most national Democrats. We felt confident the ads were not fatal.

Instead of spending campaign money, we fought back with the powers of incumbency. Hunt would go anywhere to announce a new plant location, break ground for a factory, or cut a ribbon at a grand opening. We cooked up a series of one hundred county economic-development conferences, prominently sponsored by the governor and culminating in a grand statewide conference. We had an aggressive press operation, though it was never aggressive enough for Hunt.

John Bennett became the campaign's finance director and built one of the nation's premier political fundraising operations. Arthur Cassell of Greensboro, a longtime supporter of Hunt who was active in the national Jewish community, opened doors there. Helms had been hostile to Israel during his tenure on the Senate Foreign Relations Committee. Jewish leaders detected a hint of anti-Semitism in him. Cassell introduced Hunt to Jewish leaders around the country. Hunt studied the issues they cared about. In dozens of fundraisers Cassell arranged, Hunt talked about how moved he was by the people and nation of Israel during his economic-development mission there. He decried Helms's insensitivity and intolerance. The money rolled in.

Bennett set up fundraising events across the country. Many were tagged onto official trips. In the summer of 1983, I went with Hunt on an economic-development trip to California. Along with the official events, we scheduled fundraisers in San Diego and Los Angeles. We needed the money but worried about a political backlash. While Helms attacked Hunt as too liberal, there we were raising money from some of the most prominent liberals in America, including Hollywood types who were politically and culturally out of tune with North Carolina.

One of our events was in Beverly Hills. Most North Carolina reporters did not venture that far west for Hunt's political trips, but this one was covered by a former reporter from the *Charlotte Observer* who now worked in Los Angeles. She was friendly to Hunt, so I felt safe.

Then in walked Tom Hayden, one of the best-known radicals in America. A founder of Students for a Democratic Society, Hayden was a vocal opponent of America's involvement in Vietnam. Even worse, he had married Jane Fonda; "Hanoi Jane" was then about as popular with salt-of-the-earth Americans as Ho Chi Minh. I could see the headlines back home. I could see Hunt's campaign crashing and burning.

I did something I had never done before. I went to the reporter and asked her—as a favor to me, as a favor to Hunt, and as a favor to everybody who hated Jesse Helms and wanted him out of the Senate—to not mention Hayden in her story. "Don't worry," she said. "I won't." And she didn't.

The Helms campaign missed that, but it didn't miss much else, thanks to Bob Harris. Harris had run the Congressional Club's direct-mail operation and done research for John East in 1980. His physical disability made it difficult for him to perform some tasks, but he had a brilliant mind, a photographic memory, and an instinct for the political jugular. He went to work reviewing news clippings about Hunt. He found no shortage, as our press operation was in the business of generating a lot of them. Soon, Harris spotted a weakness. Given the wealth of public statements by Hunt—and the constant political balancing act between liberals and conservatives, left and right, black and white, business and labor—his positions showed inconsistencies and sometimes contradictions. Harris zeroed in on them. "Flip-flops," he called them. He noted a series of issues on which Hunt made statements that one day sounded liberal and the next day conservative.

As political opposition research became a growth industry in later years, the search for flip-flops was always job one. Most politicians over long careers said and did things that—when put beside each other—looked inconsistent. Most campaigns sought to portray their candidates as paragons of principle running against undependable politicians who would tell people what they wanted to hear. The reality, of course, is less cut-and-dried. Statements can be taken out of context. Situations change, circumstances change, and minds change. New events, new developments, and new perspectives not only explain why politicians change their views but also make it wise and responsible for them to do so. But that takes a lot of explaining. Usually, a politician who gets pegged as a flip-flopper is doomed.

We even attacked Helms as a flip-flopper. Under heavy pressure from President Reagan and Senate Republican leaders, both Helms and Senator East voted in 1982 for a deficit reduction bill that included an increase in the federal tobacco tax. Helms had positioned himself as an opponent of higher taxes, especially on North Carolina's king crop, but he had flip-flopped. We arranged for the state Democratic Party to run a full-page newspaper ad attacking Helms and East as "the tobacco tax twins." Tobacco had been under siege for years, the ad noted, and "with friends like this, tobacco doesn't need any more enemies."

The flip-flop label did not stick to Helms, who was a model of negative and reactionary consistency. But the charge went to the essence of Jim Hunt. He was a pragmatic politician. He was a learner. He grew, developed, and changed his mind. He also had a propensity to sound liberal before one group and conservative before another. Over eight years in office, as the political winds changed, he changed with them. He always had a set course, but he tacked back and forth to get to his destination.

Helms, on the other hand, was never one to seek out new information, learn new ideas, or explore new positions. He was consistent. He said exactly the same things in the 1980s in the Senate that he had said in the 1960s at WRAL and in the 1950s when he served as executive director of the North Carolina Bankers Association and wrote editorials for its magazine, *Tar Heel Banker*.

In December 1983, the Helms campaign was searching for a way to respond to a series of ads the state Democratic Party had run attacking him on Social Security. Bob Harris faxed over three or four radio scripts, Carter Wrenn recalled. Each script had three examples of Hunt's alleged flip-flops. The campaign's pollster, Arthur Finkelstein, loved the scripts. Since the campaign did not have much cash on hand for TV ads, Finkelstein suggested breaking them into individual ten-second spots. Ten-second spots were almost unheard-of then.

The tag line for the spots came from Harris. It was the same question at the end of each spot. It came attached to every alleged flip-flop, whether it was the Panama Canal treaty, Reagan's budget cuts, school prayer, "forced busing," aid for "communist Nicaragua," or tax increases. Every ad demanded, "Where do you stand, Jim?"

Almost by chance, the Helms campaign had found gold. It would make the campaign not about ideology but about character. It would compare Hunt's flip-flops with Helms's consistency. It would define the choice as one between an untrustworthy politician, Hunt, and a man of principle, Helms.

Most of all, it would make the contest about race. As Helms said in one ad, "I oppose the Martin Luther King holiday. Where do you stand, Jim?"

In the fifteen years since Martin Luther King was assassinated—and since Jim Hunt joined that biracial procession in Wilson after the murder—a growing national movement had pushed for a national holiday honoring King. In October 1983, a bill establishing the holiday came before the Senate. It had passed the House overwhelmingly, by a 338 to 90 vote margin. Senator Howard Baker of Tennessee, the Republican leader, supported it. President Reagan said he would sign it. Even Strom Thurmond of South Carolina said he would vote for it. But not Helms.

Helms proclaimed he would fight the King holiday. He threatened to filibuster against it. His threat touched off a storm of criticism—from Democrats, from North Carolina newspapers, from civil-rights leaders, and even from some Republicans. The reaction put Br'er Helms right in the briar patch where he wanted to be. He knew small-town and rural North Carolinians. He had seen race work in elections before. He had mastered all the code words in his years as a journalist, writer, and television commentator.

Helms was "playing the race card," Carter Wrenn said a quarter-century later. David Flaherty, chairman of the state Republican Party in 1984, said later in an oral-history interview that "we used race . . . because we knew we couldn't beat Jim Hunt on issues." The King holiday debate gave Helms the perfect opportunity at the perfect time to put

A flier from the Helms campaign linked the senator to President Reagan and Hunt to Jesse Jackson. While less blatant than the leaflet from the 1950 Smith-Graham campaign, the theme was the same: race.

race in the middle of his battle with Hunt.

On October 3, Helms gave a long speech on the Senate floor against the holiday. He estimated that another federal holiday would cost the nation $12 billion in lost productivity. He accused King of promoting "action-oriented Marxism" that was "not compatible with the concepts of this country." King's associations and activities proved that he "welcomed collaboration with Communists." The late civil-rights leader had associated with communists, Helms charged, and those associations "strongly suggest that King harbored a strong sympathy for the Communist Party and its goals." King's legacy, Helms said, was one of "division, not love." He said King was "a source of tension" in society. His use of nonviolence was a "provocative act to disturb the peace of the state and to trigger, in many cases, overreaction by authorities." In other words, Helms said King and his supporters were to blame for the police dogs, fire hoses, and beatings in Selma and Birmingham.

Helms's speech touched off a torrent of criticism. The *Greensboro Daily News* called it "Sen. Helms' smear against King." The *Fayetteville Observer* accused him of dragging out the "old red herring" of communism that "thousands of racists used in the Fifties and Sixties . . . to discredit the civil rights movement."

Helms raised the persistent rumors about King's extramarital affairs and questioned the civil-rights leader's morality. He said he could not reach an "informed" judgment about the King holiday unless FBI surveillance tapes of King were unsealed. He filed a lawsuit to get access to the tapes, but a federal judge dismissed the suit.

In one speech, Helms said the Senate, instead of honoring King, should establish a holiday for Thomas Jefferson. King, he said, represented "elements of the far left and the Communist Party USA." New York senator Daniel Patrick Moynihan denounced Helms's speech as "filth" and "obscenity."

Helms dragged his favorite foil, Senator Ted Kennedy, into the fray. Kennedy denounced Helms for a "smear campaign." Helms shot back that Kennedy's argument was not with Helms but with "his dead brother who was president and his dead brother who was attorney general." John and Robert Kennedy had authorized the wiretaps and warned King against his left-wing associations. Ted Kennedy was "flushed with emotion," news accounts reported. He replied that if his brother Robert were alive "he would be the first person to say that J. Edgar Hoover's reckless campaign against Martin Luther King was a shame and a blot on American history."

The Senate brushed aside Helms's opposition and passed the King holiday by a seventy-eight to twelve vote. President Reagan signed the holiday into law. But Helms knew he had won the battle he picked with Hunt.

Helms always dressed his racial views in the robes of principle, not prejudice. He claimed to have many black friends. He hired a black press secretary, Claude Allen, who would absorb years of criticism and ridicule for his work as Helms's spokesman. Allen would later serve as a White House assistant to President George W. Bush until he was arrested for shoplifting in 2006. He pled guilty to a misdemeanor charge of theft.

Helms had a private nickname for blacks: "Freds." In 1981, when an African-American from Durham asked to meet with him about the Voting Rights Act, Helms replied, "I's ready when you's ready." One reporter said that when he interviewed Helms in his Raleigh home, the senator took down from his wall a framed picture of "a grinning, toothless black man on a porch, with a drink in his hand," saying, "This is what me and Martin Luther King had in mind." Helms told the reporter, "That'll get me in trouble." In 1998, when newly elected senator John Edwards and his wife, Elizabeth, had dinner with Helms and Dot, Helms lamented that he could not understand why "colored people" didn't like him.

In 1995, Helms was being interviewed on CNN by conservative columnist Robert Novak when a caller to the show said Helms deserved the Nobel Peace Prize "for everything you've done to keep down the niggers." Helms paused, then responded, "Whoops, well, thank you, I think." Not until he was prodded by Novak did Helms say he had been spanked as a child for using the "n-word." Helms added, "I don't think I've used it since." But as one observer noted, Helms did not take issue with "the caller's main point—the virtue of keeping down blacks."

Helms was quick to use his fight against the King holiday in his campaign. In October, he sent out a five-page fundraising letter that repeated his criticisms of King and said "the left-wing black establishment and the liberals in the news media have branded me a 'racist.' That's how they smear anyone who disagrees with them." He added, "That's how they intimidated their opponents and rammed the King Holiday through the Senate."

We watched Helms's performance on the King bill with a mixture of fear and fury. We knew what he was doing. We hated it but were afraid to call it racism for fear of white backlash. Hunt said later, "If we were worried about whether to call him a racist, we made a mistake. Because we should have."

Hunt recalled a meeting he had late in the campaign with a group of voters in Charlotte who were leaning toward Helms. They were business people from the North who had recently moved to the state. "These people weren't racist," Hunt said. "They were just Republicans, conservative Republicans. It became clear to me, and it was really surprising, that they didn't know his background, didn't know his racist background, how he'd played the race issue through the years. They voted for him just because he was a conservative Republican."

For all our belief that the coming election was a battle between the racist Old South and the progressive New South, we understood how strong the Old South still was. Hunt knew it in his bones. He had felt the hostility of racists in Wilson County. He had seen what happened to Frank Porter Graham in 1950. He remembered what happened to Richardson Preyer in 1964. It was like watching an old movie again.

But Hunt had long ago decided which side of that line he stood on.

One afternoon during Helms's filibuster against the King holiday bill, Hunt and I had a short meeting with Joe Pell. Hunt was getting ready to leave town for a speech. Pell had been receiving calls from supporters around the state who were worried about the issue. Hunt had not yet taken a public position. Pell wanted him to know what some of the callers were saying.

Pell knew that Hunt would support the King holiday. And he agreed that was the right thing to do. But he thought he had to tell Hunt the bottom line: "This is the issue that could lose you the election."

Getting up to leave, Hunt replied, "Well, in that case, I'll just have to lose."

Chapter 12

A Campaign Divided

Helms's attack on the Martin Luther King holiday—and the drumbeat of ads attacking Hunt—dramatically changed the contours of the Senate race. Although Hunt had led by 20 points a year before, Peter Hart's poll for our campaign near the end of 1983 showed that the lead had closed to 3 points, 46 to 43.

Helms had a clear strategy and message: Attack Hunt. Our campaign had neither. We were hopelessly divided. Old divisions surfaced between the Bert Bennett approach to politics and the Joe Grimsley approach. Older and generally more conservative keys around the state who were close to Joe Pell clashed with the younger and more liberal activists who staffed much of the administration and the campaign. Within the campaign itself were different camps, one staff member later recalled: "People close to Joe Grimsley, people close to John Bennett, people close to Gary Pearce."

Also divided were the professional consultants who had helped Hunt win in 1976 and 1980. Peter Hart, the pollster, was a quiet, steady, and experienced Washington hand. He believed the 1982 elections had given us the winning formula: a reliance on the bread-and-butter economic and education issues that had worked so well for Hunt. Social

Security was a vulnerability for Republicans like Helms, Hart believed. So was the environment. From Hart's polls, the campaign developed an issue formula called "the Four E's": education, the economy, the environment, and the elderly.

Where Peter Hart was Democratic orthodoxy and Washington establishment, David Sawyer, our media consultant, was Manhattan glamour. Sawyer had started out making documentaries, then migrated to politics. Suave and sophisticated, he rode a bicycle to his black-paneled studios in the city and decked himself out in expensive suits. Sawyer was ambitious and visionary. He wanted to export his brand of political consulting worldwide, and his firm would become one of the first to do that successfully. He was impatient with Hart's approach to the campaign. Sawyer thought the race needed to be bigger than the Four E's. It was good versus evil, New South against Old South, Southern progressives against what Sawyer's associate Jack Leslie, who had been an aide to Ted Kennedy, called the "Evil Empire"—Helms's web of associations with not only conservatives around the country but right-wing dictators around the world. That was a tempting siren song for many of us in the campaign. We truly believed we were in a battle of good against evil.

It didn't help that Hart and Sawyer supported different candidates for president. Hart and his firm worked for Walter Mondale. Jimmy Carter's vice president was the establishment choice after Ted Kennedy passed on the race. Sawyer, true to his high-flying nature, was helping former astronaut John Glenn, then a senator from Ohio. Hunt-Helms may have been "the Race of the Century," but a presidential contest was still a big prize for consultants.

Hart and Sawyer had so many other commitments across the country that they used associates to help with our race.

Hart brought in Geoff Garin, who was to remain his partner for decades. The two bore a startling physical resemblance to each other. Both were stocky, dark haired, bespectacled, and beginning to bald. One friend joked, "Their DNA match is almost identical. If one of them committed a murder, a blood test could convict the other one." Both were cautious and skeptical of Sawyer's "Evil Empire."

Sawyer brought in Jack Leslie and Mandy Grunwald, later known for her work with Bill and Hillary Clinton. They arranged a set of focus groups conducted by Ned Kennan, a former Israeli intelligence officer who had gone into the business of advising corporations on human behavior. The bearded, intense Kennan, who looked and sounded like a Viennese psychiatrist, probed the focus-group participants on their feelings about Hunt and Helms. When the group sessions ended, he burst into the room where we were watching and announced in his thick accent, "The campaign *iss* all about religion! Religion!" Hunt, he concluded, was the prim and proper minister at the local church, delivering the weekly sermon and ministering to the sick and aging in the congregation. Helms was an evangelist condemning sin and evil and calling on all to repent.

It sounded good, but we struggled to figure out how to translate that insight into a political campaign in North Carolina. Still, Sawyer's

The Hunts hosted a rally for his Senate campaign at their home, located on the Rock Ridge farm where he grew up.
Photo from Governor Hunt's personal collection

charisma was compelling and contagious. In strategy sessions, Hart was sober and academic. He went through the poll numbers and urged us to stick with the basics. But it seemed so much more, well, *exciting* to run the campaign the way Sawyer saw it.

The Helms campaign had no such division or confusion. Tom Ellis was in charge. Ellis, said Carter Wrenn, always listened to different ideas and opinions. He was open to the wildest of suggestions. But in the end, he decided. Hunt had no Tom Ellis, no one forceful enough to handle all the strong minds within the campaign.

Joe Grimsley, who by now had moved to the campaign as director again, was torn. Those of us who had worked with Joe for years sensed he did not have his usual self-confidence. He seemed worn down by the years of campaigning and all the battles inside the administration. Mike Davis, who was close to Grimsley, said later, "I just think he got overwhelmed. I remember him telling me, 'You know, this thing is so much bigger than I thought it was.'"

I was one of Grimsley's problems. Although still in the governor's office, I constantly meddled in the campaign. One afternoon in April 1984, Grimsley invited me to join him at a hotel bar across the street from campaign headquarters. After we talked for a while, Joe made me an offer: "Why don't you come over to the campaign? You can oversee the media and communications side." I didn't have to be asked twice. But Joe was sensitive to the fact that the campaign already had a press secretary and a communications director. He wanted to give me a good title. He was campaign director. He offered to make me co-director. It was a ludicrous arrangement, one guaranteed to wreak havoc in any chain of command. But I was raring to go. I accepted.

Early in 1984, we produced and began running a series of ads that split the difference between Hart's strategy and Sawyer's. The ads showed Hunt in fields and factories talking with average North Carolinians, trying to show that he was closer to their day-to-day concerns than Helms was in Washington, where he was spending time on conservative ideological crusades and issues like fighting communism in Central America. In one ad, Hunt said, "Well, you see, I think the job of the senator from North Carolina—he's not the senator from New York or California or somewhere, he's the senator from North Carolina."

Helms researcher Bob Harris caught the irony we missed. Months before, Hunt had held a fundraiser in New York. It was sponsored by "the New York Committee to Elect Jim Hunt." Within just a few days—warp speed in that era—the Helms campaign put up an ad juxtaposing Hunt's statement with the New York committee.

Hunt replied weakly that the New York event was sponsored in large part "by young people from North Carolina who live in New York." That was true. Unfortunately, it was also sponsored by New York governor Mario Cuomo. People were starting to laugh at Hunt. Nothing is more devastating in politics than ridicule.

At the National Governors Conference in Washington in February, Hunt voted for a resolution calling on the federal government to balance its budget through a combination of spending cuts and tax increases. The Helms campaign quickly obtained a videotape of the vote showing Hunt raising his hand in favor of the resolution. The tape was grainy, lending it an air of intrigue and suspicion. In the hands of Earl Ash, the campaign's television producer and an old Helms hand from WRAL, Hunt looked like he was caught doing something almost criminal. "Actual news footage of Jim Hunt voting to raise your taxes," the ad declared. It was to run thousands of times in the months ahead.

We were stung—and determined to fight back. Our campaign press secretary was a tough, aggressive Virginian, Will Marshall, who later was instrumental in establishing the Democratic Leadership Council and the Progressive Policy Institute in Washington. Marshall introduced us to a friend of his, a consultant he had worked with on a Senate race in Virginia. His friend was James Carville.

Politics is full of characters, but there never was a character like Carville. Unknown in 1984, he would become the most famous political consultant in the country when he ran the Clinton war room in 1992. He looked, acted, and talked like the survivor of a nuclear test explosion. He was tall, lean, and maniacal. When he got wound up and the words started spewing out in his Cajun accent, he was unstoppable and hilarious. Once listeners got past his persona, they realized that he added sound judgment and sometimes sheer genius to campaigns.

We brought Carville in to consult with us on several occasions and wanted to hire him full-time. Unfortunately, he was tied up in a Senate primary in Texas. His candidate looked like a sure loser, so we figured we could get Carville later in the summer. But he guided his Texas candidate, Lloyd Doggett, later a congressman, to an upset victory in the primary. Doggett went on to lose in November, and we lost out on Carville.

All the while, the Helms assault continued on television. Joe Pell's warning stuck in our heads: "Can you imagine anything worse than getting to October 1984 and running out of money?" We began to imagine something worse: losing control of the campaign in May.

The ads, the national attention, and the pressure wore at us. We were all working hard. But no one worked harder than Hunt. And he had a day job as governor. He still spent many hours in the Capitol meeting with his staff and cabinet, seeing visitors, and juggling issues ranging from the budget to the legislature.

We were desperate to change the momentum. Reporters, fundraisers, and our own supporters bombarded us—and the governor's office—with questions, criticisms, and complaints. Peter Hart's polls showed the race closer and closer.

We challenged Helms to a series of debates—a ploy of candidates who fear they're falling behind. It was an old trick, but it worked. We became the aggressors. After some hesitation, Helms appointed Tom Ellis and Carter Wrenn to represent him in debate negotiations with our campaign and the state broadcasters' association. Hunt named me and Phil Carlton, who had stepped down from the North Carolina Supreme Court to join a Raleigh law firm and was now active in the campaign.

Coincidentally, Carlton and Ellis had their offices in the same building on suburban Glenwood Avenue in Raleigh. Carlton was on the ground floor and Ellis the floor above. We alternated our meetings between the two offices. The first session was such an event that it was covered by news reporters and cameramen. Joining us was Wade Hargrove, the counsel for the broadcasters who had made Ellis so mad in the 1980 campaign.

As we met behind closed doors, an odd dynamic developed. Despite our mutual enmity and suspicion, the two campaigns found agreement with each other more often than with the broadcasters. The broadcasters wanted to showcase their announcers and reporters. The campaigns wanted a more free-flowing debate between Hunt and Helms.

So we threw the broadcasters out of the room. The four of us—Ellis, Wrenn, Carlton, and I—realized that, without us and without the candidates, the broadcasters would not have a show. We informed them that we would negotiate the rules we wanted. They could take it or leave it. They didn't like it, but they had no choice. From then on, in an atmosphere that was a mixture of tension and growing familiarity, the four of us spent long hours together working out the shape and schedule of the debates. We agreed on a series to be held around the state during the summer, each one with plenty of opportunities for Hunt and Helms to address and question each other directly.

As the first debate neared, the campaigns were like locker rooms before a heavyweight championship fight. Determined to do well, Hunt set aside plenty of time to prepare, as he had done from his days practicing FFA speeches on his tractor. He spent hours poring over briefing books and quizzing a parade of policy experts. And he got ready to go man-to-man with Helms.

To play Helms in our debate practice sessions, David Sawyer brought in Harrison Hickman, a pollster in Washington who later became a key adviser to Hunt. Hickman had grown up in Wake Forest, the son of schoolteachers. He lived down the street from I. Beverly Lake, Sr., and watched Helms on television through high school and college. He knew the small-town South and understood Helms's appeal. Hickman had a quick mind and an acerbic personality. He was better prepared for the first practice session than Hunt was.

Like a prize student, Hunt wanted to show off how much he knew. Hickman deflated him with a pitch-perfect imitation of Helms's country cunning and barbed rhetoric. At one point, they got into an exchange over what "Helms" called rampant communist influence in Europe. Hunt took a shot: "Jesse, all of these people you call Communists, most of them are just Socialists." Hickman shot back, "Oh, yeah? Name two." Hunt, stunned, couldn't name one.

At the end of the session, Hunt was uncharacteristically subdued. He knew he wasn't ready. But he made up his mind to get better. He plunged back into studying his briefing books, filling pages of a legal pad with notes, and sparring with Hickman.

Helms had much the same experience but a different reaction. When "Hunt"—a young man named David Tyson—got the better of Helms in their first practice, Helms shut down the rehearsal, stalked off, and angrily told Carter Wrenn he was done with debate prep. He never did another rehearsal.

Helms and his campaign team may have started to believe their own attacks on Hunt. Wrenn said later, "I had pictured him as a milquetoast." But he had a different reaction the night of the first debate, July 29. "When I walked in," Wrenn recalled, "Hunt was standing between the two podiums. He was reading a piece of paper, and he was rocking back and forth on his heels. He looked athletic. I remember thinking, 'Tennis player.'"

Hunt was agile and aggressive once the debate started. Helms had been coached to not seem mean, since his campaign was concerned that his public image could appear cruel and churlish. He even carried pictures of his grandchildren into the debate to remind him to keep his sharp tongue under control. He was surprised by Hunt's aggressiveness.

Helms defended his vote for the tobacco-tax increase, saying, "I had to cast one for my country, because that vote saved an estimated thirty billion dollars to forty billion dollars in a combination of taxes and spending."

Hunt pounced: "Jesse, you may have done one for your country, but you sure didn't do one for North Carolina, and for the tobacco farmers and their families and the cigarette factory workers in this state."

Helms criticized Hunt for making a trade trip to "communist China." Hunt responded that he was promoting North Carolina's foreign trade interests in that country, just as two Republican presidents—Nixon and Reagan—had done for United States interests.

At the end of the debate, Hunt surprised Helms with a challenge. He proposed that both candidates pledge not to accept any out-of-state campaign contributions. Helms huffed, "Governor, are you having problems raising money out of state?" But he was clearly knocked off balance.

The reaction was summed up in a story in the *News & Observer* the next day headlined, "Political experts give Hunt the edge in debate."

"I think Hunt really whipped him. I didn't think it was even close," said Merle Black, an expert on Southern politics who was then an associate professor of political science at UNC–Chapel Hill and later a professor at Emory University in Atlanta.

Years later, *Charlotte Observer* columnist Jack Betts, a reporter covering the campaign in 1984, wrote that, for Helms, "it was a disaster. Hunt put Helms on the defensive from the outset with a skillful attack on his Senate record. Hunt demonstrated a command of the issues. Helms appeared flustered."

The debate went so badly for Helms, Wrenn recalled, that Ellis decided there would be no more, no matter what he had agreed to. Ellis relented, but Helms's team knew it had to repair the damage. It turned to what had worked so well so far: television ads.

Within days after the debate—while we were still high-fiving and congratulating ourselves—Helms began running a series of ads that took clips from Hunt at the debate and contrasted them with seemingly contradictory statements the governor had made at other times. Once again, Hunt looked like a flip-flopper—or worse, a liar. The Helms campaign was stealing our triumph.

Helms was determined not to lose another debate. He abandoned the grandfatherly approach in the subsequent three and went back to the aggressive polemical skills he had honed on WRAL and the debating skills that infuriated his opponents on the Senate floor. His performances steadily improved. Hunt never backed off, but the

Hunt and Helms brush past each other after one of their bitter debates during the 1984 Senate race. Helms never debated another opponent after Hunt.
PHOTO COURTESY OF THE *NEWS & OBSERVER*

momentum we had at the end of the first debate dissipated.

What I remember most is the crackling tension, especially during the two debates when, by agreement between our campaigns, the only people in the production room were Hunt, Helms, the moderator, the camera crews, and the four of us from the campaigns. Sitting there watching Hunt and Helms go at each other, I wondered how I would react if I were in their shoes. Would I be able to get a word out? Would I be shaking so badly I could hardly stand? "It's tense, and it's tough work," Hunt later recalled. "You've got to, first of all, remember what you're going to say. You've got an opening and a closing statement that you've pretty well committed to memory. But you've got to stay flexible enough to be able to respond to a point or to maybe look for an opportunity to upstage your opponent, to be strong and aggressive, to answer the question but also make your points."

Hunt's discipline slipped one time. In the third debate, on September 23, he criticized Helms for not adequately supporting veterans' benefits. Helms responded, "And which war did you fight in, Jim?"

It was the only time I recall Hunt losing his cool in public. "I don't like you questioning my patriotism," he shot back. That exchange dominated news coverage of the debate.

I cringed inwardly when Hunt made the statement; I thought he looked oversensitive. But Carter Wrenn said later he thought it was a strong and effective reply. Years later, Hunt said Helms had made him genuinely angry. "It was a lousy low blow. But it's the kind of thing you expected out of Helms." What was especially galling was that Helms had spent World War II safely stateside as a navy recruiting officer.

To me, Hunt's best moment came when Helms criticized him for supporting the Martin Luther King holiday. Hunt was prepared for that: "Jesse, this is 1984. This is a progressive state. We're not going to go back now and open those old wounds."

Helms's reply echoed his televised reporting on Richardson Preyer's "black bloc vote" in 1964: "Governor, I want to congratulate you on a fine political speech. That's typical of you. You're proud, you say, of your support of a national holiday for Martin Luther King, notwithstanding all of the aspects against it. Now you're doing the same thing about the so-called Voting Rights Act extension. Let's bear in mind that Senator Sam Ervin described that legislation as the most atrocious assault on constitutional principles ever committed by Congress. Now, which is more important to you, Governor: getting yourself elected with the enormous black vote, or protecting the Constitution and the people of North Carolina?"

Hunt shot back, "Jesse, which is most important to you, getting re-elected or having the people of this state upset and fighting and set at odds against each other? My gracious, how far back do you want to take us? Hey, this is a state that is making progress, Jesse. You're just out of touch with it. And the reason we're growing and making progress the way we are is because people are working together; they care about each other, and they're not following the kind of negative, divisive leadership that you've been giving."

Although he did better in the later debates, Helms clearly didn't like the combat. After Hunt, he never debated an opponent again.

For all the efforts of both campaigns, the Senate race was heavily influenced by the national political climate—and the governor's race in North Carolina. Hunt had to tread carefully in the Democratic primary for governor. The field was crowded with politicians who had postponed their ambitions when Hunt was reelected in 1980. Among them was Lieutenant Governor Jimmy Green, Hunt's nemesis for eight years. Green had been weakened by accusations of corruption but still had a following of conservative eastern Democrats. Another candidate was Eddie Knox, Hunt's friend from N.C. State and political ally since. Tom Gilmore, another member of Hunt's political group at N.C. State, was running. So was Lauch Faircloth, Hunt's commerce secretary. And Rufus Edmisten, a boisterous, colorful mountain boy who had launched his political career by arranging to sit just behind Senator Sam Ervin during the televised Watergate hearings. Ervin insiders sometimes dismissed Edmisten as a publicity hound whose skills were limited to setting up the chairs in a meeting room. But he was canny enough to parlay that job into two terms as North Carolina's attorney general.

Of all the candidates, Hunt was closest to Knox. But as always, he was mindful of Bert Bennett's rule: One campaign at a time. Hunt studiously stayed out of the first primary. Edmisten led Knox by 31 to 26 percent. In the runoff, pressure grew on Hunt to help Knox. Joe Grimsley urged him to get involved. Hunt said later, "I liked Rufus, but I and everybody in my family voted for Knox." He thought Knox would be a better general-election candidate and a better governor than Edmisten. "I think if Eddie had gotten the nomination he would have won the election and would have been a good governor, would have been a progressive governor. He would have had a strong Mecklenburg County base, and he had a rural temperament and outlook on things and was very good with rural people. I think he would have done pretty well statewide."

Still, Hunt remained neutral. "I followed the rule I always had, which was not to endorse in the primary." Edmisten won the runoff.

Knox and his family were bitter over Hunt's lack of support. Knox thought he had taken a risk backing Hunt for governor in 1976. He was from Charlotte, where Hunt's support for the East Carolina University School of Medicine had been unpopular. But Knox had stood by Hunt. He was already in the State Senate when Hunt became lieutenant governor, and Knox worked hard for him there. Didn't he deserve Hunt's help?

Knox got his revenge. President Reagan made a campaign trip to North Carolina in the summer. The arrival of Air Force One was always a big event. One of the perks was inviting local politicians to fly from Washington with the president. To no one's surprise, Jesse Helms was there with his friend "Ron." To everybody's surprise, Eddie Knox was also at the top of the ramp.

While Knox endorsed Reagan, he never specifically endorsed Helms over Hunt. But his wife, Frances, and brother Charlie did endorse Helms in a series of press conferences across the state. Mrs. Knox claimed that Hunt had changed from a sincere person to a master politician. "North Carolina can no longer afford politics for a politician's sake," she said.

Hunt was stunned—and stung. "It hurt me personally," he said years later. "Eddie was a good friend. Gosh almighty. We'd gone to N.C. State together. He had been one of the people I brought along behind me as student body president." At N.C. State, Hunt and Carolyn had been close friends with Eddie and his first wife. "We didn't have any money. We'd get together and barbecue a chicken on Friday night, and we thought we owned the world. We were close."

Hunt later thought he might have made a mistake not endorsing Knox. Did he regret the decision? "That's a good question," Hunt said. "I do have some regrets about it." Hunt and Knox didn't talk again until they bumped into each other at a legislative fundraiser in Charlotte in 1998. "We just had a chance to talk probably five minutes, just kind of checking on the family and things like that," Hunt recalled. The two old friends never discussed 1984.

Chapter 13

Flip-flopping to Defeat

Years later, Jim Hunt said that the most damaging attack the Helms campaign made against him was that of flip-flopper. As much as that perception hurt Hunt with voters, the reality crippled his campaign from within.

Our campaign was bitterly divided between those who objected to Hunt's running Helms-style negative ads and those who were determined, sometimes to a fault, to attack Helms just as hard and effectively as he attacked Hunt.

The internal debate raged throughout the campaign. Like me, most of the press and communications staff wanted to attack. Staffers working in field operations, finance, and administration resisted. Early in the 1980s, when negative TV ads were new, some Democrats still felt voters wouldn't believe that kind of stuff. Unfortunately, polls showed that people did believe it unless they heard to the contrary. The objectors argued that negative ads were beneath Hunt, that he was giving up the clean-politics image that had made him successful. They weren't privy to the campaign's polls. Nor were they knowledgeable about media strategy. But their numbers and their attitude were strongly felt within the campaign. Across the state, Hunt's supporters were divided, too. Half called headquarters demanding that we hit back harder. The other half called just as insistent that Hunt stay positive.

Joe Grimsley was torn. From one day to the next, he wavered. His uncertainty was worst at Monday-morning staff meetings. Joe would spend the weekend agonizing about the course of the campaign. He might come in first thing Monday determined to press the negative attacks—or just as determined to back off.

Hunt himself never resolved the debate. Years later, he decided that "you have to fight fire with fire," that a candidate should never let an opponent attack without counterattacking. But he was not so certain in 1984. As he kept his exhausting schedule of stops around the state, the conflicting advice he heard from supporters led him to grow ever more conflicted. He would call one day to tell me about a county chairman who had told him, "Take all the negative stuff off the air and go totally positive." Days later, he was just as likely to conclude we had to step up the attacks on Helms.

The debate came to a head in July. The spark arose not from Helms but from Bob Windsor, a gadfly newspaper publisher from Chatham County. Windsor, a hefty man who wore bib overalls, published a one-man paper, the *Landmark*. He made no pretense at objectivity—and no bones about whom he liked and whom he detested. At first, Windsor had a polite relationship with Hunt and his administration. As the campaign wore on, his sympathies became clearer. His coverage of Hunt grew acidic, while he could not say enough nice things about Helms.

But no one was prepared for the *Landmark* story that appeared on the Fourth of July. "Jim Hunt is Sissy, Prissy, Girlish and Effeminate," the headline screamed. The story began, "Is Jim Hunt homosexual? Is Jim Hunt bisexual? Is he AC and DC? Has he kept a deep dark political secret in his political closet all of his adult life?"

No sane person believed Hunt was gay. But no reporter or editor in the state ignored the charge either. The story appeared on the front page of the state's papers the next day. The *News & Observer* headline blared, "Pro-Helms newspaper publishes rumor that Hunt had gay lover." Hunt threatened Windsor with a libel suit. "I'm not going to take it," he told an interviewer. "When I got into this campaign I knew it was going to be rough, but I never really had an idea it would get this mean and vicious."

Hunt was knocked off stride by the charge. He was already under one of the longest and most expensive negative-advertising assaults in the history of American politics. He was trying to do two jobs—to be both governor and candidate—at once. His campaign was clearly lagging. On top of that, he had teenage children and didn't want them upset. Years later, he said, "I was keeping a stiff upper lip, which I'd always been taught to do. Pressing ahead, you know. People take their cues from you, your family and your associates." But all the while, "you had this barrage coming at you that you thought was misleading but darned clever and effective with people, with a ton of money behind it." Now came this "bolt out of the blue, this damn gay charge."

At first, Hunt was so shocked he didn't know how to respond. "Your initial inclination is to say nobody will believe that stuff from that fool. And, second, do you want to even acknowledge it by answering it?" Worst of all, Hunt remembered, was being asked about the charge by reporters at the front door of the Executive Mansion. "I recall we had some kind of event at the mansion and I said goodbye at the door and the press was there. I remember them congregating around me at the front door of my house, the mansion where I lived, asking me all these darned questions about this thing."

Hunt shook his head. "It was pretty humiliating. It's one thing to have a humiliating experience when you've done something wrong. You deserve it. But this was the damnedest . . ." His voice trailed off.

At one of our debate negotiations, Tom Ellis made a point of telling Phil Carlton, "I'm really sorry that happened, Phil." Carter Wrenn told me years later that the Helms campaign had nothing to do with Windsor's charge. But Wrenn did say he suspected one of Helms's supporters paid Windsor.

Hunt never accepted that the Helms campaign was innocent. "Hell no," he said years later when I asked if he believed the denials. After all, the Helms campaign had bought ads in Windsor's paper. A Helms supporter in Rocky Mount, Jack Bailey, had earlier run an ad in the *News & Observer* asking, "Governor Hunt, did you or did you not accept a $79,000 donation from Gay Activists?"

Two weeks later, in the next edition of his paper, Windsor retracted his story and apologized to Hunt. "This apology is given sincerely and humbly and reflects the true feelings of the *Landmark* and its editor," Windsor wrote. "A further apology is given to the wife and family of Hunt." Windsor also retracted another charge his article had made, one that received less attention. He claimed that Hunt had a girlfriend in the governor's office. Betty McCain said years later of Windsor, "Look, honey, you're going to have to make up your mind. Was it a boy or a girl?"

But our anger at the smear—and our uncertainty about how to respond—led us to make a big mistake.

For months, David Sawyer had been pressing us to make the case against Helms's "Evil Empire." The point, Sawyer said, was that Helms was not paying attention to North Carolina. Sawyer wanted to go beyond Peter Hart's argument that Hunt, not Helms, would be the better candidate to respond to voters' immediate concerns: education, the economy, the environment, and Social Security. Sawyer wanted to expose the *reason* Helms wouldn't address those issues—namely, he was in bed with a sinister network of characters around the country and the world such as dictators in Central America, the apartheid government of South Africa, and even some pseudoscientists who claimed black people were genetically and intellectually inferior to whites.

Bob Havely, our researcher, spent hundreds of hours tracing the intricate ties of finances and friendship to shady organizations and individuals. His research filled several thick notebooks. What was the point of having all that information and not using it?

In the wake of Windsor's gay charge, the internal debate heated up among our media team. It came to a head one weekend when several of us—including Grimsley, Stephanie Bass, and me—attended a

Democratic Senatorial Campaign Committee retreat outside Washington. James Carville was there with his "campaign kids" from Texas, as were staffers from Senate races all over the country. As always happens when campaign operatives get together, the barroom talk grew more and more combative. Soon, everybody was trying to prove they were the toughest SOB in the neighborhood. We were infected by the aggressive mood.

That night, a breaking news story set off our already-taut nerves. Roberto D'Aubuisson, a right-wing politician who had been linked to notorious death squads in El Salvador, was planning to visit the United States. Helms was one of D'Aubuisson's most vocal supporters, calling him a bulwark against communism in Central America. This time, even Grimsley didn't hesitate.

David Sawyer's team sprang into action in its New York studios and produced what came to be called the "dead bodies" ad. It began by flashing pictures of murdered Salvadorans, accompanied by the sound of machine-gun fire. "This is what they do," the voice-over intoned. "Death squads in El Salvador. Men, women, and children—murdered in cold blood." Next was a picture of D'Aubuisson: "This is the man accused of directing those death squads." Then Helms's photo appeared beside D'Aubuisson. "And this is the man whose aides helped D'Aubuisson set up a political party in El Salvador. This is Roberto D'Aubuisson's best friend in Washington, maybe his only friend."

The ad was true. But it was shocking. And it eclipsed Bob Windsor. Some reporters and political observers thought we had gone too far. Carter Wrenn said later he thought we overreacted. Internally, our campaign was again divided. Half of us thought the ad was exactly what we needed. The other half were appalled. The debate spread across the state, inside the Democratic Party, and in the media. In 2007, Mike Davis would say of the ad, "It was one of those ideas that looked great on Sunday, then not so good on Monday."

The debate over the ad raged on long after the campaign. Hunt later said, "It was a good ad. Accurate and necessary. We probably should have stuck with it longer. We didn't quite have the stomach to do the tough stuff and then to stick with it when people got squeamish about it."

I always felt defensive about the ad. I maintained for years that we should have stuck with it. But I later concluded we had made a big mistake. We gave the voters something they couldn't understand: Why was Jim Hunt showing dead bodies in a North Carolina Senate race? Worst of all, we lost the moral high ground. From the day we ran the ad to the end of the campaign, our attacks and Helms's were viewed as essentially equivalent. The ad let Helms act the injured party. As he said sarcastically about Hunt, "Now he's accusing me of murder, implicitly, and of course that's not a negative ad. I thought better of the governor than that."

In retrospect, a better strategy might have been to tie Helms to Bob Windsor, not Roberto D'Aubuisson. The sheer outrageousness of Windsor's charge—and the possibility that the Helms campaign was paying him—might have led voters to suspect Helms was not exactly the man of principle he presented himself to be.

But the unrelenting pace of the campaign made calm consideration impossible. Every week—almost every day—presented a new crisis. More ads picked away at Hunt's vulnerability. I was in a hotel in Atlantic Beach late one night before giving a speech to a Democratic group the next morning. As I watched television, I saw a new Helms ad. Bob Harris had found stories in which Hunt took two different positions on whether the school day should be longer or shorter. "Hunt supports longer school day," one headline read. "Hunt supports shorter school day," said the other. I felt like I had been punched in the stomach. I didn't have the heart to call anybody at the campaign that late at night to alert them.

As the summer wore on, the national political climate turned dramatically against us.

During Jimmy Carter's presidency, Hunt had grown close to Vice

President Walter Mondale. He had been friendly to the Mondale forces during the deliberations of the presidential nominating commission in 1981 and 1982. Mondale—who was from Minnesota and was a protégé of Hubert Humphrey, one of Hunt's heroes—was the kind of responsible, establishment politician Hunt always respected.

In 1983, it had seemed that John Glenn—whom David Sawyer worked with—would be Mondale's competition. Hunt also liked Glenn, who would campaign for him in the fall of 1984. But the old astronaut never got his presidential campaign off the ground. Gary Hart, the senator from Colorado who had run George McGovern's campaign in 1972, emerged as Mondale's main opponent. Hart was not Hunt's cup of tea. Hunt thought him too liberal, too much a maverick, and, above all, too much a part of the McGovern crowd that had yanked the party to the left in 1972.

Hart stunned Mondale in the early primaries. But the superdelegates—who had been created by Hunt's commission—rallied around the establishment candidate, and Mondale had the nomination in hand as the party held its convention in San Francisco.

Democrats couldn't have picked a worse place to meet. San Francisco was the nation's gay capital. At a time when Americans were worried that the country was losing its moral and cultural moorings, Democrats seemed to be captives of the far-out left. Hunt himself was hardly comfortable. While at the convention, "I remember one night I went out to eat with my family. I don't know if our security picked out the place or we just walked in off the street. But it was apparent pretty quickly it was a gay facility." Nothing outrageous was going on, he recalled, "but it sure surprised all of us, I'm telling you. We were a pretty protected crowd, I guess."

Nothing could protect Hunt from the debacle that developed on the convention floor—or from the gamble Mondale took in his acceptance speech. Some Democrats had long believed Reagan was vulnerable because his tax cuts had ballooned the federal deficit. Peter Hart, who was also Mondale's pollster, told us, "We're going to ram the deficit down Reagan's throat." But just as Hunt's governors' conference vote for a balanced budget led to the charge he wanted to raise taxes, anyone attacking Reagan on the deficit had to confront the question, What will you do about it? Mondale decided to face the issue and tell the truth. He said in his speech, "Mr. Reagan will raise taxes, and so will I. He won't tell you. I just did."

I was standing on the convention floor during the speech, amid the usual noise and chaos. When Mondale spoke his line and the crowd roared in approval, I wondered, Did I hear that right?

Hunt had the same reaction, he said later: "When Mondale said the words, 'He won't tell you. I just did,' I just did choke. My first reaction was, 'That was clever.' My second reaction, about thirty seconds later, was, 'Oh, hell.' That's where humor and cleverness get you in trouble in politics."

For the rest of the campaign, the Helms ads hammered Hunt as a "Mondale Liberal." Helms was a "Reagan Conservative" running against "Mondale-Hunt." The ads were so pervasive that the young daughter of one supporter thought Hunt's first name was Mondale.

The lines, clearly drawn, hardened throughout the fall. Our polls showed Helms with a stubborn single-digit lead that we couldn't close. We tried everything. We continued to debate the tone and content of our ads. Hunt continued to waver over strategy. Finally, in October, David Sawyer tried to cut through our growing uncertainty and dwindling confidence. We needed a fresh perspective, he decided. "I want to bring down a fellow from New York who might help," Sawyer said. "He's a little bit strange, but he's very creative."

At that point, we were listening to anybody and everybody. Bring him down, we told Sawyer. We convened a meeting of the minds in the Executive Mansion, around the same big dining table where Hunt had held his cabinet meetings for eight years. The size of the group was one measure of our campaign's problem. More than two dozen people were there—Hunt, Carolyn, Joe Pell, Betty McCain, Joe Grimsley, Phil Carlton, Peter Hart and his crew, David Sawyer and his people, and our campaign's communications and research staff.

Sawyer introduced Dick Morris. Like James Carville, Morris would later become famous as an adviser to Bill Clinton. He rescued Clinton after the 1994 election debacle and put the president on the path to reelection in 1996, only to become enmeshed in a sex scandal that involved toe sucking and White House gossip with a prostitute. Before that, he worked both sides of the political street. In 1990, he was part of Helms's reelection campaign against Harvey Gantt. Morris would eventually turn against the Clintons and the Democrats, becoming a prolific author and a ubiquitous television commentator on the right-leaning Fox News channel.

Morris was an unknown in 1984 but quickly made an impression on us. Small and slick, he wore a dark suit. He had a jerky, fast-talking manner that screamed New York. He gave us the results of a poll he said he had done. Later, we learned there was always skepticism among some of Morris's clients about whether he actually conducted the polls or just made up the results.

Whichever the case, his "poll" had picked up what everybody knew was Hunt's problem. "The voters think you're a flip-flopper," he told Hunt cheerfully. Morris began reading comments from a pile of papers in front of him. "Flip-flop." "He's a flip-flopper." "You don't know where he stands."

Everyone around the table grew uncomfortable. Finally, Sawyer cut him off: "Okay, Dick, we get the picture. What do we do about it?"

"Abortion," Morris chirped. "Make the race about abortion. Helms is against abortion even in cases of rape and incest. When women find that out, they don't care about Hunt's flip-flops. They turn against Helms."

The abortion issue was one we had debated internally throughout the campaign. Helms had built a reputation as the most antiabortion member of the Senate. His position was just what Morris said: no abortions, even when a woman was a victim of rape or incest.

Hunt had struggled with the issue in the 1970s. When I first worked for him in 1976, he developed a tortured explanation of his position. Scientists, he said, had concluded that life began with the "quickening" of the fetus. Therefore, abortion should be allowed up to that point but not after. Later, as Hunt was influenced by the women in his administration and his family, his position grew more liberal. In fact, he withstood political pressure for years and supported state Medicaid financing of abortions. Poor women, he said, should have access to the same health care as wealthier women.

But the issue scared us in conservative, churchgoing North Carolina. And Morris's recommendation rekindled the debate.

Phil Carlton delved into the law. He decided we could take the argument even farther: Helms's position would not only outlaw abortions but make many forms of birth control illegal. Convinced that the issue could be the dynamite that broke our logjam, I prevailed on Carlton to hold a news conference explaining his conclusion. He would never let me forget how uncomfortable he felt, a former North Carolina Supreme Court justice lecturing the press corps about birth-control methods.

Both Grimsley and Hunt were reluctant to go full bore on the issue. The reaction to the "dead bodies" ad had made us cautious. So we committed a classic campaign mistake: We did the job halfway. We didn't raise the abortion issue in a television ad. We did it on radio.

Carter Wrenn recalled first hearing the ad on his way to the campaign one morning. At first, he felt panic when the ad said Helms favored making abortions illegal even in cases of rape and incest. Then he thought we went too far when we claimed Helms would also make birth control illegal. Relieved, Wrenn felt no one would believe that.

Tom Ellis thought differently. The ad scared him. It scared him even more when a woman who had been a longtime Helms supporter called for reassurance. "Tell me that the ad's not true, Tom," she said. Unfortunately, it was true, Ellis told her.

The Helms campaign's polls quickly showed Ellis was right. "We dropped like a rock with women," Wrenn said.

Now, it was their turn to panic. Ellis rushed to Helms's house in Raleigh with a script for Dot Helms. "Jim Hunt should be ashamed of himself," she scolded in the television ad. But she didn't deny that our ad was right about Helms's position on abortion.

Still, we backed down. As always, many of Hunt's staffers and supporters objected to going negative. They had barely gotten over the "dead bodies" ad. Now, the abortion attack scared them. So we never put abortion on television. We never took advantage of the opening. We gave away what may have been our last chance to change the course of the election.

Hunt recalled that the abortion ad was "strong and powerful." He added, "It was completely accurate, and it should have been run." But "the calls really came in from our people objecting to us running that ad," he recalled. "People out in the field can't know everything you're seeing in a campaign headquarters, all the polls and everything else, but my understanding was that our people really rose up against the ad, not that it was inaccurate, but it wasn't like us, it's not the way we ought to be campaigning."

Divided and discouraged, we fought on. Unable to win on television, we put our faith in the hundred-county Hunt field organization. We hoped against hope that the people who had worked for Hunt when roads and jobs and patronage were at stake would work for him in a Senate race where the stakes were much less concrete.

Money was no problem. The national operation John Bennett had built was bringing in so much that we couldn't spend it all. We never faced Joe Pell's nightmare of running out of money in October. In fact, we would finish the election with more than eight hundred thousand dollars unspent in the bank. The Helms campaign, meanwhile, went into debt paying for its television ads.

President Reagan was headed for a landslide over Walter Mondale. The national ticket's weakness was bringing Democrats down all over the country, especially in the South. The liberal-versus-conservative lines hardened, leaving little room for Hunt's brand of moderate politics.

North Carolina became a magnet for big names. The folk trio Peter, Paul and Mary did a fundraising concert for Hunt. So did James Taylor, who grew up in Chapel Hill. Twelve years later, Taylor would sing "Carolina in My Mind" at Hunt's last inauguration. TV star Andy Griffith, a North Carolina native, made an ad for Hunt. Senators Bob Dole and Howard Baker, who had problems with Helms, swallowed their objections and campaigned for their fellow Republican.

North Carolina native James Taylor returned home to perform at a fundraising concert for Hunt during the Senate race. Taylor later sang "Carolina in My Mind" at Hunt's 1997 inauguration.
Photo from Governor Hunt's personal collection

In the closing days of the campaign, Helms began traveling around the state in a comfortable motor home, his leisurely pace a contrast to Hunt's all-out sprint. "Hunt hop-scotches across the state in a twin-engine airplane," one reporter wrote in the *News & Observer*. "And when he touches ground, he walks with such gusto that reporters and supporters sometimes have difficulty keeping up with him in mills, factories and community centers."

Hunt sought desperately to show that Helms was paying little attention to the concerns of average North Carolinians. In Rocky Mount, he said, "The choice is between Senator Helms and his right-wing agenda or a senator for North Carolina, a senator for jobs, education and opportunity for people."

Helms railed against the coalition of liberals, civil-rights leaders, big-city editors, and the "so-called gay community" that he said opposed him. He said 1984 was "a make or break year for all we hold dear. There are a lot of humanists who want to plow under our spiritual rebirth."

He hammered Hunt on an issue that nagged our campaign—the use of state aircraft for political travel. For years, Hunt had taken the state airplane and helicopters when his schedule included both state business and political business, then repaid the state for the political travel. After months of newspaper stories and an investigation by the state auditor over whether the repayments were sufficient, the campaign repaid the state $186,000. In the final days of the campaign, Helms said Hunt should "confront . . . felony charges" because he "literally stole from the people of North Carolina."

Helms generally spoke to all-white audiences, except for one awkward appearance at predominantly black Livingstone College in Salisbury late in the campaign. He showed his uncertainty over how to address blacks when he told the students, "People who brought slaves over here were blacks themselves. I never owned a slave. My family never owned a slave. This system—the free enterprise system, this political system—is open to everybody." His remark elicited "whispered comments from the audience," one news account said.

To help Hunt—and defeat Helms—black leaders promised to mount powerful voter registration and turnout programs. Jesse Jackson led highly visible rallies on black college campuses. But his visibility hurt us with white voters. And the vaunted efforts to boost African-American turnout did not become a reality in North Carolina elections until Barack Obama carried the state in 2008.

Hunt said later he thought the Jackson factor hurt him "with the kind of rural conservative vote that I'd always done pretty well with before." He came from that same background and had always been able to connect with those voters on issues like schools, jobs, and roads. But "they still have strong feelings against integration," Hunt said. He was reluctant to call them racists but felt "they saw Jesse Jackson as being not just a civil-rights leader but as somebody who was kind of a leader of all the change that had them so upset and unsettled and uncomfortable, as the main leader in America who had changed their lives and upset their lives. And they didn't like it."

He added, "The Helms people knew that, and that's why they were very clever in picking out the Martin Luther King holiday issue and by trying to tie me to Jesse Jackson." The Helms strategy, he concluded, was about "building hate and resentment against people who were different."

Countering Jackson was Jerry Falwell's Moral Majority. Falwell targeted North Carolina in turning out conservative voters who attended the state's thousands of small fundamentalist churches. "Helms played the Jerry Falwell fundamentalist crowd like a banjo," Hunt said later, "and I think it was probably the first time they had been galvanized that way." The fundamentalists liked Ronald Reagan, but they had a passion for the North Carolina senator. "Helms was their man down the line. On every single issue, he was their man," Hunt recalled.

Only later, Hunt said, did he realize Falwell and his allies "tried to make it a question of, 'Are you a Christian? Unless you share our position on all these issues, you're not even a Christian.'"

Helms said he was proud of the support of Falwell and the Moral Majority. "I'd rather have them on my side than the ones the governor has, and that includes the homosexuals and the labor unions," he said.

Just days before the election, Hunt had to face a crisis in the governor's office that further complicated his political situation: the execution of a fifty-one-year-old grandmother named Velma Barfield. Barfield had been convicted in 1978 of murdering her boyfriend by poisoning him with arsenic. During her trial, she admitted also poisoning her mother and two elderly men who had employed her as a nurse and housekeeper. After her appeals dragged on for years, her execution finally was scheduled for the Friday before the Tuesday election.

Immediately, pleas for clemency landed on Hunt's desk. Although Barfield was white, the North Carolina Association of Black Lawyers asked for a delay and a review of the case, saying it would inevitably be tainted with politics. Five professors from the University of North Carolina asked Hunt to issue a reprieve so as to avoid "political taint." Newspapers editorialized against her execution.

Hunt also heard from the families and friends of her victims. He reviewed the case, as he did all death-penalty cases. He decided that no evidence justified overturning the verdict and the appellate-court decision.

The execution took place as scheduled. Aside from our feelings about Barfield and her crimes, people in the campaign disagreed about whether the political impact would hurt or help Hunt. But we all agreed it was one more problem we could have done without.

In the final days, Hunt knew he was behind but refused to give up. "I don't think we ever had a poll showing us winning" at the end, Hunt recalled. "I knew Mondale was having a hard time, a real hard time, in the South. But I just couldn't believe that the people of North Carolina would vote for Jesse Helms against me. And I had faith that if we kept at it, kept working right down to the last minute and we had good work on Election Day, we might pull it out. It's hard to say that I expected to win. But I certainly hadn't conceded we'd lose."

On Election Day, Hunt lost by 86,300 votes out of 2.2 million cast, a margin of 51.7 to 47.8 percent. That night, he gave his concession speech. In elections past when Hunt won, we had arranged for him to be onstage with only his family. This time, many of us from the staff joined him. It wasn't planned. It felt like we were doing all we could to back him up. In an echo of his 1981 inaugural, Hunt told the crowd, "Yes, we have suffered disappointment, but we are not beaten in spirit. We have fought for what we believe. We have given our all. We have carried the torch forward, and that flame will never, never die."

He said later of conceding, "It's one of the hardest things I ever had to do. You've got to be brave, got to keep a stiff upper lip, but I just couldn't believe it happened." After eight years as governor—"a good administration, a lot of good things for the state"—he was beaten by what he saw as Helms's "negative attitude, his exacerbating the race issue. To think that the people had voted for it again, especially against our record of progress and opportunity, was just awfully hard to take. But you take it, and you keep moving."

It wasn't just the loss that was hard to take, but the encounter Hunt had that morning with the young woman who told him that she and her husband were "voting for the Christian."

Hunt realized then that—for all his effort, for all the money, for all the time spent studying issues and preparing for debates, for all the television commercials—he had not only lost but had failed to show North Carolina voters who he truly was. The image Jesse Helms painted of him—the flip-flopper, the untrustworthy and ambitious politician—had stuck. And Helms, not Jim Hunt, would go on representing North Carolina.

In the early-morning hours after Election Day, I went back to my apartment. I was worn out, but I couldn't stop watching the election returns. Hour by hour as the final precincts reported, the margin between Hunt and Helms grew closer. But the gap was far too big. Victory was tantalizingly close but would never be ours. I sat up until dawn thinking of everything we might have done differently.

Chapter 14

Picking Up the Pieces

Even winning campaigns are hard. Candidates and staff alike work to exhaustion. Many get too wound up to sleep right. Family life disappears. There is no hope of a healthy lifestyle. Everyone lives on caffeine and sugar. Some people overeat and put on weight. Others stop eating; by Election Day, their clothes hang loose on them.

Losing is even worse. We were devastated. We hadn't just lost, we had lost "the Race of the Century" in the full glare of national and international attention. We had let down the Democratic Party, the progressive tradition in North Carolina, and the hopes of the New South.

Hunt had tasted failure only once before, when he flunked the bar exam twenty years earlier. But this was a test he couldn't retake. There was no hiding from the fact that he had been rejected by the voters. And it hurt. "You're a little numb, frankly," he recalled years later. "How could this have happened? It helps you, I guess, to be a little numb. And afterward, you just go through the motions. I went through the motions."

A few weeks later, Hunt had a melancholy gathering with his staff in the governor's office. "I didn't think it would end like this," he told them.

The strain and disappointment of the 1984 election showed on Hunt's face during an interview in late December, days before he left the governor's office.
Photo by Greg Gibson, UPI

Republicans exulted. Ronald Reagan was reelected in a landslide. He carried North Carolina by 62 to 38 percent. Republican Jim Martin was elected governor to succeed Hunt, beating Edmisten by 54 to 45 percent.

Helms was riding high. He crowed in his victory speech election night, "We have sent a signal throughout the world that North Carolina is a conservative, God-fearing state. The cruel hoax of liberal politicians has run its course for the last time."

Bert Bennett had a way of summing it up: "When you win, everything you did was right. When you lose, everything you did was wrong." So it was for us. Our campaign was roundly criticized by the media, political insiders, and fellow Democrats. We had made a mistake going negative. No, we waited too long to go negative. We never should have run the "dead bodies" ad. No, we should have stayed with it. We never should have raised the abortion issue. No, we should have pressed it harder. We distanced ourselves too much from Mondale. No, we were too close to Mondale. We were too close to black voters. No, we didn't do enough to energize them.

We second-guessed ourselves endlessly. One staffer said later, "We let Helms set the agenda, and we let the campaign become about who Jim Hunt was and was not." Another said, "Helms did a better job articulating what was wrong with the Democratic approach to issues. He was better at framing issues." Another: "We tried to answer emotional appeals with logic."

Years later, Hunt said, "We had an awful lot of things that were just dragging us down." The biggest problem was Mondale, who lost everywhere to Reagan but his home state of Minnesota. Hunt ran ahead of Rufus Edmisten, the candidate for governor, and 13 points ahead of Mondale. That wasn't enough. "But it's nobody's fault," Hunt said. "Against all odds, we probably should have won, and if we'd run a perfect campaign we could have."

We did not run a good campaign. We were divided and indecisive, at first reluctant to attack Helms and then, in the end, overreaching. We did not have a Tom Ellis, a commanding general with stature and self-confidence who could knock heads, resolve internal divisions, and enforce strategic discipline on the campaign.

No one replayed the campaign more—or blamed himself more—than I did. I knew we had lost the battle on television. We had not been prepared for Helms's onslaught. "I don't think we were as clever as they were," Hunt said. I never escaped the feeling that if I were smarter or had done more, Hunt would have won—and perhaps gone on to challenge for the presidency.

Hunt himself was not at his best in the campaign. He never seemed comfortable as a candidate, unlike every other campaign I watched him in. He had trouble adjusting from being governor to running for the Senate. He struggled to translate his agenda in Raleigh—jobs and education—to issues in Washington.

Hunt thought the campaign would be about issues, just like his campaigns for lieutenant governor and governor. That's why he spent hours reading briefing books and thinking through his positions. Polls showed that most voters agreed with his approach to the issues. But in the end, image—especially the image of a flip-flopper—trumped issues.

Too often, Hunt seemed to be running because he wanted to be in the Senate, rather than because he wanted to do something for North Carolina. That reeked of raw ambition. In truth, Hunt might have run simply because he despised Jesse Helms and all he stood for.

Beyond all that, though, one factor stood out. It was there from the beginning of the campaign to the bitter end. After the election, we spent some of our leftover campaign money to commission a poll by Harrison Hickman. We wanted to know exactly why we had lost—and to start looking at the future. Hickman concluded from the poll that the single best predictor of how people voted was how they felt about the Martin Luther King holiday. If they supported it, they voted for Hunt. If they opposed it, they went with Helms. The correlation was nearly 100 percent.

The campaign was, at bottom, about race.

Helms had known what he was doing when he filibustered against the King holiday bill in the fall of 1983. The race card had played out again. It was just like 1950, when Frank Porter Graham lost, and 1964, when Richardson Preyer lost.

Bill Friday, who had been with Frank Porter Graham on election night in 1950, said Hunt learned the same lesson in 1984: "Good people can be misled."

Whatever the reason, Hunt lost. His reputation was shredded. Perhaps no other politician before had more negative TV ads dumped on him. The Helms campaign spent nearly $17 million—a record for a Senate race then. In 2010 dollars, that would have amounted to more than $35 million. We had spent just under $9.5 million.

Hunt felt stigmatized by some Democrats: "You get some feelings that people kind of blame you. Some of the party people. 'Well, if you'd done good enough, you wouldn't have lost.' And sometimes, particularly in the Democratic Party, if you've said anything negative, that was seen as a mistake."

He feared that his record as governor would be forgotten. He seemed to be finished in politics. And he faced a wrenching personal adjustment. After being on the public payroll for twelve years, he had no financial wealth. He had to find a job and make a living for his family.

Hunt's therapy was to go back to work. "I had two more months as governor, and I was determined to give it all I had. Keep working every day, every night, just like I always had. Don't just quit right then and start boxing it up, but keep working on all the issues we were working on . . . in the administration."

One task was the transition to a new governor. Jim Martin had been a congressman from the Charlotte area before 1984. He was conservative, but he was no Helms. "He was a moderate Republican," Hunt said later. "I thought he'd be a pretty good governor."

Ever the student, Hunt learned all he could about how to manage a smooth transition. "We were going to be the experts on transition, the model," he said later. He ordered his cabinet to amass mounds of briefing material for Martin and his team. But "my feeling was that Martin wasn't too interested in getting a lot of help," Hunt said later. "And maybe he didn't trust me to be trying to do what was best for him." He thought he could help Martin. After all, nobody had been governor longer than Hunt.

He recalled one meeting when he and Martin discussed the touchy issue of hazardous waste disposal. The state was looking for a central site to handle all kinds of hazardous waste from all over the state. Hunt warned Martin that the decision would be difficult. He offered to take the burden off the new governor's hands. "I recall saying to Governor Martin, 'We've done a lot of work on this, I'm fixing to go out of office, and I don't have anything to lose. If you'd like for me to, I'll take the lead and see if we can't get this thing finished, so you don't have to come in and make an unpopular decision right at the beginning.'"

But Martin, filled with all the confidence of an election winner, declined the offer. He told Hunt, "No, I'll handle that."

Eight years later, Martin was still trying to handle it. No site ever opened. "He certainly did not understand how tough it was going to be," Hunt said.

Hunt took on one last big initiative. The idea came to him during a meeting with Raleigh mayor Avery Upchurch. Upchurch was a small-town mayor in a big city. Easygoing and soft-spoken, he owned a popular service station at a busy intersection. Raleigh residents delighted in taking out-of-towners to Upchurch's Exxon, where the mayor pumped gas and cleaned windshields.

During 1984, Upchurch brought a delegation of the city's developers to meet with Hunt. The developers had their eyes on several hundred acres of open land that the state owned just south of downtown. The parcel had long been part of a farm at the Dorothea Dix mental hospital. But a trend toward deinstitutionalizing patients was emptying the hospital, and mental-health leaders felt it was no longer appropriate for the remaining patients to work on the farm. Dix didn't need the land, and Mayor Upchurch and the developers thought it would be ideal for houses, shopping centers, and offices.

"I listened to them politely," Hunt recalled, "but the whole time, I was thinking, 'This is not what we need.' The minute those people walked out of my office, I thought, 'I know what we ought to do with that land. We ought to use it for a big new research campus for North Carolina.' It was one of those light-bulb moments."

The idea came out of the same belief in research and technology that had led Hunt to create the microelectronics center and the biotechnology center. Now, he made up his mind to give the land to North Carolina State University. Hunt's alma mater was next door, and it was landlocked and unable to grow. But Hunt had only two months before he was to leave office, so he needed to move fast. He got on the phone to N.C. State's chancellor, Bruce Poulton, who embraced the idea. He called Agriculture Commissioner Jim Graham, who wanted the land for a farmers' market and wasn't too keen on Hunt's taking it away. But the two men worked out a plan that would give most of the land to

N.C. State, which was also Graham's alma mater, and set aside some acreage for the market.

Hunt quickly pushed the land grant through the Council of State and signed an executive order giving more than three hundred acres to the university. He set in motion plans to provide even more land. Years later, Ferrel Guillory, then an editorial writer with the *News & Observer*, recalled that the newspaper's editors were stunned by what Hunt was doing and published an editorial raising questions. Hunt summoned Guillory and editor Claude Sitton to a meeting. As he explained the idea, the two editors saw the value of what he was proposing. Guillory recalled it as an example of how forcefully Hunt used the powers of the governor's office when he got his mind set on doing something.

Hunt's idea soon became the separate, new Centennial Campus at N.C. State. After he left office, the legislature transferred another seven hundred acres to the university, which built textile and engineering buildings, labs, and classrooms on the new campus. Private companies like Red Hat software located there. The old farmland eventually became what Hunt envisioned: a magnet to attract high-tech industries and research organizations to a sprawling campus where scientists from private industry could work side by side with the university's faculty, researchers, and students. In 2010, the university broke ground for a signature building on the campus, the James B. Hunt Jr. Library.

The Centennial Campus deal and some final judicial appointments kept Hunt working up to his last day in office.

Inauguration Day, a Saturday, was difficult, watching Republicans take over state government. Carolyn Hunt told a friend that the drive back to the farm that day was the longest she had ever taken.

The next Monday, Hunt was at work at a new job in Raleigh. He joined the law firm of Poyner & Spruill, where his old friend Phil Carlton worked. Carlton recalled that "Hunt backed up his black Ford to the front of the Poyner & Spruill building the Monday after he left the governor's office. He had all his desk stuff in the car." Hunt had no assistant. Unused to driving and parking himself, he took up two spaces in the lot. He moved his things into his new office.

After a few days, Hunt told Carlton that something was bothering him: "It's driving me crazy that the phone's not ringing." He was used to being frantically busy and having people lined up to see him. He didn't know what to do.

"I said, 'Make a list of all the CEOs and corporate counsels you know,'" Carlton recalled. Hunt made the list and began recruiting companies for Poyner & Spruill, the same way he had done for North Carolina. "He wasn't really a lawyer, he was a rainmaker," Carlton said.

Soon, Hunt brought the firm one of its biggest clients: PepsiCo. The drink got its start in New Bern, North Carolina, but had grown to become an international behemoth. Based in New York, it was legally incorporated in Delaware, like many big companies. But now PepsiCo was trying to stave off the corporate raiders roaming Wall Street in the 1980s. Hunt, Carlton, and other attorneys at Poyner & Spruill solved PepsiCo's problem. They persuaded the legislature to rewrite North Carolina's incorporation laws to protect state-chartered companies against hostile takeovers. Once the new law passed, PepsiCo changed its state of incorporation to North Carolina.

While Carlton never had Hunt's political drive, he had an entrepreneurial turn of mind. Carlton came up with the idea of a nationwide network of law firms that had offices in state capitals and did extensive state government work. Again, he asked Hunt to make a list, this time of the former governors he knew who had gone to work in firms like Poyner & Spruill. Hunt came up with Dick Riley, the former governor of South Carolina and later Bill Clinton's secretary of education. Also, Carl Sanders of Georgia, Scott Matheson of Utah, Pierre du Pont of Delaware, Charles Thone of Nebraska, and a half-dozen others. And Hillary Rodham Clinton in Little Rock, Arkansas. She was the state's first lady and a lawyer working with a capital-city firm.

Soon, the network became a nationwide—and later an international—organization called the State Capital Law Firm Group. The firms referred business to each other. They studied issues facing the states. They held annual meetings in fine resorts around the nation and the world. More than twenty years later, Carlton was still operating the group. Its headquarters was in an old bank building he owned in his little hometown of Pinetops, just east of Rock Ridge.

Hunt and Carlton always had a rivalry. Carlton was one of the first people in Raleigh to own a car phone, a status symbol in the days before cell phones became cheaper, smaller, and more common. A few months later, Hunt got a phone in his car. On the way to Raleigh one morning, he phoned Carlton, whom he always called "Judge." When Carlton answered, Hunt boomed, "Judge! I've got my own car phone now."

Carlton, determined to one-up him, replied, "Hold on a second, Jim. My other line is ringing."

Hunt hadn't lost the political itch. North Carolina had another Senate election coming in 1986, for the seat John East had won from Robert Morgan. East was no Helms. He kept a low profile. He voted almost exactly like Helms. Since he was confined to a wheelchair, he inevitably was called "Helms on Wheels."

The race looked inviting to Hunt. He would face a weak opponent. It was an off-year when Reagan would not be on the ballot. The national climate looked better for Democrats. Hunt had not yet turned fifty years old. He still had a chance to get to the Senate.

But the long battle against Helms had left him politically bloodied. Those of us on his staff were spent, physically and emotionally. One consultant who met with us thought we needed psychiatric help, not political advice. In the summer of 1985, Harrison Hickman and I arranged a set of focus groups in Greensboro to test how voters felt about Hunt's running again. Hunt went with us. What followed were four of the most painful hours of my life. With Hunt beside me, I sat behind a one-way mirror as voters vented their spleen against him. "Flip-flopper." "Nothing but a politician." "You can't trust him." "Just out for himself." "Flip-flopper."

The ever-optimistic Hunt found hope. He had armed Hickman, who moderated the groups, with a series of issue ideas. After trashing Hunt, the participants responded with some interest to the issues. "They really liked some of those worker-training proposals," he told us enthusiastically on the ride back to Raleigh. We didn't have the heart to argue. It was all too clear—from what we heard that night and what

Hunt and lifelong friend Phil Carlton in 1985
Photo courtesy of Phil Carlton

Hunt's friends all over the state were hearing—that North Carolinians were tired of Jim Hunt. There would be no comeback in 1986.

In September 1985, Hunt announced he would not run. He portrayed it as a family decision. "I really believe it's time to put my family first," he said in a letter to supporters. The *Charlotte Observer* interviewed "a relaxed Hunt," who said, "What I think my decision means is that I've found out there's something important in life besides politics." He talked about enjoying the freedom of private life, driving Baxter to graduate school in a van that broke down on the way back, eating out at restaurants, planning family vacations without worrying about matters of state. "It's really great," he insisted.

In truth, Hunt bowed to political reality. Joe Pell told a reporter, "The majority of people closest to him advised him not to run. Who have we got to run a campaign? We would have had to have found new people. Is the organization tired? It seems to me it's only been two weeks ago. How would his family feel about being exposed to another race against the Congressional Club?"

Hickman and I did our best to paint a rosy picture. I told reporters Hunt could have raised enough money and won: "It was not a political decision, but a totally personal one." Hickman argued that Hunt's political scars were healing with time. He told a reporter, "The further you get away from the 1984 election, the greater appreciation there is for Hunt's skills as Governor."

But 1984 was not far away enough yet—for the voters or for Hunt.

Years later, Carolyn Hunt said her husband took a long time to recover from the loss to Helms. He didn't show it much. As Phil Carlton said, "He's so good at hip hip hooray." But Carolyn saw it: "I think it took him a long time to get over it, really quite awhile. Longer, really longer than I let myself know or sense at the time. He took it so hard personally, that it was against him."

She added, "You know, you've done all these things, you've worked your head off, you really feel like you've done for North Carolina all you can do, and for the people. And then it's a letdown. You feel like they ought to think of all the good things and really want you to go ahead and represent them in Washington."

Hunt recalled feeling "still a little numb" for months after the election. But he soon came to terms with losing. "Sometime after probably about nine months or so, I was shaving one day at home on the farm. And the thought occurred to me, 'Well, you know, sometimes the people just make a mistake.' And I figured they'd made a mistake in that vote, and it just happened. You've got to move on. And so then I began to deal with it."

Part III
Comeback

One of Jim Hunt's favorite photos with Carolyn. With her husband often working and traveling, she took care of the children, ran the Executive Mansion, oversaw frequent public events, and volunteered in the schools.
Photo from Governor Hunt's personal collection

Chapter 15

The Road Back

After Jim Hunt left the governor's office and he and Carolyn made that long drive home to Rock Ridge, he was out of politics for the first time in almost twenty years. He had been campaigning since he got back from Nepal in 1966—organizing the Young Democrats in Wilson County, running for state YDC president, speaking at the Democratic National Convention, chairing the state party reform commission, running for lieutenant governor, running for governor, passing his programs in the legislature, running for governor again, passing the gas tax, pushing his vision of a high-tech economy, chairing the national party's presidential-nomination commission, and, for nearly two years, battling Jesse Helms.

Now, he was a lawyer again—not a small-town attorney this time but a partner in a big-name Raleigh firm. Every weekday, he commuted between his farm and Raleigh, a forty-five-minute drive each way. He began traveling around the country, recruiting clients. He said years later, "I was making the first real money in my life." And he couldn't help boasting, "I often billed more hours than anybody else in the firm, including those young bucks in there."

I took an office on the first floor of his law firm's building and started a public relations practice. Phil Carlton and I worked together on several projects. Most mornings, I spotted Hunt as he came rushing in, just as he had at the Capitol. He rarely carried a briefcase. He would have a stack of documents under his arm, with notes about things to do and people to call scrawled on scraps of paper.

Other partners in the law firm spent weekends relaxing, playing golf, or going to the beach. Not Hunt. And not Carolyn. The Iowa farm girl thrived in Rock Ridge, getting up every morning at five, managing the farm, and, very soon, helping with grandchildren.

The Hunts started raising a herd of beef cattle. Why? "I always liked cattle," Hunt said. "When I was a boy, I'd show my cattle at the State Fair." Carolyn grew up on a cattle farm. "I thought I'd just ease into it, just a few heifers," Hunt said. But he never eased into anything. "Then I wanted to get purebreds, and then I wanted to get the best purebreds. It just started building up."

Eventually, the Hunts amassed a herd of seventy purebred cows. In 1990, they had the champion Simmental female at the State Fair. "When they're purebred, they get special attention," he explained. "It's not just, 'Put them out there on the land and I'll see you once a year.' Carolyn artificially bred them all. We paid particular attention to all the shots and all the health care and made sure the calves came okay. It's, 'Keep your eye on it all the time.'" Carolyn admitted, "It got to be a lot."

"The worst was in the wintertime," Hunt said, "when we put out those big bales of hay with a tractor and a big front-loader." The bales weighed over a thousand pounds. It was muddy and cold. When calves were born, the Hunts had to be there. When the calves wouldn't eat, "you've got to get in there and put them up to those tits." When they got sick, "you've got to doctor them several times a day." In the end, "we were just working ourselves to death."

Literally. One cow almost killed Hunt. She was Starlet, "probably the most expensive cow I'd ever bought." He spent four thousand dollars on her at a sale in Virginia. Hunt was eager for Starlet to have her

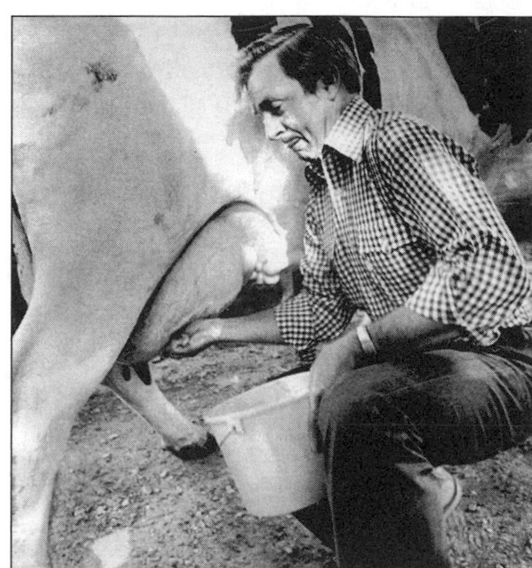

Hunt shows off his skill in a cow-milking contest with then-Lieutenant Governor Jimmy Green at a dairy industry event in 1980. Hunt won. After he left the governor's office in 1985, he and Carolyn started raising beef cattle on their farm. Carolyn did most of the work.

Photo courtesy of the *News & Observer*

Hunt on his cattle farm in 1985. He worked at his law firm in Raleigh during the week and on the farm weekends.

Photo courtesy of the *News & Observer*

first calf. He wanted heifers, not bulls, because he could breed heifers. "One day, she was missing when the others came up for water, so I knew she probably had that calf," he remembered. He walked several hundred yards from the house until he found her. "I kind of sneaked up to see if it was a heifer calf. And I got up closer than I should have. That darn cow bolted at me and knocked me flat on the ground."

Hunt found himself lying on the ground beneath the cow. "I thought she was going to stomp me to death." Luckily, Carolyn and a neighbor, George Smith, came up, and Starlet ran off to protect her calf. Hunt had a broken collarbone and ribs. He was "hurting like hell, bloody all over." They got him to the emergency room. It took a year for his collarbone to heal, and his ribs hurt for months. Later, Carolyn told the ever-impatient Hunt, "If you wanted to know what sex that calf was, all you had to do was wait until it peed."

The incident got a lot of news coverage. When he went to the State Fair, cattlemen kept coming up and telling him about similar things that had happened to them. "I got more stories than you can shake a stick at." It was the first time in a while that people saw him as a regular human being instead of a politician.

In 1986, Carolyn Hunt—the woman people in Raleigh thought hated politics—ran for a seat on the Wilson County School Board. Her husband became her campaign manager and head volunteer. "I learned to put up signs again," Hunt said. She won.

Carolyn ran, she said years later, because "I didn't think our representative was really getting into the schools. I think a school-board member has to go visit all the schools, be in constant contact with people, and listen to teachers, principals, parents, and superintendents."

She knew something about schools. Carolyn earned her teaching degree at UNC–Chapel Hill, taught for a year in Nepal, and was a substitute teacher in Wilson County. She had started volunteering in the Wilson schools years earlier, when one of their children had a teacher who wasn't very good. She kept volunteering through all the years she was first lady. In the end, she would be a school volunteer for thirty-five years.

Carolyn Hunt working as a school volunteer, as she did for thirty-five years. She earned her degree in teaching at UNC–Chapel Hill and taught in a school in Nepal. In 1986, she was elected to a four-year term on the Wilson County School Board.
Photo courtesy of the *News & Observer*

One of Carolyn's first causes on the board was pushing for more school nurses. Years later, she said, "A lot of these students, once they have their vaccinations and get into kindergarten, they do not go to a doctor for years, for years!" She sounded like Jim Hunt when he pounded the table, angry about having to wait three hours as a boy to see a doctor.

Carolyn wasn't the outgoing politician he was, but the Hunts had shared backgrounds, shared values, and shared religious faith. She also shared his politics. She was "always thinking things can be better, that there are ways to improve things," she said later.

She plunged into the tricky issue of redistricting and racial balance. The county had to shift students to avoid slipping back into segregated schools. The courts required it, but a lot of whites didn't like the policy. "We knew it was very risky for her to support that plan, but she did," Hunt recalled. Carolyn paid the price when she ran for reelection in 1990. One prominent member of the community, angered that his son was transferred to a different school, supported Carolyn's opponent. And Wilson County still had its share of racists. On Election Day, one of them let Carolyn know how he felt. At a polling place, he threw a penny at her to show his contempt.

Carolyn lost her race for reelection. But Hunt said, "I was never prouder of her, for standing up for what was right for all the children in our county, even though it was politically risky and costly."

Even after Hunt passed on the Senate race in 1986, he had no doubt he would get back into politics. He and I talked frequently about a rematch with Helms in 1990—and what we would do differently this time.

Hunt's old hero Terry Sanford had been elected to the Senate after Hunt stepped aside in 1986. It was a triumphant comeback for Sanford. His four years as governor in the early 1960s had won him a national reputation as a progressive innovator. But he left office unpopular, politically damaged by his sales tax on food. He made two failed runs for president, in 1972 and 1976. In 1972, he even lost the North Carolina primary to George Wallace.

But in 1986, Sanford trounced a group of lesser-known Democrats in the primary. Then it turned out to be a good Democratic year. And he drew an inept Republican opponent in Jim Broyhill, a long-term congressman from western North Carolina. Broyhill's protégé, Governor Jim Martin, had appointed him to the Senate after John East committed suicide. A multimillionaire furniture-industry executive, Broyhill lacked anything resembling a common touch. And he wasn't conservative enough to suit the Congressional Club. The club backed hardline conservative David Funderburk, a former ambassador to Romania in the Reagan administration, in the Republican primary. Broyhill won, but the party was split. Sanford won the fall election by 52 to 48 percent.

Although Hunt was happy to see Sanford in the Senate and Democrats coming back, he had been eclipsed. Sanford was the new

Democratic hero. Even Democrats delighted in kicking Hunt while he was down. As 1990—and a potential rematch with Helms—neared, the *Charlotte Observer* quoted one "longtime Hunt supporter" as saying, "Politically, Hunt is out of step. The electorate is changing and people are tired of him. . . . The time is right for a new face."

In August 1989, Hunt announced he wouldn't run against Helms in 1990. I helped him work up a statement in which he said, "I especially believe I would win if the campaign focused on the issues and on the future of North Carolina. But, given the experience of 1984, that probably would not be its nature." We laid it on thick: "Further, given the result of 1984, it is clear that I do not enjoy or perform well in a campaign that emphasizes negative ads and character attacks."

As in 1986, Hunt told reporters he had family considerations. He said in one interview that his parents' health, not political analysis, shaped his decision. His eighty-five-year-old mother was bedridden after suffering a heart attack and a stroke. His father, who was seventy-eight, was also ailing. Hunt said, "We just have responsibilities we have to meet."

In truth, just as in 1986, calculation shaped the decision. A race against Helms would have been a bloody rematch. Phil Carlton thought that "Hunt had had enough of Jesse Helms." And even if he ran and won, Hunt would have been starting late in the Senate, where seniority counts above all. The White House was out, too. Other moderate Southern Democrats like Bill Clinton and Al Gore were eyeing the presidency. Hunt recalled that, at one point, David Broder of the *Washington Post* "wrote that if I'd won in '84 I'd have been president." But now, Hunt knew, "that was over."

Besides, Hunt was beginning to glimpse another comeback road, one he knew well—the governor's office.

The 1984 campaign damaged Hunt in North Carolina, but his national reputation fared better.

His education proposals in his second term—as well as his national work on the subject—thrust him into the debate about education and America's economy. His national profile was enhanced, not diminished, by his loss to Helms. He had spent two years raising money and making friends in the stratosphere of America's business and political circles.

After leaving the governor's office, he started working on education reform with the Carnegie Corporation of New York, a prestigious philanthropic foundation. He and the foundation's president, David Hamberg, had long talks about America's schools. They decided to convene a one-day meeting in New York of "the Group of Fifty"—leaders from business, science, and education. Out of it came the Carnegie Forum on Education and the Economy's Task Force on Teaching As a Profession. Hunt served on the task force with a number of national education and business leaders. In 1986, it issued a report called, "A Nation Prepared: Teachers for the 21st Century." The report recommended the creation of a national board with the mission of dramatically improving teaching. The National Board for Professional Teaching Standards was created, and Hunt was appointed to chair it. The role would dramatically impact the teaching profession—and Hunt's political career.

Hunt had a long and complicated relationship with teachers. He was a certified teacher himself, though he had never taught. He enjoyed the support of teachers in his campaigns in 1972, 1976, and 1980, but the love affair turned cool when he froze teachers' pay in his second term. Teachers marched on the Executive Mansion. The North Carolina Association of Educators publicly dithered over whether or not to endorse him for the Senate. A delighted Helms mocked Hunt's education credentials.

But Hunt had a remarkable capacity not to hold a grudge. And he was a true policy wonk. He genuinely believed that the key to America's future was education, and that the key to education was teachers. He was ready to put aside hard feelings. And he sensed that the National Board for Professional Teaching Standards was a way to rebuild burnt bridges.

For ten years, even after he was elected governor again, Hunt would chair the teaching-standards board. He led the board to what Jim Kelly, its president, called "a historic breakthrough." Kelly said later, "It was the first time in history that teachers were paid more money because they demonstrated that they are excellent teachers." That is to say, not because they had tenure and not because they had this or that degree, but because they had gone through a rigorous process to demonstrate their qualifications. "There were no standards for what good teaching was," Kelly said. "And nobody was working on it. The nation's policy leaders had never met in a room to talk about it."

Hunt led what could have been a fractious board. The sixty-three members included school superintendents, principals, university deans, scientists, and business executives from companies like Dow Chemical and Xerox, as well as governors and legislators. Among the members were John Gardner, the founder of Common Cause, who had been Lyndon Johnson's secretary of health, education, and welfare; Lewis Branscomb, chairman of the National Science Board and chief scientist at IBM; and Republican governor Tom Kean of New Jersey.

Thirty-two teachers were on the board. They included the presidents of the nation's two rival teacher unions—the National Education Association and the American Federation of Teachers. The NEA and AFT were at war then. "They fought like cats and dogs," Hunt recalled. "They were bitter, bitter enemies. They shouted at each other."

Hunt believed both teacher groups had to be represented, and that teachers had to be the majority of the board. He made sure the heads of national English, science, and math teacher groups were there. "Most groups do things for teachers or to teachers," he said later. Not this board. "For it to be successful and authentic, it had to be run by teachers."

Jim Kelly noted that not everybody shared Hunt's view about the teachers' role: "There was little acceptance of the idea that teachers were experts on teaching and should be involved, let alone be a majority of the board."

It was an exhausting, exacting task. As always, Hunt was an active and aggressive leader, not a figurehead. He chaired every session. The board met four times a year, and the meetings lasted two or three days.

Kelly recalled, "Hunt attended every meeting, even when he was governor. And there were no photo ops the first seven years. It was not a Jim Hunt show." Hunt always did his homework. "He read the stuff, and he was prepared," Kelly said. "Meetings started and ended on time. There were long agendas. He stuck to them and got them done."

Every meeting, Hunt spent thirty or forty hours presiding, listening, and learning. "I worked my head off to do it," he said years later, "but what an opportunity to learn." Especially from teachers. Hunt got to know the presidents of the nation's math teachers and science teachers, as well as other accomplished teachers. "I sat at their feet for years listening to them tell what teachers needed to know and be able to do," he said. That variation on a phrase coined by Governor Kean—"what highly accomplished teachers need to know and be able to do"—became Hunt's mantra about the teaching board's mission.

He came to appreciate the complexity of teaching, of having to deal "with students of different backgrounds, different levels of intelligence and aptitudes, who learn in different ways. You've got all of them in the classroom." The experience reminded him of good teachers he had in school, like D. B. Sheffield and Onnie Cockrell, his history teacher and football and basketball coach. "Teaching is like conducting a symphony orchestra. You've got to know them all, every note they're supposed to be playing, what they're good at, how to blend it all together, and how you lead them all at the same time. That's what good teaching is like."

First, Hunt's board hammered out a statement summarizing what teachers needed to know and had to be able to do. Then it created a framework for some thirty fields of certification, by student ages and subject areas—English, history, art, and so on. Then the board had to create the standards and decide how teachers would be assessed. Eventually, it developed a comprehensive system that required teachers seeking certification to do a portfolio of their work, take a rigorous test, and videotape their teaching so evaluators could see them in the classroom.

Only after laying that groundwork well into the 1990s did the board begin certifying teachers, just as lawyers and doctors are board-certified. Then came the challenge of persuading governors, legislators, and the political community to recognize board-certified teachers with higher pay. Always before, Kelly said, the only way the best teachers could make more money was to move into administration—and out of the classroom.

It all got done—and with the board's unanimous approval. That unanimity was critical to building political support for what the board was trying to do with the profession of teaching. Hunt painstakingly built consensus, especially among the teacher members. He proselytized fellow politicians to pay board-certified teachers more money. "He was in good with the Southern mafia of governors" who cared about education, Kelly said.

Hunt helped secure federal funds for the project, especially after Bill Clinton became president. He even got a measure of revenge with Jesse Helms. "Helms fought us tooth and nail" when the board sought money from Congress, Hunt recalled. When he went to Washington to lobby some of his old Democratic friends, he told Congressman Steny Hoyer from Maryland, a member of the Democratic House leadership, that Helms opposed the program. Hoyer replied, "You mean this will upset Jesse Helms? Where do I sign up?" Congress approved the money.

By the time the board began certifying teachers, Hunt had been elected governor again. He made sure North Carolina was the first state to adopt a plan to pay board-certified teachers more money. Soon, Governor George Voinovich of Ohio, who replaced Tom Kean on the board, followed suit in his state. Hunt constantly pushed governors around the country to reward board-certified teachers. It got competitive. Hunt heard that one Midwestern governor said, "We're going to out-Hunt Hunt."

By 2010, more than eighty thousand teachers were board-certified across the country. North Carolina had fifteen thousand, the most of any state.

The bylaws originally limited the chairman to two two-year terms. But after four years, the board changed those bylaws. Hunt remained chairman. Upgrading the teaching profession was a consuming passion.

He had become the nation's expert on teachers. And the teachers who served on his board loved him.

Hunt was also passionate about another subject: early-childhood education.

He had some history on the issue. As lieutenant governor, he had helped start North Carolina's universal kindergarten program. In his second term as governor, he and Joe Grimsley came up with an early-childhood initiative called "Raising a New Generation." But the program stalled when fundamentalist preachers—some of the same people who fought the Equal Rights Amendment—condemned it as government interference in the family.

Now, Jim and Carolyn Hunt had grandchildren. Carolyn spent a lot of her time taking care of them. And Hunt was home with his grandchildren more than he had been with his own children.

"Having grandchildren really affected me," he said later. "Grandchildren are a gift, an amazing gift. Having grandchildren is like another dimension to your life. The awe, the amazement, the thankfulness for them."

Carolyn added, "I think somewhere around then, he started thinking that we're starting too late" in educating children. "We're talking about high school and college, but we also need to focus on these little ones and their little minds."

Another venture Hunt had launched—the Emerging Issues Forum at N.C. State—accelerated his focus on "little minds." After Hunt left the governor's office, Chancellor Bruce Poulton asked him to chair a forum on public policy and public issues at the campus. Hunt, who loved a good talkfest, accepted. He brought in Betty Owen, who had been his education adviser in the governor's office, to manage the project. She recalled, "He and Poulton decided they would call a big meeting in February 1986 and call it the Emerging Issues Forum. They sent invitations to every list they could come up with. It was free, and Jim Hunt was going to be there." The crowd was bigger than expected. "It was total bedlam," Owen said, "but everybody had a great good time."

The forum was such a success that it became an annual event. The next year, Hunt got Texas billionaire Ross Perot to give the keynote speech. Perot had just led a highly publicized study commission on schools for Governor Mark White in Texas and was enjoying his moment in the sun. He hadn't yet run for president and earned a reputation as a loose political cannon with a penchant for shooting his own foot.

Owen recalled how Hunt talked Perot into coming to Raleigh. He got Perot on the phone, leaned back in his chair, and boomed, "Ross!" As Owen told it later, "He just talked up a storm with Ross Perot. 'How great you are, and all these awards you've gotten, and I've just talked to Governor White in Texas, and he thinks you're wonderful, and we're doing something in North Carolina that I want you to come to.' Well, before he got off the phone, he had Ross Perot raring to come."

"When they rolled up" on the day of the forum, Owens recalled, "there were thousands of people lined up to the street trying to get in that place. All of the major business leaders from North Carolina were there that day to hear Ross Perot. It was incredible. All the bankers and lawyers. All the members of the legislature were there. It was a huge success."

The forum became a must every February for hundreds of people across the state. They came to hear big-name speakers from around the country and the world and to talk to each other and to Hunt; they went home fired up with new ideas and new energy. Over the years, speakers included Jimmy Carter, Bill Clinton, Paul Krugman, Thomas Friedman, Newt Gingrich, Hillary Clinton, Steve Forbes, Robert Rubin, Jay Rockefeller, Amory Lovins, Al Gore, and Paul Volcker. Hunt got big names through sheer persistence. He wouldn't take no for an answer. One of the speakers said years later, "If Jim Hunt asks you to do something, you may as well go ahead and say yes, because eventually you're going to."

The speakers all got effusive, enthusiastic, and sometimes

embarrassingly over-the-top introductions by Hunt. I had long ago learned that Hunt had an obsession about speech introductions. As the victim of many bad ones, he believed that a good introduction set the stage for a successful speech. While governor and forever after, he insisted that whoever introduced him had to know exactly what to say and how to do it right. Few measured up to his expectations. When Hunt did an introduction, he practiced what he preached. As one speaker at the Emerging Issues Forum said, "You've never really been introduced until you've been introduced by Jim Hunt."

Of all the forum's speakers, perhaps none had a greater impact on Hunt than astronomer-author Carl Sagan. Sagan spoke at the forum in 1990 and mesmerized Hunt with a talk about the development of human intelligence—especially how people are affected by experiences in their early years. At the same time, Hunt "was beginning to see these articles about brain development in infants and little children," he recalled.

In 1990, as he began thinking about running for governor again, Hunt reminded me of the candidate I knew in 1976. He would go on and on about his ideas for teaching and early childhood the same way he had gone on and on about his Primary Reading Program in 1976. Never one for small talk, he would veer off into a lecture about how "little minds" had the capacity of advanced computers and how "if you had great care as an infant and small child, a lot of your brain cells connected up, and you got this fully wired computer." His eyes would light up as he described what happened as a kind of "snap, crackle, and pop." His friends would look at each other and smile. Hunt would catch himself and laugh. But he was dead serious.

Hunt was thinking about what he had done as governor—and what he had not done. He said later, "I knew that just putting more money into what we had been doing was not the answer. I had figured out what was the answer. It was better teaching and starting earlier, and neither of those was happening. We were just kind of going along, doing what we had been doing, spending more money but not changing what we were doing. And I was learning what you had to do to get a different result."

Hunt still thought like a governor. He read newspapers like a governor. "I was learning about early-childhood development, and then it pops up in the paper that our infant mortality rate had shot up. We were fiftieth in the country. I see economic development sliding. South Carolina beats us for some big projects, and it becomes clear to me that we're losing our edge, that others are pushing ahead of us in economic development. I had the feeling that, yeah, we'd done pretty good" when he was governor. "But we could do so much better, and the need was so great. We had made huge progress, but we'd kind of leveled off. The curve was not as sharp up."

He paused and laughed: "Then Bob Scott called."

Hunt and Scott had reconciled somewhat since the 1980 primary. They were never close again, but they stayed in touch. In 1983, Scott got the job he had sought unsuccessfully before—president of the state's community colleges. He served in that role for eleven years and won praise for upgrading the system.

One day in 1989, as Hunt was mulling another race against Helms, he talked to Scott on the phone. Hunt was sitting at his desk, looking out on the woods behind the law building, when Scott said, "I know what you're going to do. You're going to run for governor again."

"A light bulb went off," Hunt said later. He remembered thinking, "That's exactly what I ought to do." He insisted he "had never thought about it" before. But now he did.

Maybe he couldn't be president. But he had another way to leave his mark.

"I wanted to change the country. But I figured that the best way to do that was to build a state that would be America's model. It was burning in me to change North Carolina, to make North Carolina a model state in America."

The idea of running for a third term as governor was audacious. Hunt would have to overcome doubters in his own party and among friends, reporters, and various know-it-alls in the political world. He would have to overcome the damage and the ghosts of 1984. Most of all, he would have to overcome a tough—and familiar—Republican opponent.

Chapter 16

Governor Again

The first time I heard somebody suggest that Hunt run again for governor, I didn't take it seriously. Hunt himself wasn't sure. "The idea of coming back was so far out at the time," he recalled. "I had just been the first to run for two terms as governor, and now coming back again? A lot of people thought it was totally unrealistic, outrageous."

What made it less outrageous was that the leading Republican candidate was a man who had made an unlikely political comeback of his own: Jim Gardner.

Gardner was Jesse Helms before Jesse Helms. When Gardner won a stunning upset race for Congress back in 1966, he was a new breed of North Carolina Republican—a hard-edged conservative from the eastern part of the state, not a Civil War–legacy Republican from the mountains or a country-club Republican from Charlotte. Gardner Republicans were whites who deserted the Democratic Party after Lyndon Johnson signed the Civil Rights Act.

Gardner, a restless sort, stayed in Congress only one term. In 1968, he almost became North Carolina's first Republican governor in the twentieth century, but he lost a close race to Bob Scott. In 1972, he

Running for governor again after eight years out of office, Hunt spoke to a rally of students at UNC–Chapel Hill in October 1992.
PHOTO COURTESY OF THE *NEWS & OBSERVER*

lost the Republican primary to Jim Holshouser by just a few thousand votes.

He went back into business, only to find he no longer possessed the magic touch he had at Hardee's. After suffering a string of reverses with hotel and restaurant ventures, Gardner settled down to running a chicken-and-barbecue restaurant in Rocky Mount. Old political rivals delighted in seeing him serving customers on the buffet line—dishing out the food, smiling, and charming folks.

But he never lost the political itch—or the good looks and smooth tongue that made him a formidable candidate. In 1988, Governor Jim Martin ran for reelection. Looking for a strong candidate for lieutenant governor, Republicans turned to the now silver-haired Gardner. Just as in 1964, Gardner pulled off an upset victory, beating Democrat Tony Rand, a highly regarded state senator.

More than that, Gardner destroyed Rand in a televised debate.

Rand was a consummate inside operator, a smooth, back-slapping deal maker and a power in the Senate. But he was no match for Gardner onstage. Gardner blistered him for being part of a "gang of eight"—a small group of key legislators who decided the state budget behind closed doors. Rand replied weakly, "There were not eight people there. There were six or seven people there." John Drescher of the *Charlotte Observer* wrote, "Rand said the comment with a straight face, but many in the audience laughed."

As 1992 neared, Republicans were confident. Rob Christensen of the *News & Observer* recalled covering a fundraiser at a restored white-columned mansion in Rocky Mount. Christensen wrote that Gardner "stood on an oak staircase and laid out his dreams of a Republican era—a generation of GOP control of the executive branch that would change the state's political culture." That era would encompass eight years of Jim Martin, then eight years of Jim Gardner. Gardner told the crowd, "What you have is an opportunity this year to have a Republican administration in Raleigh for sixteen years. This is a big [election] that could change the political landscape of the state."

His audience believed him. Democrats believed him, too. And they were worried.

Later, Hunt said, "Some people thought I ran to stop Jim Gardner. That's not true. I wasn't in heat to run. I'd been governor." But he was in heat about where he thought the state was headed—and what he could do. "I was consumed with my ideas about how to move North Carolina forward and make things work well."

It was about issues, not politics, he said. "I was concerned about the state and where it was headed—education, children, infant mortality rate highest in the country, SAT scores very low, losing out on economic development to South Carolina and other states. Instead of making progress, we were going down."

After my initial uncertainty, I grew excited about Hunt's running again. Throughout the 1990 campaign, we made a point of scheduling him at Democratic events around the state. More and more, we heard encouragement. Early in 1991, Hunt told me to start planning a race for governor.

His enthusiasm wasn't shared by all those around him, Phil Carlton especially. Like all of us close to Hunt, Carlton was scarred by the loss in 1984. And he thought 1992 looked like a bad year for Democrats. President George H. W. Bush had just presided over the first Iraq War. Carlton asked me over and over, "How are you going to beat Jim Gardner when President Bush is running with 90 percent approval ratings?"

Nationally, Democrats had suffered three consecutive losses in the presidential race. In North Carolina, they had lost two straight governor's races. And Helms had won a third term in 1990. He faced an African-American candidate, Harvey Gantt, who ran a spirited campaign. Helms won, characteristically, with two brutal attack ads at the end. One said Gantt had used his status as a minority to win a television-station license, then sold it for a big profit. More famous was the "white hands" ad, cooked up by Tom Ellis and his team in a Washington hotel late in the campaign. A white man in a work shirt was shown reading, then ripping up a notice turning him down for a job. The narrator intoned, "You needed that job, and you were the best qualified. But they had to give it to a minority because of a racial quota." Ellis hired a limousine to deliver the spot to North Carolina television stations the next morning. Once again, a Helms campaign came down to race.

Faced with doubts about 1992, we sent out a letter to assess Hunt's chances. Signed by Carlton, Bert Bennett, and Joe Pell, it went to Hunt's old keys who had led the campaigns in 1972, 1976, and 1980. Their responses echoed Carlton's pessimism. It was clear the keys didn't have the heart for a Jim Hunt comeback. They didn't think he could win.

But sometimes in politics, people overlook the obvious. We overlooked the fact that we shouldn't start a campaign in 1992 with a letter signed by three white men—no women, no minorities, no young people. We also overlooked the painful fact that the old keys were just that—people tied to old ways and attitudes. A generation gap was emerging in the Hunt organization. Many of us who had been in our twenties and thirties in the earlier races were ready to move up. We were chafing under the old guard.

The campaign team had broken up after 1984. The staff had

scattered—to Washington, to law and business, to various forms of public service. Joe Grimsley was now president of Richmond County Community College and wasn't interested in returning as campaign manager. But Mike Davis, who had worked with Joe through four campaigns and two administrations, was ready for the job.

We had split with our old team of campaign professionals. Media producer David Sawyer was building an international consulting firm. Harrison Hickman, the North Carolina native who had skillfully played Helms in debate prep, was our new pollster. Hickman had worked with Sanford's Senate campaign. He had a native's feel for the state's history and rhythms.

Hickman suggested a more scientific test than the Carlton-Bennett-Pell letter: another series of focus groups, just as we had done before 1986. So in April 1991, we went back to Greensboro and the kind of blue-collar voters who had turned against Hunt in the Senate race.

Hunt didn't go with us this time. Behind the mirror again, I braced for the assault. But it never came. The bitterness toward Hunt had dissipated. In fact, voters thought he looked pretty good in retrospect. By now, the state was in a budget crisis. Headlines said that North Carolina was losing industry-recruiting battles to other states.

"Hunt was a good governor," one participant volunteered. "We didn't have this budget mess when he was there," another said. They thought that, compared with Hunt, Governor Martin was too low-key and even disengaged from managing government. Nobody ever accused Hunt of being low-key or disengaged.

Hickman pressed: What about the things Jesse Helms had said about Hunt's being too liberal, too wishy-washy, a flip-flopper? "Oh, that's just Helms," laughed one woman. "He'd probably call my grandmother a liberal," a man chimed in.

For those of us around Hunt, the 1984 loss had been the most important event in our lifetimes. For voters, it was a lifetime ago. They had forgotten the Senate race. And by now, they were used to Helms's tactics.

Carlton wasn't convinced. So we did another session with blue-collar voters, near Charlotte this time. The results were the same. The voters had positive memories of Hunt as governor. They laughed at Helms's attacks on his opponents. This time, even Carlton was a believer.

The voters had changed. And so had Hunt. He now had the private-sector experience he lacked his first time in office. He had made some money. He had moved smoothly in the top circles of business and education. Most of all, he had learned his lesson about tough politics: "I wasn't going to let anybody start early on me. I was not going to let anything go unchallenged," he recalled later. "You fight fire with fire."

He had none of the wishy-washiness of 1984. "I had learned that I couldn't be my own campaign manager," he said later. He drummed his mantra into those of us on his staff: Be ready to fire back when attacked. Rachel Perry recalled that when Hunt hired her as campaign press secretary, "he got in my face." Would she be tough enough? Aggressive enough? "Don't take any crap," he told her, pounding the table. "Set the record straight. Never let a charge go unanswered. But stick to the message. Don't get rolled."

Hunt made it clear there would be no internal debates this time about whether or not to attack his opponent. He wanted to keep a positive image. But "we'd also learned that we needed to tell the facts about the opposition that the public needed to know, about character and things that went to the issue of whether Gardner would be a good governor," he said later.

One thing hadn't changed from previous campaigns. Hunt spelled out in detail his ideas on issues—education, early childhood, economic development, crime. We packaged them in a campaign report called "An Agenda for Action." He held up his agenda in campaign ads.

In the Democratic primary, Hunt's main opponent was Attorney General Lacy Thornburg. Thornburg had been a respected judge and was a solid public servant. But he had little instinct for big-time politics.

Just as our campaign had been before we organized the recent focus groups, Thornburg was a captive of 1984. He knew that many of the old Democratic keys were tired of Hunt. He didn't know the old keys had little clout in the new world of politics. He knew that teachers had been mad at Hunt. He didn't know we were aggressively courting the teacher association's leaders. And he didn't know how much credibility Hunt had gained with teachers through his work with the national teaching-standards board.

Worst of all, Thornburg neglected to raise money. We overwhelmed him financially. Hunt had new entrée in the business community. His finance chairman was Ed Shelton of Charlotte, who had made a fortune in construction with his brother Charlie. Charlie had been Jim Martin's finance chair. The Shelton brothers understood politics. They needed a friendly ear in Raleigh, so they made sure to cover all the bases.

Although some of his old keys were out of politics now, Hunt organized his fundraising the way Bert Bennett had taught him. We got the best people in every county—community leaders, business people, successful people who were respected and took time for public life. We appointed a statewide finance committee with a board of directors. We picked finance chairs in each county and gave them a quota of money to raise. The system worked; the campaign exceeded its fundraising goals.

Big donors and business leaders across the state could smell a winner, and Hunt looked like a winner. He even signed up Republicans who knew Gardner's checkered reputation in business. Phil Carlton and Jim Phillips, the appointments aide from the first term who was now the campaign finance director, organized a "Business Roundtable." Phillips said later, "We made the point that Gardner might be the business candidate, but that business people supported Hunt."

After Hunt won the Democratic primary with more than 65 percent of the vote, Gardner and the Republicans blustered that they were ready for a rerun of 1984. "I believe we are better off running against Jim Hunt with his record, which he must live or die with, than running against a candidate with no record and who would talk a good game," said Jack Hawke, the state Republican chairman.

Like Thornburg, the Republicans didn't realize how much both Hunt and the political climate had changed in eight years. They found out in late August when Gardner ran his first ad attacking Hunt for the gas-tax increase in 1981. To Gardner's team, the attack made sense. George Bush had won the presidency in 1988 by pledging, "Read my lips: no new taxes." But Bush had gone back on his pledge, and we knew from our polling that voters didn't hold the gas tax against Hunt.

We were poised to respond. We probably had been poised since 1984. We had researched Hunt as thoroughly as we had Gardner. We had anticipated every possible attack—every one Helms had made in 1984 and every one our high-strung imaginations could think of now.

We had also hired a new media producer skilled in the political jujitsu of taking an opponent's attack and turning it against him. He was Frank Greer, an Alabama native who had a big consulting firm in Washington. Greer was a master of the counterpunch. His formula was simple: First, deny the charge—quickly, in just a few seconds—and then accuse your opponent of something even worse.

That's what we did when Gardner ran his first ad against Hunt. We came back fast and hard. "Behind in the polls, Gardner's falsely attacking Jim Hunt," our ad said. It recounted some of Gardner's business reverses. It noted that, after beating Tony Rand, Gardner had been forced to apologize for one of his ads. The ad had tied Rand to a drug dealer. Rand sued. Gardner eventually settled the lawsuit and had to apologize publicly to Rand. Press secretary Rachel Perry summed up our credo for reporters: "We are not going to be distracted from our positive message for North Carolina. But we are not going to allow Jim Gardner to distort Jim Hunt's record or hide his own record."

We came back so fast and hard that even Hunt temporarily got cold feet. He told Carlton to keep a closer eye on Davis and me. "The financial leadership of this campaign wants to see some gray hair in here," Carlton told us. Davis laughed years later that the message was, "Let the kids do it, but keep an eye on them."

We never let up. We organized an aggressive communications war room—before the Clinton campaign made war rooms fashionable. Rachel Perry bedeviled Gardner by going to his news conferences, collaring reporters afterward, and responding on the spot.

Our research on Gardner had found dozens of court documents tracing bankruptcies, unpaid debts, and, most damaging of all, unpaid taxes. We targeted a hundred thousand swing voters statewide with a series of mailings about Gardner's business failures and unpaid debts. Our direct-mail consultant, Dave Gold, had an apt description of the mailings: "An ice pick to the forehead."

Gardner had minimized his business problems to his staff. Nothing to worry about, he assured them; he could explain it all. But he had no explanation the voters would buy.

Hunt and Gardner debated twice. The first time, in Charlotte, Gardner almost did to Hunt what he had done to Tony Rand four years earlier. He ran through a long list of prison inmates paroled while Hunt was governor, all of whom had gone on to commit violent crimes.

Hunt landed a few punches. When Gardner said state government should be run like a business, Hunt shot back, "I hope you don't get to run it like one of your businesses." But Hunt was caught off guard by Gardner's aggressiveness.

The debate stalled our momentum. The media and the political establishment declared Gardner the winner. Hunt was on the defensive. But Frank Greer steadied us. He suspected voters saw the debate differently. We set up a focus group in which voters watched a replay of the debate and recorded their responses in real time. Greer was right. The voters did not respond to Gardner's attacks or even think they were relevant. They did respond, however, when Hunt started talking about jobs and education and teachers and children's little minds. We feared he overdid it, but the voters ate it up. "They love that positive bullshit," Carlton laughed.

Still, we had to change the tone of the news coverage. So, in the second debate, held in Winston-Salem, Hunt was the aggressor. Gardner tried to defend his record in business. Hunt told him, "The truth is that you are the candidate who has been sued for fraud, deceit and misrepresentation. In your last campaign you were sued for libel, and you had to publicly apologize in court. And you have the gall to talk to me about truth? You need to learn to tell it."

He wasn't Mr. Positive, but the farm boy who had packed a switchblade to Iowa knew how to fight back. The media, predictably, called the more aggressive debater the winner. That was Hunt.

Unlike 1984, we had the national political wind at our backs. Bill Clinton, a moderate Southerner and an old Hunt friend, was the Democratic candidate for president. Ross Perot, Hunt's friend from the Emerging Issues Forum, was running as a third-party candidate. Perot siphoned voters from George Bush, whose once-high poll ratings had plummeted when the economy went into a recession. For the first time since 1976, North Carolina looked winnable for a Democratic presidential candidate. Clinton's campaign was led by James Carville. Clinton and Carville both had a soft spot for Hunt and his state. In the end, Clinton fell short in North Carolina, trailing Bush by only twenty thousand votes, less than a single percentage point. It was the only one of his top ten target states he lost. But at least we didn't have the burden of another Walter Mondale dragging us down.

In the final weeks of the campaign, it was clear Gardner was losing. Hunt had a positive message voters liked: "We did it before, and we can do it again." He said in his TV ads that he was running because "I love North Carolina too much to watch it fall behind." And we were pummeling Gardner with attacks on his business record. In one focus group, a man said of Gardner, "He'll be lucky if he doesn't go to jail."

It got so bad that Jim Phillips came to Mike Davis and me to suggest we let up on the attacks. We hooted him out of the room.

Good thing we did. In the final week, Gardner upended the campaign with a sensational charge. At a press conference, he accused Phil Carlton and another of Hunt's law partners, Charles Lane from Rocky Mount, of masterminding a political spying operation against Gardner. He claimed that Carlton and Lane had arranged for a Rocky Mount woman to eavesdrop on the cell-phone conversations of Gardner and key aides.

The charges were dubbed "Scannergate" because the woman allegedly used a police scanner for her eavesdropping. After the election, the affair was investigated by the FBI and the United States attorney, a

Republican. In November 1993, Carlton and Lane acknowledged they had received and read notes from the woman that she said were from Gardner campaign phone conversations. Carlton also said he had listened to a tape the woman gave him. But he and Lane said they never told Hunt about the affair and never passed the information on to the campaign. Carlton said in a statement that he viewed the information as "trivia, gossip and typical campaign chatter." Both men pled guilty to "infractions"—charges less than a misdemeanor.

Inside the campaign during those final days, we knew we had never received any information—from anybody—that gave us a strategic or tactical edge. But we fretted that the last-minute bomb would blow up our carefully planned campaign. Fortunately, the polling we conducted every night quickly made it clear that voters were skeptical about the charges. In the end, the episode had little impact on the election. Hunt won by nearly 250,000 votes, a 53 to 43 percent margin.

Our election-night celebration was muted, though, because of what was happening in another race. Even though Bill Clinton was winning the White House, Terry Sanford was losing his race for reelection to the Senate. And he was losing to his old friend and Hunt's old cabinet member Lauch Faircloth.

Faircloth had wanted to run for the Senate in 1986. But he and Sanford had always been close politically and personally. They had even shared a bed at a supporter's house one night during the 1960 Sanford campaign. Before the 1986 race, as Faircloth told it later, he and Sanford agreed that only one of them would run—and that they would talk about the subject again later. Then, according to Faircloth, Sanford jumped into the race without any warning. "I didn't know it was going to be a race to the trough," Faircloth complained. He never forgave Sanford. He vowed revenge.

A few years later, Faircloth switched parties and decided to run against Sanford. And he turned his campaign over to Tom Ellis and Carter Wrenn.

Wanting to make sure Faircloth was a true conservative, Ellis started asking him where he stood on various issues. Faircloth stopped him:

"Tom, you write the music and I'll sing it any way you want."

Together, they wrote a Congressional Club classic, the campaign's ads relentlessly pounding Sanford while Faircloth rarely appeared in public. In their one televised debate, Sanford ran rings around him. Funny and voluble in private, Faircloth was surprisingly tongue-tied in public appearances. He said only five words in his own TV ads: "We need workfare, not welfare."

But that was enough. Late in the campaign, Sanford was hospitalized with heart problems. Faircloth made a big show of suspending his campaign. He ran an ad ostensibly wishing Sanford well but also reminding voters of his opponent's age and poor health.

Sanford lost by 50 to 46 percent. Faircloth boasted that his victory would make Jesse Helms "the liberal senator from North Carolina."

On election night, I walked down the hall from where Hunt's young campaign aides were celebrating victory and stopped by the suite where Sanford's staff was sunk in gloom. I knew how they felt.

Chapter 17

A New Start

In the 1992 election—just like in 1972, twenty years earlier—Jim Hunt was the Democratic Party's fire wall. His victory meant there would not be sixteen years of Republican dominance or a fundamental shift in the state's political landscape. Instead, North Carolina stood out in the South as a Democratic island in an increasingly Republican sea.

When he gave his Inaugural Address in January—his third—he said, "Today, people ask if there's a new Jim Hunt—or if it's the same old Jim Hunt. Well, it's an older Jim Hunt, but not quite the same old Jim Hunt."

For one thing, he said, he was more skeptical about government: "I am less confident that the answers to our problems can be found in government, but I am more certain that the answers will be found in our people."

He was more confident in himself. He was fifty-five years old, no longer the young man who had faced suspicion and outright hostility among North Carolina's business elite. By now, he had become one of

Hunt and Carolyn at his inauguration on January 9, 1993, completing his political comeback after eight years out of office. Chief Justice James G. Exum, Jr., administers the oath.
Photo by Charlie Jones

them. The state's top executives were his friends and supporters. He felt comfortable picking up the phone and calling them. Asked in his first post-election news conference how he had changed, Hunt said, "I think the difference is I know the leadership of the state a lot better. As I have matured personally, I have come to feel a lot more comfortable with other people."

He no longer needed a John A. Williams or a Joe Pell beside him in the Capitol. He named thirty-five-year-old Ed Turlington, a Raleigh lawyer and Democratic activist, as his executive assistant. Most of his key staffers—legislative counsel Jim Phillips, legal counsel Brad Wilson, and press secretary Rachel Perry—were about the same age as Turlington.

Some older faces were still around. Jane Smith Patterson took on a broad role in technology matters, especially on what she called "the information highway"—the emerging Internet. Hunt didn't understand information technology, Patterson said. In fact, "he wasn't that interested," she recalled. "But he trusted me."

I didn't want to go back into the daily grind of state government. I had a family and children now, so Hunt let me work as a part-time outside adviser.

The personal pressures had eased. Carolyn Hunt said, "It was more relaxed the second eight years because we didn't have children at the mansion." This time around, the Hunts could go to their farm on weekends. They baled hay, fixed fences, and took care of cattle. They doted on grandchildren. And they went to church in Wilson on Sundays.

While Hunt's drive and energy hadn't faded, he made a few concessions to age. His first two terms, he had been an avid runner. And he was fast. I was a runner, too, and twelve years his junior, but I had a hard time keeping up with him. Now, he walked for exercise. Characteristically, he called it "fast-walking." And it was.

The once-skinny young man—always a hearty and enthusiastic eater—began developing something of a paunch. And in a step that amazed old friends and Raleigh gossips, the longtime teetotaler began allowing wine to be served at official functions at the mansion. He was even known to take a sip now and then.

Hunt had overcome the numbness of losing in 1984. Reelection as governor healed a lot of scars. And the eight years out of office—time spent reading, thinking, listening, learning, leading study commissions, and making a living as a corporate lawyer—had changed him. He may have been more conservative on some issues, but he was also bolder, more certain of his own instincts, less likely to be swayed by others' opinions.

Most of all, Hunt had tasted defeat and knew this would be his last chance to make a mark. Walter Davis, a North Carolina native who made a fortune in the Texas oil fields and became a behind-the-scenes power in his home state's politics, once said, "Everybody needs to get fired one time in their life." Now, Hunt had endured that painful education.

He was like a baseball pitcher who in his early years had depended on a blazing fastball. Now, he was a veteran with a variety of pitches—sometimes the heat, sometimes the slider, and, when the hitter least expected it, the changeup. The young man who had risen in politics by pleasing older men now had acquired something of the toughness of a John A. Williams, the smoothness of a Joe Pell, and the slyness of a Bert Bennett.

Hunt would need all those personal and political tools. He faced a dramatically changed political environment in Raleigh. And he had a different agenda, one that didn't fit neatly in the old categories of liberal or conservative, Democratic or Republican.

The new Jim Hunt was reflected in a crucial decision he made even before he was sworn in. During the transition period, a split emerged in Raleigh over what shape his early-childhood initiative would take. Children's advocates wanted him to create a new state government department for children. But the public-school establishment thought the schools should be in charge of early-childhood education.

Hunt didn't like either alternative. "I figured the public schools had about all they could handle," he recalled years later. "Plus, I was increasingly aware of how bureaucratic school systems can be, like other public bodies and agencies." And he believed that a new department could be just as bureaucratic.

He had more faith in local leadership, nonprofit groups, and the private sector. He had been impressed by the early-childhood school at his church in Wilson, where Carolyn served briefly as volunteer director. "I saw how the local people cared about it, how much loving attention and resources they gave to it, and how much good leadership they gave it."

Hunt created a program that, unlike almost any other in state government, essentially had no government structure in Raleigh. Instead of designating the money to either a new state agency or to the public schools through bureaucrats in Raleigh, Hunt sent the funds directly to local nonprofit agencies, churches, private schools, and day-care centers in communities across the state.

The local communities had to put together a coalition of people and come up with plans for how they would spend the money on early education, family support, and health care. That would not only make sure the programs met local needs, Hunt figured, but also build grassroots support for his initiative.

But something was still missing from the program: a name. Hunt was big on names. The gas-tax bill in 1981 was the Good Roads Act. A drunk-driving bill was the Safe Roads Act. There was the Primary Reading Program and, briefly, the ill-fated Raising a New Generation program. Now, Hunt wanted a name that would distinguish his program—a name people would remember.

From somewhere, I came up with the name Smart Start. Hunt jumped at it, and Smart Start became one of the best trademarks in North Carolina politics.

Of all the millions of words I wrote for him, Hunt always said those two were the best. I don't remember where I got them. I probably saw the phrase someplace. Some people later thought we got it from Kellogg's Smart Start cereal. But Hunt's program came long before the cereal. Maybe we should have sued Kellogg's for stealing the name. A big settlement could have helped a lot of children.

The name was more than symbolic. Hunt was thinking about how to make sure his program lasted beyond his time in office. He said later, "I believed that if you built support for [early-childhood programs] at the local level, it would be hard for anybody to take it away. Because the local people would own it. If you build it and root it at the local level, where it's their program, it's their Smart Start, it's their local partnership for the children, it would be hard to ever kill it. And having served as governor and gone out and seen some things killed or lost that we had started, I was thinking a lot about institutionalizing things, so they would continue and improve over the years. I wanted to root Smart Start in a way that subsequent administrations could not change."

He set up a statewide committee, the North Carolina Partnership for Children, to oversee Smart Start and dole out the money. Hunt wanted a business leader to chair the partnership. He recalled later, "I wanted it to be branded from the beginning as a public-private—especially private—endeavor. I wanted somebody who would be a strong and effective and passionate leader, somebody who would make it work well, be businesslike about it, and somebody who would help me convince the rest of the state, including the Republicans in the legislature, somebody who business people would respond to."

His choice was a surprise. Hunt picked the man who ran the television station that made Jesse Helms famous.

Jim Goodmon was the grandson of A. J. Fletcher, the founder of WRAL television in Raleigh and the man who launched Helms's career in broadcasting. But WRAL had changed dramatically since Helms left in 1970. Goodmon was building a first-class station, investing heavily in technology and the news operation.

Democrats in North Carolina had not forgotten Jesse Helms's race-baiting editorials on the station. Many of them still thought of WRAL as a Republican station. But I had discovered that Goodmon was a different cut of cloth from Helms.

In 1990, a mutual friend recruited me to help Goodmon write a commencement speech. One day as we worked on his speech, Goodmon launched into a tirade about what he saw as state government's failure to take care of poor children. He sounded to me in some ways like a raging liberal. And the speech we produced sounded like Jim Hunt.

I told Hunt about the speech. He met with Goodmon. Soon, we scored a coup in the campaign against Gardner by announcing that Goodmon supported Hunt. After the election, Hunt decided that Goodmon was the perfect person to lead the Partnership for Children. He invited Goodmon to the mansion. Sitting in front of a roaring fire in the library, Hunt pitched his early-childhood program. Goodmon took the assignment.

Just as Hunt planned, Goodmon gave Smart Start credibility. Goodmon recalled years later that he told Republicans, "Come on, guys.

It's a local program. Quit complaining. The money goes to local Smart Start committees, and they figure out how to spend it. It's the kind of program Republicans ought to support."

Goodmon was as passionate as Hunt about the subject. The more they talked to each other about early-childhood issues, the more worked up both got. When *Time* magazine ran a cover story about the importance of brain development in the early years, Goodmon went around town buying all the copies he could. He had one delivered to every legislator's office.

In the end, Smart Start was the culmination of everything Hunt had learned about politics. It was about meeting the needs of people where they lived—about changing their lives. It was about children, education, and health care. It was about getting people organized to do things. It was about coalition politics—reaching out to people in different parties and from different backgrounds. And it was about the power of persuading—and educating—the public.

Neither Smart Start nor any other initiative could get planted—let alone rooted—without going through the legislature.

The Senate was friendly. Senator Marc Basnight, the president pro tem, would keep a firm hand on the chamber through the next decade. Basnight was from Manteo in coastal Dare County and had a distinctive "Hoi Toide" accent. Although he possessed only a high-school education, he was a canny political operator who had become a power in the Senate. Hunt had launched Basnight's political career by appointing him to the Board of Transportation back in his first term as governor. Hunt knew he had Basnight's support, though Basnight had an explosive temper and could be demanding when it came to patronage and roads.

The House was the challenge. Throughout his second term, Hunt had been close to the speaker, Liston Ramsey. Ramsey, a mountain populist, usually supported Hunt's bills. But after the 1988 election, the

House had been thrown into turmoil. A coalition of Republicans and dissident Democrats unseated Ramsey. That arrangement lasted only two years. Then a younger and more liberal faction of Democrats took charge. They were led by Dan Blue, an African-American from Raleigh who was a protégé of Terry Sanford. Blue, like Hunt, was a progressive, and the two men agreed on most issues. But Blue and other House leaders had grown more assertive under Republican governor Jim Martin. They, not Martin, had taken the lead on progressive legislation since 1991. They were accustomed to moving without the governor.

Hunt and House speaker Dan Blue at a Martin Luther King holiday observance at First Baptist Church in downtown Raleigh in January 1995. Hunt's support for the King holiday—and Jesse Helms's opposition to it—played a key role in the 1984 Senate race.
Photo courtesy of the *News & Observer*

One Democratic legislator later recalled how House leaders ignored Martin, who didn't have veto power. "When he sent over a budget, they threw it in the trash can," he said.

Now, Blue and his lieutenants weren't ready to march in lockstep with Jim Hunt. They supported Smart Start but were less enthusiastic about his vision for tougher standards and more accountability in the public schools.

The House also didn't like Hunt's push for a gubernatorial veto. North Carolina was the only state in the nation in which the governor had no veto, a fact Blue and his lieutenants wore as a badge of pride. They didn't like it that Hunt had pushed through succession nearly two decades earlier. They certainly didn't want to give him veto power.

Some House Democrats also grumbled as Hunt embraced what were called "Third Way" initiatives—similar to several of President Clinton's ideas that had emerged from the centrist Democratic Leadership Council. The DLC had been formed by Southern and Midwestern Democrats in the wake of the 1984 election. It pushed policy ideas that were less about big government than about individual responsibility.

In his campaign, Clinton had promised to "end welfare as we know it"; he would work with congressional Republicans to pass a welfare-reform law. In North Carolina, Hunt started a welfare-reform initiative he called Work First. He ordered a crackdown on "deadbeat dads" who didn't pay child support. He directed the Department of Correction to begin requiring prison inmates to work on highway maintenance and other manual-labor projects. Just as he had the first time as governor, he offered up a tough anticrime program.

His crime proposals touched raw nerves among liberals and black leaders. African-Americans had seen Republicans use welfare, deadbeat dads, and crime as racial issues. They knew Hunt's record of supporting civil rights and appointing African-Americans. But some House Democrats, blacks and whites alike, viewed him as a bit too conservative, even as a man who pandered to North Carolinians' less noble instincts.

Hunt thought legislators needed to show less sympathy for suspected criminals and more for victims of crime. The crime rate had risen sharply across the state, and Hunt was adamant that state government needed to respond to the problem—and to public concern.

Tensions came to a head when Hunt called a special legislative session on crime in February 1994. He served up a list of thirty-six proposals. Many were of the get-tough variety: no parole for first-degree murderers, automatic prison sentences for third-time offenders, longer sentences for violent crimes and drug crimes. Hunt also proposed raising the statutory limit on the state's prison population.

Ever the optimist, Hunt thought he had Speaker Blue's support. He had persuaded Blue and Basnight to accompany him to a series of crime-related public events around the state. But some of Hunt's aides were wary of Blue. They sensed resistance. Soon, it came. Blue sent several of Hunt's bills to a committee chaired by an ally, Wake County representative Bob Hensley. Hensley sat on the bills. Days, then weeks, passed without action.

Stalemate set in. So did a frustrating routine. Brad Wilson, Hunt's legislative counsel, would report no progress. Hunt would call or meet with Speaker Blue and feel encouraged. "We had a great conversation," he would say. "I think Dan's going to help us." But nothing would happen. That dance went on for weeks. The session dragged into March. Hunt grew frustrated. Hensley's committee wasn't even meeting. Hunt went to the Legislative Building to meet with Blue—an extraordinary step for a governor. But Blue didn't budge.

Hunt was losing patience. He later recalled, "I was just stewing and getting madder by the day. And when this had gone on for too long, I remember entertaining the notion that if something didn't happen, if that logjam didn't break, I was going to go public. I would have severely criticized the Democratic leadership that would not let the committee meet and vote on the bills. I know there would be severe repercussions in the party. But I was ready to go at it tooth and tong, whatever the consequences, to get those bills through. Preventing the committee from even voting was wrong, and I wasn't going to stand for it."

He especially didn't like the delay in an election year that looked ominous for Democrats. Bill Clinton had stumbled early in the White House, and his plan for health-care reform died. Republicans were energized, while Democrats were dispirited. In North Carolina, Democrats worried that the long-running, fractious crime session was dividing the party. Legislators needed to get home and campaign. Eventually, the House relented, almost all of Hunt's bills passed, and the session ended. But hard feelings lingered.

That fall, disaster struck the Democrats. Nationally, the party suffered one of the most stinging rebukes ever dealt in an off-year election. Republicans took both houses of Congress in Washington. Newt Gingrich became the first Republican speaker since 1954. Incumbent Democratic congressmen from North Carolina were swept out of office. Even Hunt's friend David Price, who had been elected to Congress in 1986 and was rising steadily in the congressional leadership, lost in his Research Triangle district.

Across the nation, Democrats were in a panic. The Clinton White House was shell-shocked. Clinton struggled to prove he was still relevant in Washington.

In North Carolina, Republicans won a majority in the State House. For the first time in the century, they would run a legislative chamber. Hunt's problems with House Democrats paled beside the challenge he faced now. Whatever the disagreements on crime, House Democrats had supported Hunt on Smart Start and education. Now, he faced a House leadership that was hostile to his most cherished priorities.

Never one to hunker down and await developments, Hunt decided to outflank the Republicans. Knowing they planned tax cuts, he proposed cuts that dwarfed theirs by hundreds of millions of dollars. The legislature included much of what he asked for in a massive tax cut that added up to nearly half a billion dollars. The sales tax on food was repealed. So was the intangibles tax on stocks and bonds. Income-tax exemptions were increased, as were tax credits for families with children, charitable tax deductions, and homestead exemptions for senior citizens.

Stealing the GOP's thunder was a neat political trick, but it was also bad policy. Hunt would later admit he overreacted. He said years later that the state's robust economic growth at the time led him to think the cuts were affordable. But "we cut taxes too much," he said. He would regret the lost revenue when hurricanes and a national recession hit years later. "It's why you need to be careful how much you cut taxes, because it's easy to get lulled into thinking the money is always going to come in. And sometimes it doesn't." Hunt said some taxes needed to be cut to keep the state competitive in economic growth. And the sales tax on food had fallen heaviest on low-income families. But it was too much, Hunt acknowledged. "We really did get in a bind."

Even with Republicans in charge of the House, Hunt's approach to the legislature remained the same. He spent two or three hours every day meeting with legislators—not just the leadership, but rank-and-file members. Hunt angered some Democrats by addressing a meeting of the House Republican caucus. As before, he called legislators throughout the day and into the night. He traveled the state, visiting schools and day-care centers to highlight his programs. He invited legislators to join him. He wasn't just being polite; it was a way of pressuring them to support his programs.

Sometimes, the pressure was more direct. One legislator recalled going into Hunt's office to talk about a certain bill. The legislator expected Hunt to put on the hard sell. But he didn't expect what he saw. There sat the legislator's biggest fundraiser from back home. The fellow was Hunt's supporter, too. The message was clear: The Governor had friends in the legislator's backyard.

Just as before, we matched the inside game with an outside game. This time, our communications operation in the governor's office was more sophisticated. We had learned some hard lessons in 1984. One of them was the value of a permanent campaign.

We were ready when Smart Start ran into conservative opposition, just as the New Generation program had a decade earlier. To help set our strategy, we used leftover campaign money to conduct focus groups in Charlotte. It turned out we had nothing to worry about. Voters didn't buy the criticism that government was interfering too much in the family. If anything, they thought government wasn't doing enough. We could move on.

Hunt even picked up support from Republicans. David Flaherty, his Republican opponent in 1976, endorsed Smart Start. Flaherty had become county manager in Caldwell County. He saw the need for the program—and the money—in his county.

But not all Republicans in the legislature agreed. They wanted revenge for what they saw as decades of mistreatment by Democrats. And they wanted to bring Jim Hunt down a peg. They couldn't kill Smart Start; the Senate wouldn't go along. But they knew that even some Democrats had doubts about pumping millions of dollars into local programs. So the House put a condition on Smart Start: Hunt would have to raise $3 million cash and $3 million in in-kind services from the private sector.

Over Goodmon's objection, Hunt accepted the challenge. It was a huge task. He turned to the business executives he had courted over nearly two decades—and in his last campaign. Years later, he recalled meeting with executives from several of the state's biggest companies. "I challenged each of them to give two million dollars from each of their companies, and they all sat right there and did it. They started challenging each other. We needed the money, we needed their help, and they believed in it. They were behind it."

He raised the money and saved Smart Start. But it was a constant battle to get the Republican-controlled House to put in enough money to expand the program to all one hundred counties—Hunt's ultimate goal and one he eventually achieved.

That was one reason Hunt put so much value on his relationship with business. He thought business leaders, especially CEOs, had "a special aura or status with average people. They're considered to be successful. They have great numbers of people who work for them and look up to them. And of course, they provide jobs. When business people spoke, average citizens listened to them. People just trusted them. And so did most legislators."

Over the years, Hunt had developed a relationship with business leaders that was rare among Democratic politicians. The relationship was vital to his election victories because business people were a prime source of campaign contributions. The relationship reflected Hunt's approach of reaching out to a broad range of allies. It also reflected the nature of North Carolina's business community, which changed as the economy evolved. The old-line conservative textile and furniture executives of decades ago had been replaced by a rising class of modern business leaders—men like Jim Goodmon, Hugh McColl of Bank of America, John Medlin of Wachovia, Jim Goodnight of the software firm SAS, and Bob Ingram with Glaxo. They were conservative, but they cared about issues like education and economic change.

Hunt said later that the business community was more progressive than popular image would have it. "I give the greatest credit for that to the University of North Carolina system," he said later. He thought UNC–Chapel Hill and N.C. State especially "turned out people who became successful in business and industry, but who also were taught the humanities, who rubbed shoulders in public schools and public universities with people from all ranks of life, and who were not aristocrats or blue bloods. They wanted to help rank-and-file citizens."

Hunt found ways to get those business people involved in his administration. Their support was key to his success with Republican legislators.

While Smart Start was a struggle, Hunt found it easier getting Republican support on other parts of his program. His crime proposals fared better in 1995 than they had before. And the Republicans were for the gubernatorial veto. Their support stemmed from their frustration when Jim Martin was governor. After that experience, the state Republican Party made passing the veto a staple of its campaigns. Republicans said the veto would protect against overspending by the legislature. They even put the veto in a "contract" they proposed during the 1994 campaign, mimicking Newt Gingrich's Contract with America.

Since the Democratic leaders of the Senate had long supported the veto, the stars were now aligned. Some House Republicans had second thoughts when they realized the power they were giving Hunt. But they were stuck. Hunt pushed hard, and both the House and Senate approved the veto. It was put on the statewide ballot in November 1996, the same day as the general election. The voters overwhelmingly approved the measure.

Once again, Hunt had transformed the office of governor.

Nearly twenty years earlier, he had won the right for governors to succeed themselves. Now, he had added the veto power. But he never used it. He never needed to. It was his gift to his successors.

The Republicans' election gains in 1994 gave them hope they could beat Hunt in 1996. We feared they were right. We especially were concerned about Richard Vinroot, a tall, imposing lawyer who had played basketball for Dean Smith at Carolina, volunteered for service in Vietnam, and served as a popular mayor of Charlotte. But Vinroot never made it past the Republican primary. He was beaten by Representative Robin Hayes, one of Hunt's biggest opponents on Smart Start. Hayes, an heir to the Cannon textile fortune in Cabarrus County, attacked Vinroot as a closet moderate who was not conservative enough for the GOP of the 1990s. He embarrassed Vinroot over his past support of Planned Parenthood, which was anathema to antiabortion Republicans. Vinroot never figured out how to respond. We were happy Hayes won. Although we worried about the amount of money he might spend, we suspected he was too far right for North Carolina in 1996.

We organized an aggressive, well-funded campaign. Both Ed Turlington and Rachel Perry left the governor's office, Ed to manage the campaign and Rachel to oversee communications. A third son of Bert Bennett's, Jimmy, headed fundraising, as his brother John had in 1984. As a sign of how much politics had changed and how much North Carolina had grown since the $1.5 million budget of Hunt's 1976 campaign, the 1996 campaign cost over $10 million.

Our opposition research in 1996 was just as thorough and tough as it had been against Jim Gardner. And we were just as merciless and relentless. We uncovered a ridiculous-sounding quote from Hayes suggesting that teenagers use Lysol to clean themselves if they engaged in sexual activity. Thereafter, whenever Hayes attacked Hunt, we shot back with a rapid-response we called "the Lysol Report."

As in 1992, we had an "Agenda for Action" spelling out Hunt's goals for his fourth term, especially those for teacher pay and Smart Start.

Unlike 1984, this was one of those campaigns in which we got all the breaks. First, the House Republican leadership blundered. In the summer, the legislature held its traditional even-year "short" session on the budget. The state was running a surplus of $700 million, so Hunt proposed a budget that included pay raises for schoolteachers, a clean-up program for the state's rivers, and continued expansion of Smart Start. But Republicans calculated that they could paint Hunt's budget as a spending spree. They dug in their heels. The session dragged late into the summer. Just as in the crime session two years earlier, nothing happened for weeks. Hunt brought the leaders of the House and Senate into the library at the mansion for a day of fruitless negotiations. Finally, the House Republicans decided to leave town without passing a budget. "We're out of here," Robin Hayes said.

Hunt pounced. He flew around the state denouncing House leaders for not doing their job. Without a budget, he said, two hundred thousand teachers, university and community college faculty members, and other state employees would get no pay raise. The state would not be able to inspect hog-farm waste lagoons for possible pollution. Federal disaster money would be lost.

He held four "citizens' forums" across the state to stoke public anger at the legislature. In Wayne County, one speaker told an approving Hunt, "There's not a family in this room that, if they were sitting around a table working out a budget, would quit and go on vacation." The comment, a news account said, drew "hearty applause from the crowd."

Hunt called the legislature back into session. The House gave in and passed a budget more to his liking. Once again, the oldest of state-capital political maxims had held: A media-savvy governor will always dominate the cacophonous voice of the legislature.

By the time House Republicans realized the damage, it was too late. And the national tide was flowing our way. In Washington, Gingrich and his House Republicans tried a strategy similar to that of the Raleigh Republicans, shutting down the federal government. President Clinton, now being advised by our acquaintance from 1984, Dick

Hunt and North Carolina's four living former governors in front of the Executive Mansion in 1994. From left are Jim Martin (1985–93), Hunt, Jim Holshouser (1973–77), Bob Scott (1969–73), and Terry Sanford (1961–65).
Photo by Charlie Jones

Morris, seized the opening, put the Republicans on the defensive, and regained his political footing.

Then a natural disaster struck. Hurricane Fran hit North Carolina—and the state capital—hard on the night of September 5. At my family's house in Raleigh, we were awakened by trees crashing in our yard, one onto the back of our house. Across the state, twenty-two people died. Thousands of homes were damaged or destroyed. Millions of people had no electricity. Damage ran into the billions of dollars.

Harrison Hickman, our campaign pollster, called from Washington that morning as I surveyed the damage to our house. After expressing sympathy for about a minute, he had a brilliant idea: Cancel all our television advertising. People had no electricity, no television, and certainly no interest in politics. Why waste the money?

We did just that. Then Hunt took off his candidate's hat and put on his disaster-management hat. A hurricane—and the human suffering it caused—brought out the best of his energy and focus. He took command of the state's emergency response. He toured damaged communities. He comforted victims. He pressed Washington for disaster aid. He dominated the news cycle for weeks.

It was well into October before the state's focus returned to politics. Hunt held a comfortable lead in the polls throughout the campaign. But he wanted every vote. He angered some in the party by going after the endorsement of the National Rifle Association, which usually took aim at Democrats. He managed a tie; the NRA decreed to its members that both Hunt and Hayes were acceptable. Hunt also determinedly wooed the kind of conservative ministers who had worked so hard for Helms in 1984. Throughout his third term, Hunt had conducted an aggressive outreach program toward them. He made sure they knew that Smart Start money would go to the kind of day-care centers their churches ran. And he left no doubt about his being a devout Christian.

Hayes had no chance. Hunt coasted to a fourth term by a 56 to 43 percent margin. He was now a two-time two-term governor.

Chapter 18

"America's Education Governor"

In 1982, John I. Wilson was a self-described rabble-rouser and young militant, a leader in the North Carolina Association of Educators. He was ready to go to war when Governor Hunt froze teachers' salaries during a recession. Some of the NCAE leaders wanted to hold a rally in protest. That wasn't enough for Wilson and his cadre of young firebrands. "We said, 'No, we're marching,'" he later recalled. And so Wilson led the teachers' march on the mansion that did so much damage to Hunt in the 1984 Senate race.

In 2009, twenty-seven years after the march, Wilson was executive director of the National Education Association, the nation's largest teacher organization. He sat in a Raleigh restaurant and said teachers across America "think Jim Hunt is the best governor ever. He is the epitome of an education governor."

Jim Hunt's education journey was a long one. The road had its twists and turns. But the story of Hunt and education is, in essence, the story of his life.

In his last months in office in 2000, as North Carolinians were deciding who would succeed him as governor, Hunt decided to write a book on education. He wanted the last word about the passion that had driven him throughout his political career—that had driven him, in fact, since the day he arrived at N.C. State and realized his Rock Ridge education hadn't prepared him as well as the boys from Broughton High in Raleigh and Grimsley High in Greensboro.

Hunt asked me to help with the book. I started by getting him to tell his education story. We had several one- and two-hour sessions in which I asked questions and let him talk—and let a tape recorder run. I cut, edited, and organized the transcript. Then he took the drafts and worked painstakingly on them for hours, editing, revising, and writing out dozens of pages in his bold hand with a felt-tip pen. I had learned long ago that Hunt was a good writer. He was clear and succinct. He knew what he wanted to say. And he knew how he wanted to say it.

The result was a short book, *First in America: An Education Governor Challenges North Carolina*. The first chapter, titled "A Teacher's Son," began, "My mother was a teacher, a marvelous teacher. She taught English. She loved literature, and she loved to teach. So early in my life I saw what successful teaching was and how all students learned from it, because I saw my mother do it. I saw excellence close up."

He wrote that education "is the reason I went into politics." When he was growing up, he said, there weren't many good jobs in Wilson County. Most jobs were in agriculture, and they didn't pay well. He recalled that some community leaders didn't want good jobs; they didn't want competition for labor.

"I didn't think that was right," Hunt wrote. "I believe in helping all people have a good life, a good job, enough money for their family, and a good future. I learned early on that the only way to have those things

The cover of Hunt's book about education, which he worked on during his final months in office in 2000. The book covered his early interest in education—including the influence of his mother—and his policy ideas for the future.

for our people is through education—through the public schools."

That was the gospel Terry Sanford had preached in the first campaign Hunt worked in, back in 1960. Sanford's mother, like Hunt's, was a schoolteacher. Hunt was impressed when Sanford pushed through an unpopular sales tax on food to pay for his education program. Years later, Hunt remembered going to a rally in downtown Raleigh for the "United Forces of Education" in support of Sanford's education program. He took note how Sanford earned a national reputation for his innovation, leadership, and courage.

That was the kind of governor Hunt wanted to be when he was first elected in 1976. Soon, he was in the forefront of a group of governors—many of them young, many Southerners, and many but not all Democrats—who championed education for economic growth. Among them were Dick Riley in South Carolina, William Winter in Mississippi, Lamar Alexander (a Republican) in Tennessee, and, of course, Bill Clinton in Arkansas.

Like Hunt, they saw education as the ladder for their states to climb out of a history of ignorance, poverty, and racism. They were all avid industry hunters. They had learned that Southern states could no longer lure industry just with low wages and unionization levels. Industries were becoming more technologically driven. Companies needed skilled employees. Corporate executives and managers wanted good schools for their own children to attend.

But well into the 1970s, the South still lagged behind the nation in education. And by some measures, North Carolina lagged behind much of the South. Dropout rates in the state were high. Teacher salaries were low. Most embarrassing, North Carolina ranked forty-eighth in average SAT scores. Tar Heel educators and politicians argued that SAT scores were misleading; more students took the test in North Carolina than in other states, many who took the test were not headed for college, and the scores typically reflected parents' income and education levels. But being forty-eighth still rankled.

The dirty little secret was that—just as Hunt had seen in Wilson County—some of the state's old-line business elite thought that too much education might be a bad thing. Those mill owners, bankers, and big lawyers put a premium on the universities, which educated their sons, though not so much their daughters in those days. Public schools had never been high on the priority list of many of them. It didn't take a lot of education to run machines in a textile or cigarette or furniture factory. The owners wanted people who would work hard for low wages and who wouldn't organize unions and stir up trouble. Tellingly, North Carolina's average manufacturing wage, like its SAT scores, ranked near the bottom.

When Hunt became lieutenant governor in 1973, a consensus was growing in Raleigh—backed by an emerging group of progressive business leaders—that the state needed to invest more in education. Governor Bob Scott had pushed through tax increases to pay for higher teacher salaries and for the beginnings of a statewide kindergarten program. Hunt joined Republican governor Jim Holshouser in a bipartisan push for education. By the time their four-year terms were over, teacher pay was raised and the state established public kindergartens for all students.

Sometimes, though, Hunt took more conservative positions. School busing was a highly charged issue in the 1970s as Washington pushed Southern states to desegregate their schools. Charlotte became a central battleground when—in the *Swann v. Charlotte-Mecklenburg Board of Education* case—the United States Supreme Court upheld the use of busing to promote integration.

Hunt denounced busing. He even made a point of greeting George Wallace at the airport when the old segregationist came to a political rally in North Carolina. Some of Hunt's liberal friends were dismayed, but he believed the Democratic Party couldn't survive without conservative whites.

After he was elected governor in 1976, the state ran budget surpluses. Hunt had plenty of ideas for how to spend the money on education. His ideas were state of the art at the time: higher teacher pay, smaller class sizes, a Primary Reading Program that put aides alongside teachers in every classroom in the first three grades. Hunt was one of the first governors in the nation to push for standardized testing. In 1984, he proposed the Basic Education Program to reduce class sizes, upgrade teaching, and help schools in poor parts of the state.

But the teachers' march—and the loss to Helms—took a toll on Hunt's cherished reputation as an education governor.

The eight years he spent out of office changed Hunt in many ways, including how he thought about education. He rebuilt his relationship with teachers. More than that, the thousands of hours he spent on the National Board of Professional Teaching Standards gave him an education about teaching. He listened to teachers. And he realized that, for all he knew about education when he was governor, he had more to learn.

Hunt spent the years after 1984 thinking about what he had and hadn't done. In his first two terms, "we had done a lot of things," he said later. "We had invested right much more money. We had begun accountability and measuring how we were doing. We had put more resources into those early years. We put in kindergartens when I was lieutenant governor. When I was governor, we put in the reading program with a reading aide in every classroom in grades one, two, and three. That was a big deal. And we supported improving teaching and more money for teachers' pay."

But "we had not made big progress in student learning," he added. "We made some progress. But we didn't make a big jump."

When Hunt ran for governor again in 1992, he was determined to make that big jump. And he thought he knew the formula: A good start for children and good teachers in the classroom. First, he had to get elected. And he wanted the support of teachers.

By now, John I. Wilson was an ally. For all his rabble-rousing when Hunt froze salaries, Wilson thought teachers should have supported Hunt in 1984. "I argued that we had to hold our noses and endorse Hunt over Helms," Wilson said later. "I said he had good intentions. He had improved the salary schedule. He had given raises over time."

In 1992, with Wilson's help, we went to work securing the NCAE's endorsement. We knew that support of Hunt by the teachers would surprise the media, the political world, and, most of all, our opponents. And thanks to Wilson and some other friends, we knew Hunt's chances were better than most people thought.

Hunt spent considerable time talking with the leaders. He promised to have better communications this time around. And it didn't hurt that he had the enthusiastic support of teachers outside North Carolina, including leaders of the NCAE's parent organization, the National Education Association. "The national board teachers loved Hunt," Wilson recalled. "And Hunt was genuine when he said, 'I learned a lot on the national board.'"

The wooing paid off. The NCAE delivered a strong endorsement of Hunt in the primary that gave our campaign an early boost. Later, after Hunt was elected, he appointed a teacher advisory committee and met with it regularly. He appointed a classroom teacher, Karen Garr, to be his teacher adviser in the governor's office. A decade earlier, Garr had been one of the militant young teachers who marched on the Executive Mansion. Now, she was inside the mansion advising Hunt.

During his third term, Hunt pushed for higher teacher salaries, and the legislature went along. He also won legislative approval for more spending on instructional programs, community colleges, and the university system. At the same time, balancing as always liberal and conservative approaches, Hunt advocated more accountability standards for teachers and schools.

In the 1992 campaign, he talked about the importance of students getting the knowledge and skills they needed in life. In 1993, he proposed—and the legislature passed—a bill establishing the North Carolina Accountability and Standards Commission. Hunt named as chairman Sam Houston, an innovative school superintendent who had started the state's first year-round schools in Mooresville, near Charlotte. The commission held a series of hearings around the state, many of which Hunt attended. It heard testimony from business leaders about the skills and knowledge students needed to be successful in the new global economy. The commission called for a rigorous program of measuring students' progress through end-of-grade tests. It also proposed requiring a senior project and an exit exam for graduation.

Another focus on accountability came from Hunt's appointee as chairman of the State Board of Education, Jay Robinson. Robinson pushed through a statewide accountability system—called "the ABCs"—that issued report cards measuring student learning in individual schools and school districts. The ABC system provided salary bonuses to teachers in schools that significantly increased student learning. Hunt backed Robinson but also paid attention to teachers' complaints that they were being left out. The teachers—and many Democratic legislators—feared that minority students and schools in poor areas would be at a disadvantage. Hunt persuaded Robinson to give teachers more voice in developing the program.

"Many education people fought the end-of-grade tests, questioned how to do it, didn't really want to do it, and it took a long time to get it done," Hunt said later. Teachers "weren't necessarily thrilled" at the prospect of being measured. "But the way I always handled it was I'd say, 'Listen, here's some things you want and you should want, including higher pay, but here's some accountability and measures to make sure every kid's getting it that I have to have to go with it.' And we'd always work it out that way."

Unlike some politicians then and later, Hunt never went in for teacher bashing. "I didn't do what so many governors around the country had done, particularly Republicans, which is to just beat up on the teachers and beat the hell out of the teachers' unions. No, I said, 'Let's work together.' And we sat down together, and we talked about what they wanted and what I wanted, and we put the package together."

The culmination of Hunt's years of work on education—and his most lasting mark on the state's schools—came in his fourth term. He set a goal of raising North Carolina teachers' salaries to the national average.

This was an example of good politics leading to good policy. As the 1996 campaign neared, I scouted for issues Hunt could champion in his last race. Just as when he ran on the Primary Reading Program in 1976, he wanted a signature education issue. He already had Smart Start. He needed something for the public schools. He wanted to be able to go to the legislature after he was reelected and say, "The people want this."

Late in 1995, John I. Wilson and I had breakfast at Big Ed's, a country-style restaurant in downtown Raleigh that attracts a big political crowd. He gave me a poll showing that 88 percent of North Carolinians agreed that teachers should be paid a salary at least equal to the national average. That got my attention.

I set up a meeting between Hunt and Wilson. Hunt later recalled, "John I. Wilson came in to see me and said, 'Governor, do you realize that North Carolina has slipped to forty-third in the nation in teacher pay?' We were one place behind South Carolina! It shocked me to death. I didn't really believe it. I had to check it out. It was true."

Then Wilson asked him, "Why don't you propose raising teacher pay to the national average?"

Hunt was intrigued. "I thought about it, and I checked out how much it would cost. It would cost over a billion dollars. But as I thought about it, I said, 'Why not do that? We're putting a lot more on them, requiring a lot more from teachers. Why not raise their pay *and* raise the standards for teachers? And why not lay that out as a challenge for North Carolina? Not just the governor saying he's for it. Why not let the people decide if they're for it?'"

Hunt liked the idea of a big, clear, audacious goal—the kind Terry Sanford would have set. It became a centerpiece issue in his campaign. Just as in his first run for governor twenty years before, Hunt talked about the goal in speeches all over the state and featured the idea in his campaign ads.

Winning reelection in 1996 meant that "we had a mandate to raise standards and raise teacher pay to the national average," Hunt said later. "The people had said yes, and we'd told them how much it was going to cost. Which of course goes to my theory of what a campaign ought to be. Talk to the people about what you're going to do, take them into your confidence, get ideas from them, and together on Election Day you make a contract. They decided to do this, not just elect you, but do these things. If you'll lay your plans out to people and the focus isn't totally obscured with a damn negative campaign, then the people can decide what they want to do and where they want the state to go."

Hunt celebrated the start of his final term by holding his inauguration at Raleigh's venerable Needham Broughton High School, which three of his children had attended. "Education Is Our Future. It's Everything" was the theme. The swearing-in ceremony ended with James Taylor singing "Carolina in My Mind."

Next, Hunt plotted how to get his teacher-pay goal enacted by the legislature. He came up with the kind of name he liked: the Excellent Schools Act. And he wanted the top leaders in both houses of the North Carolina General Assembly to sponsor his bill.

Marc Basnight was still boss of the Senate. Hunt recalled, "I talked to Marc, my friend, and asked him to sign the bill. He had never signed one as president pro tem. He agreed to sign that one."

Hunt needed the support of Republicans, who still had a majority in the House. So he turned to the Shelton brothers in Charlotte—Ed, who had been his 1992 campaign finance chairman, and Charlie, who had been Governor Martin's.

Charlie Shelton was close to Harold Brubaker, the Republican speaker of the House. He called Brubaker while Hunt did his own wooing of the speaker. Since Brubaker became speaker in 1995, Hunt had spent a lot of time developing a relationship with him. Brubaker, like Hunt, had a cattle farm. Hunt went to Brubaker's farm in Randolph County a couple of times to talk cattle and education. "I talked to Brubaker and asked him to sign the bill, and, with Charlie's encouragement, he signed it," Hunt said later.

Why did Basnight and Brubaker do it? "Because the people had just said yes, and they wanted to be on the right side of the issue," Hunt said. "I mean, here I was, just reelected with a pretty big majority, good majority, and the people had spoken. And they wanted to be on the right side of that issue. They wanted to support raising standards and raising pay dramatically for teachers in North Carolina."

It didn't hurt that the state's economy was booming, revenues were rolling in, and no tax increases would be needed to pay for Hunt's billion-dollar proposal.

He mobilized his friends in the business community. "We had the big hearing in the appropriations room in the legislature, and that's when we lined up fifteen CEOs to testify." One of them was Hugh McColl, the ex-marine who built Bank of America into a national giant. Also included were top executives from Glaxo, IBM, Duke Energy, Progress Energy, Wachovia, First Union, Belk, and other big companies. "That room was full," Hunt remembered. Over half the members of the legislature were on one appropriations committee or another, "so you probably had close to a hundred legislators in that room. And when those top business people finished testifying and saying they were for this bill, the game was over."

The *News & Observer* compared Hunt's effort to pass the bill to his just-completed campaign for reelection: "Hunt left little to chance. He kept making campaign-style visits to schools—often in the districts of key legislators, who typically felt obligated to show up and rarely challenged Hunt on the wisdom of significantly boosting teacher pay." The *N&O* said, "By the time the pay plan came up for votes in both houses, few legislators seriously considered voting against it."

When Hunt left office, teacher pay in North Carolina had reached the national average. The average teacher's salary went from thirty-one thousand dollars to forty-two thousand dollars in four years. The state jumped from forty-third to the top twenty. After Hunt left office and the national recession hit, though, the state fell back in teacher-pay rankings.

Other measurements showed significant progress in the schools. Average SAT scores rose forty points, faster than in any other state, and North Carolina's ranking among the states rose from forty-eighth to thirty-eighth. North Carolinians made the highest overall gains of students from any state on the National Assessment of Educational Progress. That assessment, conducted by the United States Department of Education, was the most widely used measure of American students' knowledge. The National Education Goals Panel, formed by President George H. W. Bush and the nation's governors in 1990, said in 1998 that North Carolina had made more progress in education during the decade than any other state. *Education Week*, a national newspaper, rated North Carolina one of the top twelve states overall in education.

North Carolina and its governor were hailed nationally for what was happening in the schools.

Then and later, Hunt had little patience with critics who said the state's education system was failing. He thought they ignored the progress students were demonstrating in a wide range of assessments. Did the criticism make him mad? "Well, it makes me mad in the sense that they don't recognize the successful things we've done. But when I see the dropout rates where they are, I know that even though test scores are going up a lot and a lot of things are being done to help children more, we still aren't there. But I think you've just got to keep working at it all the time. You can't ever rest on your laurels. You'll never finish the job, and you've got to keep getting better and better."

One problem for North Carolina and all of America, Hunt said, was that "we're working against a tide of poor home situations and a lot of things in society that distract students."

As Hunt planned to deliver his final State of the State Address, he wanted to root his initiatives, especially Smart Start and better teaching, so firmly in place that no governor or legislator would challenge them. He came up with one last big idea: First in America.

When he addressed the legislature in February 1999, Hunt noted that the National Goals Panel said North Carolina was leading the nation in education progress. He said the state should set a higher goal: "I believe that if we can lead the nation in education *progress*, we can lead the nation in education—*period*. So tonight I am announcing a new initiative to set new goals for our schools. I challenge North Carolinians to raise our sights and raise our schools to an even higher level. Let's commit ourselves to this ambitious goal: By the year 2010, North Carolina will build the best system of public schools of any state in America. By the end of the first decade of the 21st Century, we will be first in education."

It was a lofty goal—again, Terry Sanford's kind of goal. And promoting First in America became the focus of Hunt's final two years' work on education.

To measure the state's progress, Hunt got the legislature to pass a bill endorsing the goal and establishing a statewide "report card" on individual schools and school districts. The measurements included getting children ready for school, setting rigorous standards, testing student progress, reporting on test results, evaluating teachers, turning around failing schools, improving discipline, and getting communities, volunteers, and mentors involved. Hunt organized an "Education Cabinet" that brought together the disparate—and often feuding—agencies of state government, the public schools, community colleges, the state university system, and private colleges and universities. He gave the cabinet the responsibility of keeping North Carolina on track with the First in America goal.

Hunt's last two years in office were a dramatic contrast to the end of his first stint as governor. Then, he had been under fire from both the left and the right. Teachers were angry about the pay freeze. Progressives thought he was trimming his sails to run against Jesse Helms. Hunt spent much of 1983 and 1984 under withering fire from Helms.

By comparison, he enjoyed something of a victory lap in 1999 and 2000. President Clinton, who wanted to be known as "the education president," praised Hunt's education initiatives in visits to North Carolina and in his State of the Union speeches. Even Republicans sang

An exuberant Hunt at an event with state education leaders in 2000. Behind him are then-UNC president Molly Broad and, beside her, State Senator Howard Lee. Partly obscured to the right of Hunt is Senator Marc Basnight.

PHOTO COURTESY OF THE *NEWS & OBSERVER*

Hunt's praises. After George W. Bush won the disputed 2000 presidential election, some speculated he might try to give his cabinet a bipartisan flavor by asking Hunt to serve as secretary of education. Hunt let it be known he wasn't interested in working for a Republican administration.

The *Saturday Evening Post* published a special issue about education. One article said about Hunt, "The past quarter century has witnessed a veritable Mount Rushmore of 'Education Presidents,' each continuously promising to rescue and revitalize our nation's schools, but for the most part—after election day—that responsibility has fallen to the chief executives of the states. Few have risen to the challenge with more determination or sincere commitment than Governor Jim Hunt of North Carolina. . . . If they ever sculpt a Mount Rushmore for governors, Jim Hunt will have reason to be smiling."

In 2007, the National Board of Professional Teaching Standards held a dinner honoring Hunt. It had been twenty years since he launched the board and began serving as its chairman. Speaker after speaker lauded his leadership on the board, in North Carolina, and nationally. "A national treasure," one called him. "A dynamo," another said. "A hero." "America's education governor."

When it came Hunt's time to speak, he had a simple message: "The most important thing we do in America is teach our children."

Chapter 19

The Art of Governing

When Jim Hunt began running for governor again in 1992, he told a friend that, if reelected, "I'm going to do it different this time. We're going to be focused."

If one word describes the difference between the first Governor Hunt and the Governor Hunt of the 1990s, that is it: *focused.*

Focused on the job at hand, for one thing. No one talked this time about Hunt's running for president or even the Senate.

Focused on the big things, especially Smart Start and the public schools. The hyperactive young governor Joe Grimsley called "Mr. Total Initiative" had learned the value of concentrating his efforts.

As soon as he moved back into the Capitol, Hunt boiled his agenda down to a list of priorities that he posted on an easel in his office. His secretary of transportation, Sam Hunt—no relation to the governor—had the list printed up on small laminated cards. Sam Hunt joked, "Nobody beats me when it comes to sucking up." Governor Hunt happily passed out the cards to his staff and appointees. Even Jim Goodmon confessed years later, "I always worried he'd catch me without the list in my pocket."

Janice Faulkner from Greenville, who had known Hunt since his YDC days, was now his secretary of revenue. She later recalled what Hunt told her when her department faced controversy and criticism: "You just sit tight and keep doing what you're doing every day. Don't pay much attention to what flies at you. This thing won't loom as large ten days from now. Stay in the groove and stay focused." She added, "He was hard to drive off the tracks. He never panicked."

By the time he left office in January 2001, Hunt's focus paid off.

He had fundamentally reshaped the office of governor, to begin with. When he took office in 1977, North Carolina was viewed as having one of the weakest governors in the nation. The state's governors were limited to one four-year term, and they couldn't veto legislation. Then Hunt served two terms, and so did Jim Martin. Next, Hunt returned for two terms, and Mike Easley then served two. And the veto Hunt pushed through in 1996 guaranteed that all governors—not just those with Hunt's persuasive powers—would be factors in the legislative process.

Hunt not only saw his decades-long emphasis on better education come to pass but also was able to cement his initiatives on economic development, crime, and human services. The progress in early-childhood programs was especially dramatic. Because of Smart Start, $240 million was flowing to local communities annually by the end of Hunt's last term to provide education, child care, and health services to children and their families. The Frank Porter Graham Institute at UNC–Chapel Hill conducted over thirty research studies of Smart Start programs. The studies found that Smart Start children had better math and language skills and fewer behavior problems entering kindergarten than other children. They also were more likely to be immunized on time and to have a primary health-care provider. North Carolina became a recognized leader in the early-childhood field. In a special session called by Hunt, the legislature set up a health-insurance program for children whose families lacked coverage. The Health Choice

Hunt with Erika Hines, age four, at an early-childhood center in Chapel Hill in March 1995. Visits to such centers—and the news coverage they received—were part of his campaign to sell his Smart Start program.

PHOTO COURTESY OF THE *NEWS & OBSERVER*

for Children program would insure seventy thousand children by the end of Hunt's governorship.

In economic development, North Carolina was successfully making the transition to a high-tech future. The state's unemployment rate was one of the lowest in the nation—and would remain so until the 2008 recession. Hunt's administration calculated that more than six hundred thousand new jobs were created in the state during his final two terms. North Carolina's economic expansion—as measured by growth in real incomes—was 52 percent stronger than the nation's in the 1980s and 34 percent stronger in the 1990s. Textiles, tobacco, and furniture were replaced as economic mainstays by electronics, automobile parts, machinery, and chemicals. The state was poised for growth in biotechnology, medicine, nanotechnology, space exploration, and energy, including fuel cells and solar power.

North Carolina was routinely cited in surveys as one of the best states for companies to do business. But Hunt found that aggressive salesmanship alone wasn't enough to keep competitive. The state lost its bid for a huge Mercedes manufacturing plant when Alabama offered a breathtaking package of tax breaks and financial incentives. Although he argued that North Carolina didn't need to match other states' "give-aways," Hunt pushed a law through the legislature allowing the use of incentives. He used the new law to recruit the state's first steel plant, Nucor, in Hertford County and a FedEx shipping hub in Greensboro.

The "information highway" initiative launched by Hunt and led by Jane Smith Patterson paid off. North Carolina was one of the first states to establish a statewide fiber-optic network, built through a partnership with telecommunications companies. Hunt may not have understood all the ins and outs, but he "demonstrated his willingness to hire good people who were tech-savvy and tech-focused," Patterson said in 2010. By that year, she said, Internet service was available to 82 percent of North Carolinians—a remarkable level, given that the state had 3.2 million citizens living in what the census defined as rural areas, second only to Texas's 3.8 million. The network helped recruit industry, supported telemedicine, and linked the state's schools, community colleges, and universities. One staffer with the Federal Communications Commission told Patterson, "North Carolina knew this was necessary before others."

In his last term, Hunt became convinced he hadn't done enough on the environment. His reputation was less for protecting the environment than for creating jobs. The soil conservationist's son decided he needed to make up for lost time. He appointed one of the state's leading environmentalists, Bill Holman of Raleigh, as secretary of the Department of Natural Resources, despite the vocal opposition of business leaders. Hunt launched a Million Acres Initiative to preserve open space and farmland. He supported a sweeping Clean Air Act developed by the legislature in 1999. He supported an $800 million statewide clean-water bond issue, which passed in 1998, and helped Senator Basnight and other legislative leaders create the Clean Water Management Trust Fund. Both the fund and the bond issue helped communities upgrade or replace water-quality systems. Some of the money was used to purchase unique water resources, including the waterfalls seen in the movie *Last of the Mohicans*.

Hunt continued his emphasis on fighting crime. During his final two terms, the state's crime rate dropped dramatically—by nearly 13 percent. While social and economic factors undoubtedly played a large role, Hunt maintained that the numbers showed the effectiveness of tougher sentences for criminals, the construction of more prisons, and stricter limits on paroles. He coupled those get-tough steps with an emphasis on helping young people stay out of crime. He set up volunteer programs to recruit mentors for at-risk young people and "Support Our Schools" (SOS) after-school programs. He established a new Department of Juvenile Justice.

Hunt could also rightly claim credit for another set of numbers: the increased presence of minorities and women in state government. He supported a raft of programs to help minority- and female-owned businesses. His office noted that 22 percent of his appointees to state boards and commissions were minorities, paralleling the state's population makeup. And in 1999, he appointed Henry E. Frye of Greensboro as the first African-America chief justice of the North Carolina Supreme Court.

For all the focus on his priorities, Hunt saw again—as he had his first time around—that no governor could dictate his entire agenda. He once again faced a string of crises and disasters—some natural, some political.

The man-made disasters often came from his own appointees. One of his closest longtime aides later said that Hunt's belief in "the inherent goodness of people, in human potential" did not always serve him well: "He trusted people too much."

Plus, Hunt was under a media microscope. The capital press corps had a deep cynicism about him. They remembered Joe Pell's efficient patronage operation. Patronage was once the way business was done in Raleigh. Now, it was a dirty word. Over the years, especially after North Carolina became a true two-party state, personnel laws were tightened to reduce political hirings and firings. To stem criticism and controversy, Hunt announced with much fanfare in 1997 that he was abolishing the time-honored governor's patronage office.

But state-capital reporters remembered Jesse Helms's attacks on Hunt as a flip-flopping consummate politician. And many never warmed to Hunt personally. Their knock on him was that he was too political, too plastic.

Reporters always asked those of us who worked for Hunt what he was really like. They didn't believe he could be the same in private as he was in public. The exuberant, ever-optimistic, ever-enthusiastic politician they saw had to have a different face. Maybe some kind of dark side, like a Richard Nixon.

No. "What you see is what you get," Jim Phillips said. Phillips had known Hunt from the early 1970s, first working as an assistant out of a hideaway office behind Hunt's big one in the Capitol, then as his legislative lobbyist in the third term. Hunt in private was the same as Hunt in public. He was never one for small talk, just an unrelenting focus on the job at hand.

Was he too political? No doubt, he was consumed with politics. But as Tom Lambeth, who had been an aide to Terry Sanford, asked, "What is too political? Does anybody ever complain that their cardiologist is too medical?"

Still, members of the press corps were convinced Hunt must have a flaw. And they were determined to uncover it.

They pounced when the Department of Transportation once again was plunged into scandal. In the 1980s, it had been bid rigging. Now, it was allegations that board members had profited personally from road decisions and that legislators and campaign contributors had too much say over DOT's priorities.

No agency in state government was more political than DOT. Its decisions on where and when the state built roads meant millions of dollars to developers, businesses, and local governments. Traditionally in North Carolina, the governor's biggest campaign donors and fundraisers were rewarded with seats on the DOT board. Sam Hunt, the secretary of transportation in Hunt's third term, had been a big fundraiser in 1992 and was finance chairman for the reelection campaign in 1996.

In late 1997, the department was rocked by a series of front-page stories alleging conflicts of interest and favoritism in road-building decisions. Some of Hunt's biggest contributors and supporters were targets of the charges. He had to force three board members to resign after newspapers reported they had pushed road projects that could benefit them personally.

One DOT official recalled, "There was a lot of legislative interference in road-building decisions, a lot of discretionary money being bandied around, and a lot of, 'Go do this in my district.'" Critics charged that transportation decision making was being driven by politics. "And to a large measure, it was," the DOT man said.

This cartoon by Dwane Powell of the News & Observer *traced how Hunt changed—and didn't change—during two decades. Over the years, Powell replaced the comb in Hunt's hair with a weathervane.*
Cartoon courtesy of Dwane Powell

Hunt had learned something about managing crises in his first term. He said later, "The danger in these situations is that you'll develop a bunker mentality. You'll deny things. You'll think it'll blow over."

That was exactly the reaction of some of Hunt's friends at DOT and across the state. They saw the allegations as politically motivated attacks by Hunt's enemies. They thought the newspapers were being unfair. But Hunt said later of the press, "They're just aggressive. And their job is to find out the facts."

That's what Hunt had to do, too. But "that is tough to do, because you'll ask your people what the situation is, and they'll always try to cover it up," he said. "They'll always sugar-coat it. But you've got to find the facts. Then you've got to decide, 'All right, what needs to be done to correct this?'"

The crisis broke just before Christmas, so Hunt had time to ponder his response. Then he called Norris Tolson.

Tolson had been part of Hunt's farm-boy political network at N.C. State. He went on to a career with DuPont, then returned home to Edgecombe County. He was elected to the legislature, and Hunt appointed him secretary of commerce in early 1997. Now, Hunt asked Tolson to meet him in Rock Ridge between Christmas and New Year's. He asked Tolson to become DOT secretary.

As Tolson recalled it years later, Hunt told him, "I don't want a transportation expert. We've got hundreds of engineers who know how to build roads. What I need is somebody who can go in there with a business focus and reorient that department and remember that it is the people's transportation department and not the secretary's and not the governor's. It is the people's business that we're trying to run at DOT."

Tolson took the job. He asked Hunt, "What's my charge, what do you want me to do?" Tolson said Hunt "got a piece of paper, a blank piece of paper, and put it on the desk and said, 'That's your charge, go do it. I'm not going to tell you what to do. You go create the plan, and I want you to tell me in forty-five days what you think you ought to do to revamp that department.'"

Tolson came back in March with a package of reforms. The longtime state highway administrator, Larry Goode, was replaced. New procedures were established to govern spending decisions. The power of individual legislative leaders and Board of Transportation members to direct where money went was curtailed. The process of setting statewide priorities was opened to more public scrutiny.

The reforms angered key legislators and some of Hunt's financial backers. But Tolson said the governor backed him up: "We did some things that really angered some people. To me, that's an indication of the moral fiber of the guy."

It was also—in the long run—smart politics and media relations. It defused the crisis. Years later, Hunt won praise from one of the hardest-nosed reporters in North Carolina, Pat Stith of the *News & Observer*. Stith was a legendary investigative reporter, a bulldog of a man who uncovered dozens of scandals in state government. He broke so many DOT scandals that he joked, "DOT is God's gift to investigative journalists."

When he retired, Stith said in an interview that Hunt was one of the few politicians he respected: "I may have interviewed him six or eight times, always about problems in his administration. He didn't duck, and I like that. He would see you. And he'd do something about problems, too."

The DOT affair was an echo of the bid-rigging scandal in Hunt's first two terms. And he faced another repeat controversy—another fight with a Democratic White House over tobacco.

Last time, the villain was Joe Califano. This time, the trouble came from our old acquaintance in the 1984 campaign, Dick Morris. Morris had been an on-again, off-again adviser throughout Bill Clinton's years as governor of Arkansas. But he also played both sides, advising Jesse Helms in 1990 when Helms defeated Harvey Gantt.

After the 1994 election debacle, Clinton reached out to Morris again. Morris was nothing if not cunning. In 1984, he had spotted Jesse Helms's rigid position on abortion as a potentially winning issue for

Hunt. Now, he found a hot-button issue for Clinton: the health dangers of tobacco. Tobacco might be politically sacred in North Carolina, and Clinton might have a soft spot for Jim Hunt and the state, but Morris thought tobacco—and especially big companies like R. J. Reynolds and Philip Morris—were perfect political targets for the president.

Clinton and Hunt were friends and had been governors together, but the president was never one to let personal friendships stand in the way of his political fortunes. He called on Congress to ban all tobacco advertising and give the United States Food and Drug Administration the power to regulate tobacco like a drug. The Republican Congress, which was well funded by Big Tobacco, wasn't about to go along. That was fine with Clinton and Morris. They had their issue. And Hunt once again was caught between his farmers in North Carolina and his friends in Washington.

By now, Hunt knew how to walk the tightrope. Publicly, he railed against Washington. Yes, he said, people—especially children and teenagers—should be told the health risks of smoking. But adults should be allowed to make their own choice, he said, and the FDA should spend its time approving medicines that could save lives. Privately, he acknowledged the health risks of smoking. He understood what Clinton was doing and why. Hunt didn't want to burn his bridges with the White House.

Although FDA regulation didn't pass, tobacco was well on its way to becoming a national villain. Eventually, NASCAR's annual Winston Cup Series—named for the R. J. Reynolds cigarette—became the Nextel Cup and later the Sprint Cup. In years to come, even North Carolina would ban smoking in offices, stores, and restaurants.

Hunt escaped significant political damage, though his critics saw the episode as one more example of political pandering. But was it pandering or smart politics? Tobacco was king in the North Carolina he came from. But it was anathema to the kind of people his education and economic-development policies—and his national reputation—were bringing to the state. Hunt was trying to balance the two worlds. Above all, he wanted to maintain his political strength—his approval ratings routinely topped 60 percent—and keep his friends in Washington. He knew he might need the White House sometime. Soon, he did.

In September 1999, eastern North Carolina was slammed by the worst hurricane in its history. Over the years, North Carolinians have learned the hard way that hurricanes often do the greatest damage not along the coast but inland. Now, Hurricane Floyd swept across the eastern half of the state, dumping record levels of rain on the flat, low-lying landscape. Floyd inundated dozens of counties, including Hunt's own Wilson. More than fifty people died. Thousands were homeless. Farms, factories, businesses, and stores were devastated.

As soon as the rain slowed and the state helicopter could fly, Hunt headed east. "The first thing I saw, down here close to my home, was a brand-new lake filled up with brown water. Well, that was the lake that the city of Wilson had built for its water supply, and the day before it had been empty. It filled up in one day." Flying along Interstate 95, Hunt discovered that a section of the highway was under water. Even the North Carolina Highway Patrol didn't know that yet. "We called it in, nobody knew it. We said, 'Stop traffic, the road is flooded.' We got on down to Trenton, and we saw caskets were coming up out of the ground."

Hunt believed that the governor—or any leader—had to be on the scene in a crisis. "You've got to get out there and see firsthand. First of all, it gives you real knowledge of the extent of the disaster and what things are happening where. Every day, I saw the water get higher and higher, because I was out there every day, sometimes more than once a day." By being there, he showed victims of the floods that somebody in Raleigh cared about them and was determined to help.

The governor had another responsibility, he said: "You've got to require the maximum that everybody can give, and only the governor can do it. You're not in charge of the day-to-day stuff, but you're in charge of the overall response, getting the resources and making them available and driving it and not being satisfied with ordinary actions."

He added, "Two words: Take charge."

That meant prodding the bureaucracy in Raleigh. The state's disaster-management agencies, along with the National Guard, the highway patrol, and federal agencies, had an emergency center in the basement of the Administration Building. But Hunt believed it was in the nature of bureaucracies to find reasons why things couldn't be done. So he made it a point to be in the command center regularly. The agencies did their jobs, he said later, "but the governor has to give it the sense of urgency. The governor needs to be seen as in command and requiring everybody to give their fullest and make all the resources available that are needed."

Hunt made sure people in Raleigh knew what he was hearing from citizens down east. "People would call me, from Pitt County and all over, and they'd tell me their situation. So not only was I hearing it

Hunt took President Bill Clinton and Federal Emergency Management Agency head James Lee Witt on a helicopter tour of flood-ravaged eastern North Carolina after Hurricane Floyd in 1999.

Photo courtesy of the White House

through the regular channels, but all of our political people out there would call. I had so many ties around the state—the organization and the political contacts, the friends, everything. And those people would call up, and they'd tell me things that nobody had told me before."

Then Hunt would press the agencies to help. He made up his mind that the federal government should give direct grants to people who lost their homes. Federal officials told him they could do only loans, not grants. "I pushed them to make ten-thousand-dollar grants to those people, and they worked it out."

Just like after Hurricane Fran in 1996, he pushed all the way to the top—to Congress and the White House. He went to Washington at least once a week for seven straight weeks to press for disaster assistance. He took a yardstick with him: "This is how much rain we got. A whole yard." He pressed President Clinton's aides and administration daily. He hauled Clinton and James Lee Witt, the director of the Federal Emergency Management Agency, around in the state helicopter to survey damage.

Hunt then met with the president at the White House. He recalled later that John Podesta, Clinton's chief of staff, "took me downstairs to a room below the level where the Oval Office is." When Clinton came in, he asked Hunt, "How much is this going to cost?"

Hunt replied, "Mr. President, I think it's going to take four billion dollars."

"Well," Clinton laughed, "what's four billion dollars between friends?"

North Carolina got the money.

Back home, Hunt wanted to give a televised speech appealing for private help for hurricane victims. In his first two terms, especially after his Wilmington Ten address, he had become a fervent believer in the power of such speeches. Afterward, whenever he had a big initiative to announce—an education program, the gas tax, Smart Start—he wanted to be on statewide TV.

But these were no longer the days of just three networks and the public-broadcasting channel. More and more cable channels were available, and television viewing was fragmented. But Hunt paid no more attention to the objections raised by his media advisers than he did when disaster-management officials told him they couldn't do something he wanted.

So his communications office arranged a one-minute talk by Hunt at the beginning of nearly every North Carolina station's 6 P.M. newscast. Going on the air live, Hunt described the damage and appealed for contributions to a relief fund. His talk was an emotional one; he knew many of the people who had lost their homes, farms, and livelihoods in the storm, some never to recover. "They're at the low point of their lives," he said. "We must be their high ground." Donations poured in.

For much of the remainder of the administration, Hunt's focus shifted to rescuing his home region. For once, his main legislative priority wasn't education; it was storm relief. He called a special session of the legislature, which approved $800 million in disaster assistance. He considered asking for a temporary tax increase to provide even more money but didn't think he could get enough support. Later, he regretted that decision.

The damage wrought by Floyd was one factor in Hunt's increased focus on environmental issues. The floods highlighted pollution problems caused by the explosive growth of the hog-farming industry in eastern North Carolina. Back in 1995, the *News & Observer* had published a Pulitzer Prize–winning series about the industry and pollution.

Hunt was in a ticklish situation. He was close to many hog farmers—especially Wendell Murphy, a fellow N.C. State alumnus who had built a billion-dollar hog-growing empire and become one of the richest men in the state. While Hunt never went as far as editorial writers and environmentalists wanted him to in regulating hog farms, he went far enough to strain relations with Murphy and other friends in the industry.

In 1997, he had successfully urged the legislature to place a moratorium on new farms and the growth of existing farms. The state mandated tougher permitting, increased buffer requirements, and annual inspections of farms. Hunt also pushed scientists and the industry to develop more effective waste-treatment processes. After Hurricane Fran, he used state funds to buy out hog farms in flood plains and to eliminate waste lagoons.

Before leaving office, Hunt threw himself into another election battle, this one to restore the Democratic Party to power in the state legislature. Republicans had kept their majority in 1996 when Hunt was reelected. And they kept bedeviling him on Smart Start and his education programs.

For Democrats, 1998 turned out to be a good year. I spent most of it working with the United States Senate campaign of John Edwards. Edwards had never run for office. Sometimes, he hadn't even voted. But he made a fortune in the courtroom as a trial lawyer and had a legendary reputation for his ability to connect with juries. He showed the same magic touch on television and was willing to spend $6 million of his own money to put himself in campaign ads.

I sensed throughout the campaign that, while Hunt accepted Edwards's sudden rise with good grace, he was more concerned with winning back the State House. That's where he worked the hardest. Democrats did capture the House, ensuring that Hunt would have a friendlier legislature his last two years in office.

As the 2000 elections neared, the political spotlight shifted away from Hunt. Edwards quickly became a national political star. In North Carolina, Democrats began focusing on the primary race for governor between Attorney General Mike Easley and Lieutenant Governor Dennis Wicker. Both were moderate-to-progressive young politicians in the Hunt mold. As usual, Hunt stayed out of their primary battle.

Inevitably, our team began to scatter. I went to work in Dennis Wicker's campaign. Ed Turlington worked for Bill Bradley, who was planning to run for president in 2000. Rachel Perry left for a job with a public relations firm in Raleigh. Jim Phillips and Brad Wilson had departed earlier for jobs in law and business.

Hunt pressed on. Through the final days of December 2000, even as the inaugural platform was being built on Capitol Square for Governor-elect Easley's swearing-in, he never slowed down. Wayne McDevitt, Hunt's last chief of staff, recalled that even then, "he was still working. He'd call and say, 'I've got an idea.'"

Unlike sixteen years earlier, in the dark days after his loss to Helms, Hunt went out this time on a wave of public approval. Jim Hunt stories—some true, some exaggerated, some apocryphal—made their way around Raleigh. Jim Hunt impressions—keeping an iron grip on a listener's elbow while making a fervent appeal on behalf of "the little children"—became a cottage industry.

He began to show a side apart from the familiar serious, driven figure. One reporter wrote, "He can be less stiff and more relaxed than he often appears in public and on television." Hunt even went to the annual party put on by the capital press corps. A highlight was usually someone's imitation of Hunt. This night, no one volunteered to take the stage—until Hunt, who had been prepped by some of his younger aides, stood up. Said one news account, "Hunt brought down the house with an over-the-top impression of himself."

Newspapers published glowing tributes to his sixteen years in the governor's office. "He has been the most influential governor in this century in North Carolina," said one.

Hunt's old adversary-turned-friend John I. Wilson said, "Once you get his attention on an issue, you know he's going to come through. This man is a master at selling the state on any issue he believes in. Nobody else even comes close."

Chapter 20

"The Eternal Governor"

In January 2001, just as he had after leaving office in 1985, Hunt started commuting from Rock Ridge to a law office in Raleigh. This time, he joined the state's largest firm, Womble, Carlyle, Sandridge & Rice. He moved into a suite of offices on the twenty-first floor of one of Raleigh's tallest buildings. His corner conference room overlooked the Capitol.

He was aggressively recruited by Burley Mitchell, whom Hunt had appointed chief justice of the North Carolina Supreme Court. Mitchell was now a partner at Womble Carlyle. The firm made Hunt a financial offer that would in time bring him and his family enough wealth and financial security to help pay for the college educations of their ten grandchildren. Hunt had another offer from an out-of-state company that would have paid more. The difference was that Womble Carlyle encouraged him to pursue his public-policy interests. "You do good, and we'll figure out how to do well," Mitchell told him.

Hunt plunged into doing good works—and helping the law firm recruit clients. His frenetic pace barely slowed. He put in sixty-hour weeks for the firm. He traveled around the country and the world

Jim and Carolyn Hunt, their four children, the children's spouses, and all ten grandchildren at the family farm in December 2009

Photo from Governor Hunt's personal collection

speaking, serving on study commissions, and joining in policy-fests. By 2010, he had made twenty-five trips to Japan.

He founded the James B. Hunt Jr. Institute for Educational Leadership and Policy at UNC–Chapel Hill. The institute focused on educating governors and legislators from across the country on improving public education. Hunt addressed joint legislative sessions in other states, conferred with experts, and met with education and business leaders across the country. His clout continued in North Carolina. A briefing the institute held in January 2010 drew more than seventy members of the legislature, from both parties.

The Emerging Issues Forum at N.C. State grew into the year-round Institute for Emerging Issues. Whatever the hot issues facing the world—energy, the environment, taxes—Hunt's institute was in the middle of the action. He continued to preside over the annual forums in February, which still attracted crowds and big-name speakers. The institute began offering up policy ideas, like a sweeping tax-reform plan for North Carolina.

The institute put on its twenty-fifth annual forum in February 2010. The topic was simple: "Creativity." After interviewing Hunt about the forum, Jack Betts of the *Charlotte Observer* wrote that, "true to Hunt's nature, he had a lot of thoughts about innovation, creativity and thinking about things in different ways."

His image became that of statesman, rather than politician. Frank Daniels, Jr., the former publisher of the *News & Observer*, told him, "You're the new Bill Friday. You're the one person in the state who can rally everybody around a cause."

Tom Lambeth dubbed Hunt "the Eternal Governor."

On July 4, 2008, Jesse Helms—aged and feeble in a Raleigh nursing home—died. The obituaries largely downplayed his record on racial issues. He was hailed as a leader of the national conservative movement, a key figure in the rise of the Republican Party in the South, and the champion of the New Right. Vice President Dick Cheney came to his funeral. Even old critics in North Carolina bit their tongues. The *News & Observer* ran front-page tributes that, Democratic die-hards complained, overlooked the past and overdid the praise.

Publicly, at least, Helms and Hunt had put aside the hard feelings from 1984. In 1993, Jim Goodmon of WRAL got both men to attend his fiftieth birthday party. The old foes smiled and shook hands for a picture and inscribed it warmly for Goodmon. As senator and governor in the 1990s, they made a great show of working together on issues important to the state—tobacco, highways, economic development, and hurricane relief. Hunt publicly thanked Helms for that help at the groundbreaking ceremony for Wingate University's Jesse Helms Center in 1999.

But Hunt held back when reporters called him for a comment after Helms's death. He didn't want to say what he really thought. Nor did he want to mouth platitudes that masked his true feelings. He decided to say nothing.

At age seventy-one in 2008, Hunt threw himself into an election campaign as eagerly as he had for Terry Sanford nearly a half-century earlier. He helped recruit Democratic candidates for Congress and the state legislature. He raised money. He campaigned all over North Carolina—two or three stops a week, a fundraiser here, a rally there. He campaigned for Beverly Perdue for governor and peppered the candidate and her staff with advice.

Hunt was active in the United States Senate race against the Republican incumbent, Elizabeth Dole, a Republican superstar. Married to former presidential candidate and former senator Bob Dole, she had run for president herself in 2000 and had beaten Erskine Bowles in 2002 to succeed Jesse Helms in the Senate. To run against her, Hunt recruited Kay Hagan, a state senator who had co-chaired his campaigns in Greensboro.

He stayed scrupulously neutral in the Democratic presidential race, dutifully endorsing John Edwards as a favorite-son candidate. After Edwards withdrew, some of Hunt's children and younger friends pressed him to endorse Barack Obama over Hillary Clinton. Hunt was impressed by Obama—especially his ability to inspire young voters and African-Americans—but he didn't take sides. He was still close to Bill Clinton. Some of his best and oldest friends, like Betty McCain and Jeanette Hyde, were passionate supporters of Hillary Clinton. Hyde had known Hunt since his YDC days, raised money for his campaigns, and served as United States ambassador to Barbados and the eastern Caribbean in the Clinton administration.

Hunt was neither surprised nor disappointed when Obama won North Carolina's primary by more than 15 points and went on to the Democratic nomination.

In the fall, Hunt grew increasingly energized as polls showed Obama had a chance to carry North Carolina. He contributed money out of his own pocket so the Wilson County Democratic Party could hire an organizer for Obama and the Democratic ticket. The young man didn't know what he was getting into, working for Jim Hunt in his home county.

Wilson went Democratic, and so did North Carolina. Perdue was elected the state's first female governor, and Hagan unseated Elizabeth Dole. Democrats won solid majorities in both houses of the state legislature and some closely contested congressional races.

And Barack Obama carried North Carolina by just sixteen thousand votes out of more than four million. It was the first time the state had cast its electoral votes for a Democratic presidential candidate since Jimmy Carter in 1976.

Hunt wasn't on the ballot, but he was a big winner. And he saw the decades-long struggle over racial issues come full circle. In 1960, he had watched Terry Sanford dance around questions about race and integration. Through the 1960s and 1970s, he watched as Republicans used racial appeals to rise to power across North Carolina and the South. In 1984, he lost a Senate race in large part because he supported a national holiday honoring Martin Luther King.

Now, the state that had elected Jesse Helms helped elect an African-American president of the United States.

No one was happier than Hunt. And no one was more realistic. Inevitably, the election honeymoon faded. Obama's poll ratings drifted downward through a painful national recession in 2009. So did Perdue's. A number of prominent Democratic politicians and fundraisers were caught up in political-corruption scandals. Hunt cautioned friends that the 2010 and 2012 elections could turn out very differently from 2008. Politics, he knew, offered no final victories—and no final defeats.

Hunt's reputation grew steadily after he left office in January 2001. He became the standard against which other North Carolina politicians were measured—and found wanting.

At first, Raleigh welcomed a break from Hunt's hyperkinetic style. His successor, Mike Easley, was a far different personality. Where Hunt was driven, Easley was laid-back. He routinely ducked public appearances. But where Hunt could be stiff, Easley had a deep reservoir of personal charm with a quick, ironic wit. He could do a dead-on impersonation of Hunt. And Easley naturally wanted to escape his predecessor's long shadow.

Although not as ambitious, Easley's agenda as governor built on Hunt's. He developed a More at Four early-childhood program along the lines of Smart Start. To address the high dropout rate, Easley led a nationally recognized effort to reform high schools and link them with community colleges. Faced with a slowing economy and falling state revenues when he took office, he had the courage to push the legislature for higher taxes. He expanded the use of state incentives, which Hunt had begun, to recruit industries. North Carolina's robust growth continued until the national recession hit in 2008.

But as he left office, Easley became ensnarled in scandal and controversy. He was accused of accepting free airplane flights, arranging a high-paying job for his wife at N.C. State, and getting a sweetheart deal on a valuable piece of coastal property. Soon, he faced investigations into his campaign finances by the State Board of Elections and, more ominously, a criminal investigation by the United States attorney's office.

When Beverly Perdue succeeded Easley, she had a rough start. Perdue had been in the legislature since 1986 and was a state co-chair of Hunt's campaign in 1992. She saw herself as an education governor like Hunt, but a deep national recession and a growing budget deficit even worse than the one Easley faced forced her to cut spending on human-services programs and education. Just as with Hunt twenty-five years earlier, teachers made her the target of protests. Her poll ratings fell.

Other Tar Heel politicians were tarnished. Jim Black, who was House speaker from 1999 to 2006, went to prison for accepting a bribe. Commissioner of Agriculture Meg Scott Phipps, the daughter of Bob Scott, was removed from office and sent to prison in 2003 for violating campaign-finance laws in her 2000 race. Several Democratic legislators were caught up in a witches' brew of ethics controversies.

John Edwards suffered one of the most spectacular falls of any politician in American history. He went from being a rising star—he was almost picked to be Al Gore's running mate in 2000 before becoming John Kerry's in 2004 and a leading contender for the presidential nomination in 2008—to having his reputation shredded over an affair with a campaign videographer.

Amid the wreckage, Hunt looked better and better. Reporters contrasted his openness with the media—and his willingness to clean up rather than cover up—with what they viewed as Easley's evasiveness and stonewalling. Legislators compared Hunt's relentless salesmanship to Easley's arm's-length approach and Perdue's initial uncertainty. Business leaders complained that under Easley, the state lost the aggressive edge Hunt had given to economic development.

He had navigated his way through nearly thirty years of public life with his integrity intact. He maintained a reputation as an effective public leader in an age when few people believed government or politicians could do anything right. He survived an election defeat that would have ended many a politician's career. He came back to be reelected governor twice. He left North Carolina one of the most Democratic states in the country. In no other state had Democrats won five straight gubernatorial races, held majorities in both houses of the legislature, and elected so many Democratic United States senators and representatives.

Most important, it became clear as the years passed that Hunt had presided over a dramatic transformation of North Carolina. The state where he grew up would not have recognized the state North Carolina became.

Imagine North Carolinians being told in 1950 what was to come: the decline of textiles and furniture, the onslaught of overseas competition, the demonization of tobacco. Imagine them hearing it would eventually be illegal to smoke a cigarette in a store, a restaurant, or a workplace in North Carolina. They might have expected economic disaster lay ahead.

The opposite happened. North Carolina boomed. Its economy was revolutionized. The state became a magnet for highly educated, ambitious, entrepreneurial people from across the country and around the world.

Without Jim Hunt, it might not have happened that way.

How did he do it? How did he succeed where so many North Carolina politicians fell short? How did he adapt to the rapid, dramatic changes of his time and impose his vision, goals, and ideas on the state's direction?

Through four decades working in and writing about North Carolina politics, I saw the best and the worst. I worked with Hunt, the most successful political leader of his time, and with John Edwards, the most disgraced. I spent thousands of hours with politicians, dozens upon dozens of them: members of Congress, legislators, county commissioners, city council members, and would-be candidates for every conceivable office.

I came to see the wisdom in James Carville's statement, "There are two kinds of politicians: Those who want to *be* something—and those who want to *do* something."

In truth, all politicians are a combination of both impulses. The difference is the relative weight of the two. At one extreme was John Edwards, who seemed in the end to want only to be something. At the other extreme was Hunt. Yes, he wanted to be governor. He wanted to be a United States senator. Deep down, though he never said it, I believe he wanted to be president.

But for Hunt, *being* something was a means to *doing* something—doing something for people. Helping kids get a good education, helping their parents find good jobs, helping North Carolinians have a better future.

And he was absolutely driven to do it. Everybody who worked with him said he had more determination and energy than anyone they ever met.

Darren Clark, who worked as Hunt's personal aide before becoming a government-relations executive with Pepsi-Cola, said, "He had an inborn drive to do things. If he'd been a stockbroker, he would have been the richest stockbroker ever." Clark remembered what Hunt said when a friend retired with a golden parachute at age sixty-two: "I couldn't imagine ever retiring." Clark asked why not. Hunt said, "Because there's a lot more to do. I couldn't sit around doing nothing."

Stephanie Bass, who was deputy press secretary in Hunt's first term and later a policy adviser, said, "He had a missionary zeal, like his circuit-riding great-grandfathers. His father had it about improving the land. His mother, tutoring the farm boys everybody else had given up on. He believed that everybody can improve, and your job is to help them. There's just something in his DNA."

Carolyn Hunt saw that side of her husband from the day he sat beside her at the National Grange Youth Conference in Hamilton, Ohio, in 1955: "He's always wanting to make things better for people. This has been since day one. He probably talked about this when we first met, what he could do to help folks and to bring about equality and all those things. It goes way back, way back. He's always thinking things can be better. There are always ways to improve things. And I think that never stops. The older we get, I keep saying, 'You've got to slow down a little bit.' He knows that, and I know it, but it's hard. It really is. Because there are so many ways he thinks he can help other people and help the state. It's never-ending."

The drive came first of all from the way he grew up. Both James Hunt, Sr., and Elsie Brame Hunt were visible in him. He had his father's confidence and competitiveness, his impatience and frugality. But that toughness was leavened by his mother's loving and compassionate nature.

His father was stubborn enough to prove he could make a sorry piece of land productive. His mother believed every one of her students could learn. They both had college degrees and a near-religious fervor for education. They were Franklin Roosevelt–Harry Truman–Kerr Scott Democrats. They believed in farmers working together politically to get things done that improved their lives.

They imbued both their sons with an ethic of public service. Robert pursued a career as a social worker. All four of Jim and Carolyn's children ended up in some type of public service. Rebecca became a nurse. Baxter worked for the State Department in Washington and overseas. Rachel got involved as a political volunteer in Charlotte and in 2010 was thinking about running for school board one day. Elizabeth became a social worker.

His country upbringing explained a lot about Jim Hunt. He grew up believing country people deserved a better chance—better jobs, better roads, better schools, better health care. He got so mad about how people in the country were shortchanged that, sixty years later, he was still angry about how long it had taken him to see the doctor at age thirteen.

Hunt's religious faith shaped him. He found comfort sitting in the pew and intellectual stimulation arguing scripture in Sunday school. But he was never one to make a show of his faith while campaigning. Later in life, especially after leaving office, he grew more willing to talk publicly about his faith and how it influenced him. In 2009, when he made his customary appearance at the Democratic Party's annual Sanford-Hunt-Frye dinner, he told the crowd members they had a duty "to do as Jesus would do—to care for 'the least of these.'"

For Hunt, being a Democrat was close to being a Christian.

His faith helped him see that racial discrimination was wrong. Not everyone from his time and place came to that realization. For Jim and Robert Hunt, it started with their mother telling them the way black people were treated wasn't right. Hunt realized the full import of what she said when he went to college.

Hunt was shaped by N.C. State during four years as an undergraduate and two more pursuing a master's degree. He came to believe in the importance of technology and scientific research.

He was shaped by law school—and by failing the bar exam his first try. He mastered the grind of studying the law and learned as a young lawyer how laws touched people's lives.

He was shaped by the two years he and his family spent in Nepal. He learned of the wider world, grew comfortable with it, and accepted that changes would come with an increasingly globalized economy.

Hunt was shaped by his political family—the Kerr Scott–Frank Graham–Terry Sanford–Bert Bennett family. They were the progressives—the "Go Forward" crowd of Scott, the "New Day" crowd of Sanford. Without them, Hunt never would have been governor.

Politicians like Edwards and Easley didn't come up in politics the way Hunt had. Politics changed as North Carolina changed. Television and a mobile population killed the county-by-county, precinct-by-precinct politics ingrained in Hunt. In many ways, he was the bridge between the old and the new politics; he came up in the old politics in the 1960s and 1970s and mastered the new politics in the 1990s.

But something was lost in that change. Edwards, Easley, and other modern politicians didn't have Hunt's rigorous apprenticeship of driving thousands of miles to every community, winning over old Sanford keys and Lake supporters, speaking to the Young Democrats, patiently and painstakingly building an organization of thousands of people. Days, weeks, months, and years of campaigning took Hunt to every corner of the state and put him face to face with hundreds of thousands of North Carolinians.

Nobody knew the state like he did. He said once that if a person named any location in North Carolina, "I have a picture of that place in my mind's eye. I know the people there. I know what their lives are like." He said that, often as not, when people told him their names, he could guess what county they came from.

That rootedness ultimately enabled Hunt to change the state. He knew what North Carolina was like, so he knew it had to change. He knew what North Carolinians were like, so he believed they would change. And he knew how to talk to them, so he was confident he could persuade them to embrace change.

Hunt saw in the 1970s that the old economy of textile plants and small tobacco farms was in trouble. He knew North Carolina was going to have to prepare for new industries, new technologies, and new sciences. He knew that global economic forces offered both challenges and opportunities for the state. He knew that North Carolinians had to be smarter, more skilled, and better educated. He knew that government and society had to open the doors to women, young people, African-Americans, and, in later years, Hispanics.

He wasn't by any means the only one who understood North Carolina had to change. But he was the only one who was governor for sixteen years. And not every politician possessed or acted on that same knowledge. Some, like Helms, built their careers appealing to people's fears about change, rather than their hopes.

Hunt didn't fear, fight, or flinch at change. He embraced it. He got excited about it. He got other people excited. He got legislators excited. He got business people from around the world excited about coming to North Carolina. He got North Carolinians excited about getting ready—getting the schools ready, getting the next generation ready.

He preached the message relentlessly, year after year. People heard him; they couldn't help hearing him. Sometimes fitfully, sometimes reluctantly, sometimes enthusiastically, they listened. A lot of them responded.

And a lot of us joined him—in campaigns, in his administrations, and in whatever projects he dreamed up that caught our imaginations.

Hunt wasn't tall or physically imposing; he was a couple of inches under six feet. Some people were surprised when they met him, expecting a bigger person from seeing him on TV. But he had a spirit about him that was almost a physical force. Betty Owen, his education adviser in his first two terms, said, "He's unexpected. He looks ordinary—until you talk to him."

Part of it was sheer energy and enthusiasm. It came out at N.C. State football and basketball games. A rabid lifelong fan, he was often spotted in the stands wearing his red blazer, chomping down on a hot dog and cheering for the Wolfpack.

He did everything at top speed, and he did a dozen things at a time. He lived—and thrived—in a blizzard of public appearances, meetings, phone calls, newspapers, and memos. Staffers were as likely to get a note from him scrawled on a napkin or a stray scrap of paper as on an official notepad. Howie DeVane, one of his assistants at Womble Carlyle, once received a tiny note from Hunt on an empty yellow packet of Splenda sweetener. "See me" about something, it said.

He could be disorganized. His desk was always buried under papers, reports, books, and notes. He overscheduled himself, jamming too much into too little time. He gave aides and cabinet secretaries conflicting and differing directives. But as hard as he drove himself and everyone around him, he remained—as John A. Williams, Jr., described him in his first term—"an exacting man to work for, but not demanding."

Rachel Perry was his communications director in the 1992 campaign and his third term. She often caught the brunt of his whirlwind activity. She said later, "I always thought that he had the highest standards and the highest expectations of anybody I've ever met, yet he also had the highest regard for people, the highest level of support for his staff. It was an odd combination."

Ultimately, Hunt knew people—and how to motivate them.

Bert Bennett explained why he was glad three of his sons worked for Hunt: "If I had my choice, if they had the ability to go to Harvard MBA school or three years with Hunt, I'd take by far three years with Hunt. Because he was a master to work with and for. Their future in life, attitude, service, decision making, how to treat people. All the things that go into it, he was a master."

Brad Wilson, who later became president of Blue Cross and Blue Shield of North Carolina, said Hunt never lost the quality that first attracted him in the 1970s: "That was the time of Watergate, Vietnam, anti-emotions. He was the antithesis of that. He appealed to the goodness and to the positive effect of government. He always led by inspiration. He appeals to the fundamental goodness—the idea that North Carolina is able to do anything. He was a positive voice in a negative din."

He was a lifelong learner. Ed Turlington, Hunt's chief of staff in the third term, said in 2009, "To the day he left office, he was growing. He was intellectually curious. He kept a broader sense of the world. He didn't assume he knew all he needed to know. And he's still doing it."

He wasn't a particularly reflective man. Even when I interviewed him for this book, he rarely settled into the kind of rumination and reminiscence I expected from a politician looking back over a long career. He talked matter-of-factly about what he had done and why and how. But his real interest was always action. He was always Mr. Total Initiative: What's next? What's left to be done? What are we going to do now?

That's how he saw his role as a leader: "When I give a speech, I always wind it up by lifting the audience up. I may have a dozen ideas in a speech about what we need to do, but I see it as my responsibility to ask myself, 'What's going to get people to do something about it? How can I encourage them, inspire them, motivate them?'"

Often as not, a Jim Hunt speech was something like the altar call at a religious revival. His voice would rise, then fall to a whisper. He would reach his arms out like he was trying to embrace the audience, pull them to him, and literally propel them into action. He had a tendency to talk too long. When I chided him about it, he would tell me, "But I had to *educate* them." And his heated speaking style made some people uncomfortable. But especially as time went on, people realized Hunt was passionately sincere about what he said.

Above all, "he did it in good spirits," Burley Mitchell said. "He kept positive, kept an optimistic view of humans even though he had seen the seamier side. He was always an idealist."

In the end, Hunt's spirit was the quality that set him apart from so many politicians. The programs he passed, the initiatives he launched, and the successes he racked up don't paint the full picture. When he got excited about an idea or an initiative or a new fact he learned, he had a way of sweeping people up in his excitement, convincing them that great things could be done, and inspiring them to become part of it.

He made people feel like the future of North Carolina and every single soul who lived there depended on how well they did their jobs. They believed it when he said he couldn't do it without them. Phil Baddour of Goldsboro—who had known him since the Richardson Preyer days, worked in his campaigns, and sponsored much of Hunt's key legislation as a member of the House—said, "He made every person feel that he had a special bond with them."

Karen Garr started out as a young teacher who supported Hunt for lieutenant governor and governor. She became an activist who marched in a teacher protest against him. In his last two terms as governor, she worked on his staff as his teacher adviser. She summed up what it was like to be around him: "You'd knock yourself out for him. He had a way of making you believe you could do anything."

Hunt made a lot of North Carolinians believe that. That's how the farm boy from Rock Ridge transformed his state.

Epilogue

If 1984 was the low point of Jim Hunt's political life, the high point may have come twenty-five years later.

On October 23, 2009—nearly a quarter-century to the day after Hunt lost the United States Senate race—several hundred people gathered under a tent on the Centennial Campus at North Carolina State University. They were there for the groundbreaking of the James B. Hunt Jr. Library.

Jim Woodward, N.C. State's chancellor, noted that it was Hunt who arranged for the university to have the land that became the Centennial Campus. It was Hunt who had the idea of using the land for a new type of research campus, one where university scholars and private-sector researchers worked side by side. Now, the campus was home to dozens of classroom buildings, labs, and corporate offices and thousands of students, faculty members, and private-sector employees. Now, Woodward said, universities across the country were copying what N.C. State had done.

Woodward said it simply: "No Jim Hunt, no Centennial Campus."

Erskine Bowles, the son of Skipper Bowles and in 2009 the president

Hunt speaking at the twenty-fifth Emerging Issues Forum at N.C. State in 2010. The forum became a "must" event for legislators, educators, business leaders, and policy wonks every February.
PHOTO BY STEVE EXUM

of the UNC system, hailed Hunt as "the true and unequaled champion of public education in North Carolina." After the ceremony, he said, "Each of us here today is his protégé."

Senator Kay Hagan reminded the crowd that Hunt had launched Smart Start and that his commitment to education impacted everyone from young children to Ph.D.'s.

Lieutenant Governor Walter Dalton said that, thanks to Smart Start, North Carolina's fourth-graders scored among the nation's best in math assessments. He added that Governor Beverly Perdue couldn't attend because she was overseas on the kind of industry-hunting trip that had been Hunt's trademark.

Chancellor Woodward said the Hunt Library would become one of the university's two signature structures, along with the Bell Tower on the main campus. Drawings showed a design that would sweep up from the red-brick buildings on the campus and soar out toward Lake Raleigh and the woods and fields beyond.

It would be more than a library. It would house a gallery celebrating North Carolina's—and Hunt's—history. And it would be about the future. It would serve as headquarters for the Institute for Emerging Issues. It would house interactive exhibits about issues facing the state—and address the need for North Carolinians to get involved in resolving them. As Rob Christensen of the *News & Observer* wrote, the library symbolized that Hunt "still has big plans for North Carolina."

Christensen, author of a book about North Carolina's political history, added, "The library, the institute and the Centennial Campus all bear Hunt's imprint. They are among the visible parts of a remarkable legacy of the influence of one man's drive. Raised on a Wilson County dairy farm without wealth or connections, Hunt's career is a testament to the power of persistence, persuasion and an ability to make others see the virtue of his vision for the state."

Standing in the crowd that day, I thought back to the time after the

1984 election. We—the Hunt team, the North Carolina progressives who traced our roots to Kerr Scott, Frank Porter Graham, and Terry Sanford—were down, defeated, and devastated.

"We were all in shock," recalled Hunt's daughter Rachel. But Hunt was never upset or emotional. "He very rarely got down," Rachel said. "Nineteen eighty-four was the darkest time, but even then he had another game plan."

He kept working. And thinking ahead.

When it came his turn to speak at the library groundbreaking, Hunt recounted how the mayor of Raleigh and a delegation of developers had come to see him. They wanted to buy the land that became the Centennial Campus. They wanted it for houses and private development.

"The easy thing to do," Hunt recalled, "was to give them the land, take the money, put it in the state treasury, and cut taxes. But that's not how you build a great state. The right thing to do was to think about the public purpose: How does this best serve the public, the vision, what we can be?"

More than two hundred years earlier, Hunt reminded the crowd, North Carolina had established the first public university in the nation, in the village of Chapel Hill: "The universities then were the Harvards and Yales and Princetons, set up by the rich people for their own children. And here comes this poor state of North Carolina that has the audacity to set up a public university for the people—and pay for it with their tax money. And, boy, were they poor. That's how we started out. That's the kind of state we are."

Hunt talked about North Carolina's progressive tradition—about Terry Sanford and Skipper Bowles—and how it had changed the state.

He paid tribute to Carolyn: "I certainly couldn't have done this and I wouldn't have been working with you if it had not been for the woman who is the love of my life and the greatest partner anybody could have."

Then he did something customary in his speeches. He started talking about individuals in the crowd. He would spot people, call them by their names, and talk about what they had done for North Carolina. He made it sound like they had changed the world for the better all by themselves. He'd go so overboard that, while they might feel good at first about being recognized, they'd start feeling guilty because they really weren't as great as he made them sound.

Today, once again, he was pumping us up, lifting us, telling us we could be better and do more than we thought.

He told us, "This is the progressive team in North Carolina. And we've done all this together. We're proud of where we are today, but we aren't beginning to be satisfied. We know what the future can be. We believe in the future."

He said what we might just as well have said to him: "I want to thank you for what you've done, for the leadership you've given, for the way you believe, the way you care, the way you work."

Then the ever-optimistic, never-satisfied Jim Hunt added, "We're just getting started. The future's going to be great."

Acknowledgments

Thanks, first, to my family—my wife, Gwyn, our son, James, and our daughter, Maggie. An author typically acknowledges how hard it was for family members to put up with his distraction while writing the book. For years before that, my family had to endure a husband and father consumed by politics. Their love and support sustained me through it all.

Thanks to Jim Hunt for the opportunity to write his authorized biography and for the invitation thirty-five years ago to join his political journey. Thanks to members of the Hunt family, especially Carolyn Hunt, who shared their photographs, memories, and observations.

Thanks to everyone who gave me their time and answered my questions in person, by phone, and by e-mail. They are named in the Sources and Notes, and I sincerely appreciate their help.

Thanks to Lisa Pace for all she did to help with this project. I especially thank her for getting the photographs, some of them decades old, and tracking down when, where, and by whom they were taken.

Thanks to Sheila Evans and Howie DeVane, Governor Hunt's assistants at Womble, Carlyle, Sandridge & Rice, for their help throughout this project.

Thanks to Jennifer Fox Jackson, the primary researcher. She found countless news clippings, chased down elusive facts and quotations, and helped shape the manuscript. Thanks also to Katie Hughes and Mark A. Reidy for their research assistance.

Thanks to Charlie Jones and Peggy Neal at the *News & Observer* and Kim Cumber at the North Carolina Office of Archives and History for their help with photographs. Thanks to Dan Crawford of Durham for permission to use the cover photograph.

Thanks to everyone at John F. Blair, Publisher, in Winston-Salem, N.C., for bringing this book to print: Carolyn Sakowski, Steve Kirk, Debbie Hampton, Angela Harwood, Margaret Couch, Brooke Csuka, Jaci Gentile, Artie Sparrow, and Heath Simpson.

Thanks to those who shared their advice and experience about writing and publishing books: Rob Christensen, John Drescher, Bill Friday, D. G. Martin, and Kate Torrey.

Thanks to Tillman Cooley, Joyce Fitzpatrick, and Ferrel Guillory for reading the manuscript and offering their suggestions. They made the book better.

Thanks, finally, to my parents—my mother, Becky, and my late father, Jim. If they hadn't possessed the wisdom to move to Raleigh when I was a year old, I would have missed all this. My father was a newspaperman all his life—a printer, copyeditor, and writer. When I was sixteen, he helped me get a part-time job as a copyboy in the *News & Observer* newsroom. So I approached him with trepidation ten years later when I was considering leaving the paper to work in Hunt's first campaign for governor. I expected him to tell me I'd be foolish to throw away my career on such a risky venture. Instead, he said, "You'd be crazy not to take that job. You don't know where it might lead you."

He was right.

Sources and Notes

This book is based on interviews with Jim Hunt, interviews with people involved in the political times, and my own experiences and observations. With the research assistance of Jennifer Fox Jackson, I also used contemporary newspaper clippings.

The three published volumes of Governor Hunt's official addresses and papers from the North Carolina Office of Archives and History, Department of Cultural Resources, were an invaluable resource. William H. Brown, who is editing the fourth volume, was tremendously helpful. Unfortunately, that volume will be the last. Budget cuts have forced the state to suspend the publication of governors' papers. Also, *Report to the People: The Hunt Administration Record of Accomplishments, 1993–2001*, published by the Governor's Office in December 2000, was helpful in researching Hunt's third and fourth administrations. Several books cited below were invaluable as well.

I have come to appreciate how difficult it is to accurately report history—especially events from years and decades earlier. Memories fade, recollections differ, and opinions vary. I have done my best to be accurate. I relied on sources who asked not to be named only when I felt it was essential. I regret and take responsibility for any errors.

Rather than a cumbersome list of footnotes—nearly every sentence and paragraph would require a note—I provide here a guide to the people, publications, and other sources on which I relied. I express my appreciation to all who contributed to this work.

I interviewed more than fifty people, including Zeb Alley, Phil Baddour, Stephanie Bass, Bert Bennett, Jack Betts, Bill Brown, Barbara Buchanan, Phil Carlton, Rob Christensen, Darren Clark, Jack Cozort, Frank Daniels, Jr., Mike Davis, Paul Essex, Janice Faulkner, Joel Fleishman, Bill Friday, Karen Garr, Jim Goodmon, Wayne Grimsley, Ferrel Guillory, Bob Havely, Carl Henley, Jim Holshouser, Abe Holtzman, Baxter Hunt, Carolyn Hunt, Robert Hunt, Jim Kelly, Tom Lambeth, Howard Lee, Quentin Lindsey, Betty McCain, Lynda McCullough, Wayne McDevitt, Burley Mitchell, Rachel Hunt Nilender, Betty Owen, Jane Smith Patterson, Rachel Perry, Jim Phillips, Karen Ponder, Wade Smith, Banks Talley, Norris Tolson, Ed Turlington, Harold Webb, Brad Wilson, John I. Wilson, and Carter Wrenn. I regret that death and illness made it impossible to talk to some people, including Joe Grimsley, Joe Pell, Ben Ruffin, Terry Sanford, Bob Scott, and John A. Williams.

PROLOGUE

Several times during our interviews, Jim Hunt told me the story about the young woman he greeted on Election Day. I realized the impact that the encounter had on him at the end of a grueling campaign.

Regarding the statement that "Hunt was the first modern-era North Carolina governor elected to two four-year terms," Michael Hill, editor of *The Governors of North Carolina* (Raleigh: North Carolina Office of Archives and History, 2007), notes that gubernatorial succession was permitted before the Civil War; some governors were reelected. No North Carolina governor had been reelected since a new state constitution adopted in 1868 limited governors to a single four-year term.

The conclusions contained in the rest of the prologue, of course, are my own. They are based on my observations about the changes that occurred in the state where I was born and grew up. Ferrel Guillory, director of the Program on Public Life at UNC–Chapel Hill and a former reporter and editorial writer at the *News & Observer*, gave me valuable guidance on describing the scope and importance of those changes.

CHAPTER 1 FARM BOY

The description of racial attitudes in Wilson County comes from Karl Fleming's *Son of the Rough South: An Uncivil Memoir* (New York: Public Affairs, 2005), quoted by permission of the publisher.

CHAPTER 2 "BERT BENNETT'S BOY"

The race-baiting tactics of the 1950 United States Senate campaign are described in John Ehle's *Dr. Frank: Life with Frank Porter Graham* (Chapel Hill: Franklin Street Books, 1993).

John Drescher's excellent account of the 1960 gubernatorial campaign between Terry Sanford and I. Beverly Lake—*Triumph of Good Will: How Terry Sanford Beat a Champion of Segregation and Reshaped the South* (Jackson: University Press of Mississippi, 2000)—was invaluable.

Another valuable description of the 1960 campaign can be found in the documentary *Terry Sanford and the New South*, by Thomas Lennon, a production of Thirteen/WNET New York, co-produced in association with Duke University and The Center for Documentary Studies, and in association with Thomas Lennon Films and UNC-TV.

Sanford's encounter with the "redneck" supporter was confirmed to me by two people close to Sanford who heard him tell the story.

My interview with Bert Bennett about the Sanford days and the young Jim Hunt was entertaining and enlightening. I hope someone will undertake a book or research project about Bennett and the crucial role he played in North Carolina politics.

Phil Carlton provided useful—and often hilarious—insight into those early campaigns, as well as Hunt's entire career. Tom Lambeth and Joel Fleishman were helpful in recounting Sanford's 1960 campaign.

Quentin Lindsey described Hunt's time in Nepal and shared his later experiences as an adviser to Governor Hunt.

Chapter 3 Young Democrat

This chapter relies heavily on interviews with Hunt, Bennett, Carlton, and Betty McCain. Mike Davis was a great help in describing the 1972 campaign.

Chapter 4 Old Politics, New Politics

The passages about Hunt and his relationship with Joe Grimsley are based on my observations at the time, the recollections of others who knew Grimsley, and my frequent contacts and conversations with Grimsley before his untimely death.

Joe's son, Wayne Grimsley, wrote a well-researched book about Hunt's early career: *James B. Hunt: A North Carolina Progressive* (Jefferson, N.C.: McFarland & Co., 2003).

Former governor Jim Holshouser graciously shared with me his candid and good-humored observations about his relationship through the years with Hunt.

Chapter 5 Happy Days

Mike Davis helped refresh my recollections of the 1976 campaign.

The *News & Observer* story on Jimmy Carter's discussion of his religious faith is from March 20, 1976. It was headlined, "Candidates Campaign for N.C. Votes."

The quote that Jesse Helms and Tom Ellis "cut their teeth on politics" in the 1950 Willis Smith campaign is from Rob Christensen's *The Paradox of Tar Heel Politics* (Chapel Hill: University of North Carolina Press, 2008), pages 145–46.

Guillory's reporting on Hunt's whistling is from "Hunt Serenely Whistling Happy Days," which ran in the *News & Observer* on October 31, 1976.

Chapter 6 "Mr. Total Initiative"

This chapter owes much to my interview with Banks Talley, who generously shared with me a daily journal he kept throughout 1977, the year he served as Governor Hunt's executive assistant. Many times during our interviews, as we racked our fading memories, Hunt and I wished we had possessed the foresight to keep a written record.

Chapter 7 Weathervane

Jack Cozort and I lived through the Wilmington Ten episode. He reviewed it at length in our interview.

The quotes from James Ferguson ("A step backward") and Elizabeth Chavis ("He will never serve as governor again . . .") are from the January 24, 1978, edition of the *News & Observer*. The quote that Hunt "sought to please both sides and wound up pleasing neither" is from an editorial in the *News & Observer* the same day.

Chapter 8 Education Governor, CEO Governor

John I. Wilson and Quentin Lindsey were a great help in reconstructing the events described here.

Chapter 9 Against the Wind

For this chapter—and those that follow on the 1984 campaign—I am especially indebted to Carter Wrenn for telling me the story as he saw it from the Helms campaign's side. Over the years, Carter and I have gone from being bitter enemies who disagreed about most everything to good friends who still disagree about most everything. We have worked together on some nonpolitical clients, and we co-publish a political blog, www.talkingaboutpolitics.com. Carter was unfailingly generous and open in sharing his perspective about the 1980 and 1984 campaigns and about the origins and growth of the Congressional Club.

Chapter 10 Rough Seas

John I. Wilson and Karen Garr provided a useful perspective into how teachers saw Hunt.

The information about the education proposals developed by the North Carolina Commission on Education for Economic Growth comes from the commission's report, *An Action Plan for North Carolina,* released in April 1984.

Chapter 11 "Where Do You Stand, Jim?"

Richard Whittle's story "Jesse Helms Has a Problem; He's Destined to Lose in '84" is from the October 23, 1983, *Washington Post.*

Joe Grimsley's quote about the 1984 race as a battle between the New South and the Old South is from "A Battle of the Titans Shaping Up in Carolina," published in the *Washington Post* on September 24, 1983.

The quote from James B. Hunt, Sr., on the New South and the Old South is from "Jesse Helms, on Right, Faces Moderate Gov. Jim Hunt in Race With High Stakes," published in the *Wall Street Journal* on January 20, 1984.

The paragraph about the scope of the Helms campaign's ad buy is from "Ads Signal Helms-Hunt Race Is On," published in the *Charlotte Observer* on June 9, 1983.

David Flaherty's statement that "we used race . . ." is from his September 27, 1996, interview with the Southern Oral History Program of the University of North Carolina–Chapel Hill.

William Link's exhaustively researched biography of Jesse Helms—*Righteous Warrior: Jesse Helms and the Rise of Modern Conservatism* (New York: St. Martin's Press, 2008)—gives a thorough account of the senator's battle against the Martin Luther King holiday.

"Sen. Helms' smear against King" is from John Alexander's column in the *Greensboro Daily News* on October 9, 1983. The *Fayetteville Observer*'s "old red herring" quote is from an October 5, 1983, editorial.

Helms's use of the term "Freds" for African-Americans was confirmed to me by a source who asked to not be named, as was the "I's ready when you's ready" quote, which is also reported in William Link's book.

The anecdote about Helms's removing a cartoon of "a grinning, toothless black man on a porch" is from *Helms & Hunt: The North Carolina Senate Race, 1984,* by William D. Snider (Chapel Hill: University of North Carolina Press, 1985), pages 26–27.

Then-senator-elect John Edwards, with whom I worked during his 1998 campaign, told me the story about his dinner at the Helms home.

The quote about Helms's response to the CNN caller is by David Greenberg in "R, North Carolina," published in the *New York Times Book Review* on February 10, 2008.

Chapter 12 A Campaign Divided

The story summing up reaction to the first Hunt-Helms debate and quoting Merle Black ("I think Hunt really whipped him . . .") is from the *News & Observer*, July 30, 1984.

Jack Betts's assessment of the first Hunt-Helms debate is from his "Race, Religion, Patriotism" column in the *Charlotte Observer* on September 25, 1994, looking back at the 1984 campaign.

Chapter 13 Flip-flopping to Defeat

The *News & Observer* headline "Pro-Helms newspaper publishes rumors that Hunt had gay lover" is from the July 6, 1984, edition.

The descriptions of Hunt's and Helms's campaign styles and the subsequent quotes from the two are from "Hunt, Helms campaign styles as different as philosophies," published in the *News & Observer* on October 28, 1984.

The account of Helms's appearance at predominantly black Livingstone College is from "Many blacks don't listen to Helms' college talk," published in the *News & Observer* on October 18, 1984.

The quote from Helms about Hunt's support from "the homosexuals and the labor unions" is from "Battle turns nasty in Bible Belt," published in the *Globe and Mail* of Toronto, Canada, on October 22, 1984.

Chapter 14 Picking Up the Pieces

The story about how the Centennial Campus came about is from my interviews with Hunt and from contemporary news accounts. Ferrel Guillory gave me a useful perspective from what he saw as a *News & Observer* editorial writer at the time.

I relied heavily on Phil Carlton's account of Hunt's days at Poyner & Spruill, as well as my own observations.

The interview about Hunt's not running for the Senate in 1986 is from "Jim Hunt Chooses Private Life Over a 2nd Rugged Senate Race," by Tim Funk, published in the *Charlotte Observer* on September 13, 1985.

Chapter 15 The Road Back

The *Charlotte Observer* quote from "a longtime Hunt supporter" is from the February 12, 1989, edition of the paper.

Betty Owen was a great help in recalling the beginnings of the Emerging Issues Forum and Hunt's work on national education study commissions. Jim Kelly gave me his view of working with Hunt on the National Board for Professional Teaching Standards.

Chapter 16 Governor Again

Mike Davis, Rachel Perry, and Jim Phillips helped supplement my recollections of the 1992 campaign.

John Drescher's account of the Tony Rand–Jim Gardner debate is from "Gardner, Rand trade attacks in fireworks-filled debate," published in the *Charlotte Observer* on October 3, 1988.

Rob Christensen's recounting of when Jim Gardner "stood on an oak staircase and laid out his dreams of a Republican era . . ." is from *The Paradox of Tar Heel Politics*, page 235.

Jack Hawke's quote that "I believe we are better off running against Jim Hunt with his record . . ." is from "Hunt pondering gubernatorial comeback bid," published in the *News & Observer* on March 5, 1991.

Chapter 17 A New Start

Rachel Perry, Ed Turlington, Jim Phillips, and Brad Wilson were helpful in recounting Governor Hunt's approach when he took office in 1993.

Karen Ponder and Jim Goodmon helped me reconstruct the beginnings and growth of Smart Start.

Chapter 18 "America's Education Governor"

As they did for Chapter 10, Karen Garr and John I. Wilson gave me useful insights into the evolution of Hunt's relationship with teachers.

The quote about a "Mount Rushmore for governors" is taken from the *Saturday Evening Post Education Update* of September 2000.

Chapter 19 The Art of Governing

Janice Faulkner's insights into Hunt's management style were enlightening.

An excellent source on the transformation of the state's economy is *North Carolina in the Connected Age* (Chapel Hill: University of North Carolina Press, 2008), by Michael L. Walden, William Neal Reynolds Distinguished Professor at North Carolina State University.

Norris Tolson, a great source of information about Hunt's college days, also provided a useful view of how Hunt handled problems in the Department of Transportation.

John I. Wilson's quote ("Once you get his attention on an issue...") is from "Hunt: As our two-time, two-term governor, he made his agenda the state's agenda. Here's how," published in the *News & Observer* on April 1, 2000.

Chapter 20 "The Eternal Governor"

Jack Betts's description of Hunt and the Emerging Issues Forum is from "Hunt on charters, creativity and fast trains," published in the *Charlotte Observer* on January 28, 2010.

Epilogue

The quotes from Rob Christensen about the James B. Hunt Jr. Library at N.C. State are from his "Hunt's not done with North Carolina" column, published in the *News & Observer* on October 25, 2009.

Index